Child Care That Works

Child Care That Works

A Parent's Guide to Finding Quality Child Care

Eva and Mon Cochran

Robins Lane Press
a division of Gryphon House, Inc.

Beltsville, MD
www.robinslane.com

For information about permission to reproduce
selections from this book, write to Permissions,
Robins Lane Press, P.O. Box 207, Beltsville, Maryland, 20704,
or email *info@robinslane.com.*

Library of Congress Cataloging-in-Publication Data
Cochran, Eva.
    Child care that works / Eva and Mon Cochran.
        p.   cm.

    Includes index.
    ISBN 0-395-82287-4
    1. Child care — United States.   2. Children of working
parents — United States.   I. Cochran, Moncrieff.   II. Title.
    HQ778.7.U6C63   1997
    362.71'2 — dc21   97-25279   CIP

The authors are grateful for permission to reprint the
following material: Happy Day Playschool, "Our Goals and
Philosophy," *Happy Day Playschool Parent Handbook
(1996–1997).* "Head Start Builds Positive Self-Development,"
Head Start Program of Cortland County, brochure, reprinted
with permission of CAPCO Head Start Program of Cortland
County. Ithaca Community Childcare Center, "Mission,
Values, and Vision," *IC3 Handbook,* revised September 1995.
National Association of Child Care Resource and Referral
Agencies, NACCRRA Directory of Programs, 1997.

Printed in the United States of America

Book design by Joyce C. Weston

QUM 10 9 8 7 6 5 4 3 2 1

To Maria and Aaron, Monny and Marnie,
and to the memory of
Moncrieff M. Cochran, Jr., 1917–1997,
and to Thomas Gunn Cochran

Contents

Part 1.
Overview

1. Getting Started   3
2. What Are the Options?   8
3. What Is Quality Care?   23
4. How to Locate Care   38

Part 2.
Types of Care and How to Find Them

5. Family and Group Family Child Care   47
6. Center Care   73
7. Part-Day Programs   109
8. Care in Your Own Home   120
9. School-Age Child Care   135
10. Creative Alternatives   155

Part 3.
Staying in Touch with Your Child and with Yourself

11. Time Off after the Birth of Your Child   169
12. Children's Reactions to Child Care   184
13. Handling Guilt and Anxiety   192

Part 4.
Building Partnerships

14. How to Support Your Child's Caregiver   207
15. The Caregiver as a Family Resource   216

Part 5.
Economic Issues

16. Paying for Child Care   227
17. Child Care on a Shoestring   235

Part 6.
Advocacy

18. How to Improve Child Care Conditions   245
19. Employers and Public Policies   252

Appendixes

A. National Support Service Organizations and Agencies for Children in Need of Special Care   263
B. Child Care Resource and Referral Agencies   267
C. Family Child Care Forms and Checklists   297
D. Center Care Forms and Checklists   311
E. Part-Day Program Form   323
F. In-Home Care Forms and Checklists   325
G. School-Age Care Forms and Checklists   332
H. Suggested Reading and Other Resources   338
I. Questions for Potential Family Child Care Providers   339

Notes   341
Index   344

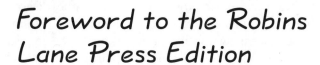

Foreword to the Robins Lane Press Edition

The first edition of *Child Care that Works* was published in 1997. Three years later, as we sat down to write this Foreword, we found ourselves wanting to give the reader a sense of how parents have used our book, and the way things have worked out for them. A number of people have told us their child care stories and described the ways in which this book was helpful. But perhaps not surprisingly we have been most affected by the child care search carried out this year by our son, Monny, and his wife, Marnie. After all, this is grandson Tom we are talking about!

The experiences of Marnie and Monny mirrored the challenges, confusions, and compromises made by so many modern American parents. Here is their story, as summarized recently by Marnie:

Late spring, 1999. Baby Cochran is due at the end of August. We just re-read your book and discussed the alternatives with you. We concluded that we'd like family day care if possible, because the group would be small and the idea of a family setting feels right.

June, 1999. Monny visits the Bright Horizons center at the local hospital and likes it. We put Baby C. on a waiting list just in case we can't find good family care. This costs $75, non-refundable.

Summer, 1999. Constantly talking with neighbors and friends about their likes and dislikes. Three families in our immediate neighborhood are all searching simultaneously. Interestingly, we all have different takes on what we want. Monny and I realize that by comparison we are pretty laid back about all this. Start wondering if we should be more worried. Read your book again and calmed down!

We call the Boston Child Care Resource and Referral agency to get the list of family day care providers living in our area. At a dollar per page, we get almost twenty pages of referrals. Where do we start?

We hear of a woman down the street who does day care and has an almost disciple-like following of parent fans. Monny introduces himself to her on a walk in the park with our dog Fenway (she is outside with kids in a great-looking garden). She tells him that she only takes 1-year-olds and up and that, by the way, she is not certified. We don't care so much about the certification from a safety perspective because she comes so highly recommended. But we know that we can't write off the expense at tax time if she is uncertified, and we simply can't afford to give up the tax break. This woman's set up is wonderful, says Monny—now we have a good baseline to which we can compare our other options.

Monny starts driving by houses on the massive referral list. Although we know that "judging a book by its cover" isn't a great way to go, what else could we do? We have to start the process somewhere. Dropping a child off at a cheery place matters to us. Monny develops a rating system. Criteria include house appearance, outside play space (that can be seen from the car), street safety, neighbor house appearance, etc. He actually makes a chart.

When Monny has about ten places picked out, I drive by the "top five." Then I start calling the ones we both like. I explain that we will need care in February, once both Monny and I have used up all our leave time. All providers tell me that we are WAY too early. They say to call back in the late fall.

For the time being, we drop the search.

August 31, 1999. TOM IS BORN!

Late October/early November, 1999. I begin to call again in earnest, and I make arrangements to go see one woman living close by. She lives in a triple-decker house that's in good shape, though it is in kind of a dreary neighborhood. Again, that's not a bad thing, but I get a little sad by it all. Could be the thought of leaving Tom anywhere, or could be the thought of leaving him there. The woman is perfectly nice, but she doesn't give me a tour of her place, and her teenage son can be heard in the kitchen slurping his way through a bowl of cereal. I try to ask the right questions (from your book), but I am a bit unnerved by her. I guess I figured that she'd be anxious to show off what she does. Instead she seems weary and doesn't offer any information that I don't ask for specifically. Again, she is perfectly nice, but I wouldn't say we really hit it off. I come away realizing that it was me, not her, who was trying hard to be liked. Why did I have to work so hard? Eventually, I will realize that day care in our neighborhood is a seller's market—lots of people are looking and most providers are full.

December, 1999. That first real visit with a real live day care provider leaves me a bit demoralized. Tom is looking tiny to me in my arms. As Christmas approaches, I turn my attention to him and to the holidays. I bury my head in the sand, as it were.

My parental leave ended in November and I am now working from home. This "special arrangement" ends this month. I'm not really nervous that we won't be able to find care, but I'm anxious to get some control over the situation. Monny is taking January off from his teaching job, so I start calling around again, this time to set him up with some possible providers. I don't get too far—they are all full! Help!

One of the providers who was full tells me about a woman who coordinates a family day care providers' group in town. She thinks that this woman will be able to tell us who has openings. I call the person and she gives me a short list. Pamela is right at the top of the list.

I drive by Pamela's house and come home announcing to Monny, "I think we've found her!" Her house looks quite elegant, and it's in a nice neighborhood, with lots of toys and green space. Dogs are in a side yard (we like dogs), and there is cheery kids' art in the windows. And it's within walking distance of our home!

One evening several days later I call Pamela and end up talking with her for an hour. She seems so loving and caring. Pamela tells me she has an opening and that she'll meet with us if we'd like. But she thinks it's best if we visit more than just one other place before coming to her, so we can make a really informed decision. I lie and tell her we'll do that. In my heart I don't want to search any more.

January, 2000. A week later Monny and I pay a visit to Pamela in the evening, and bring Tom along. We sit and talk in her living room for 45 minutes. It feels good. But afterwards, we realize that we didn't even talk about day care. Almost none of the questions we had prepared have been answered. Because we've been taught (from your book) to get certain kinds of information before making a decision, we don't just trust our gut impressions and sign up. Instead, I ask if we can come by one day and observe. This seems to make Pamela very nervous. We start to wonder why she won't let us come by during the day, when she's "in business."

Back and forth we go, trying to find a time when we can come by and when she is comfortable with having us. She admits to me that she thought we got along well in person and can't really understand what we hope to accomplish with our observation. Having us there will upset the regular routines, she says, and will distract her from her work with the kids. She seems very confident to me, but also very nervous. What's going on?

One night Monny and I agree that we'll give up the idea of observing—we liked Pamela, so we decide to give her a try. I call her and tell her we want to sign up. I also mention that "soon we'll come by to check out your outdoor space. You told us how you make use of your garage and it sounds great." Wrong move. This is interpreted as another attempt to check her out, which I guess it was. She calls back to say that she "just doesn't think this is going to work out." Again, we are in a seller's market—she doesn't want to complicate her professional life with people who don't trust her and who are as rigid as we seem. She doesn't say it like this, of course, but I get the message. The call comes to me at work and I am in tears. Rigid, us? Where did we go wrong? We're the easiest going folks we know. Don't other parents ask to observe? Don't other parents care about the safety of outdoor space? I ask her this and her response is that, "actually, no they don't." She says that other parents she has worked with like her and trust her to love their children, and she does. It's always been that simple for her. I beg her to take us on, again trying hard to be liked by the person we have liked the best. I don't mention that Monny's family leave is about to end. Pamela says, "Let's both sleep on it and talk again in a few days."

We talk to you and you urge us to try one more time, hoping to clear up what is obviously a misunderstanding. We call her and say, "We think there's been some kind of miscommunication. If you take us on, you'll soon discover that we aren't the ogres you seem to think we are. If you are willing, we want to give this a try." She agrees that the communication broke down, saying that her assistant is asking, "Why do you drive these people away when you don't even know them yet?" We agree to a two-week trial.

Once we are on board, the proverbial door is open to us. Pamela says that when Tom is with her we can come by any time, and call any time. She tells us of the schedule she keeps, what Tom will eat, where he'll sleep, her feelings about children's Tylenol, and so on— all the stuff we were dying to know beforehand! We begin to see that she feels the relationship starts with the parents getting to know and trust her as a person, and that the care arrangements are something we should have taken for granted.

January 31, 2000. Tom begins day care. I weep at the first drop-off. Pamela calls me in the car on the way to work to say Tom is doing fine. She calls me again later that day to reassure me. She gives Monny a play-by-play of the day when he picks Tom up. We find her understanding and sensitivity remarkable, and wonder how we could have ever have come so close to losing her.

February-May, 2000. We are happy with the care, and Tom is thriving. The little girls also in Pamela's care have nicknamed him "Tom Tom" and dote on him. We feel fortunate.

Looking back, I think we got a little caught up in what we "should do" because of the day care nightmare stories in the media and Tom's vulnerability at this early age. I don't think we listened to our gut instincts quite enough. At the same time, Pamela seems to be operating a bit in the dark ages with her resistance to an initial observation. As you point out, most family day care providers expect to be checked out in that way. We won't be the only family to challenge her in the way that we did—our neighbors, for instance, would NEVER have chosen her if they had met the resistance we did.

Your book was invaluable to us as we went through this process. Tell your readers, however, that while the checklists and suggested questions were expected and anticipated by the day care centers, the family providers I met were more informal, and felt intimidated by such a structured way of being judged. I believe that they shouldn't feel threatened, and that they should appreciate the value of an informed "consumer." But in the end, the operative word in family day care is *family*. When I put myself in Pamela's shoes, I realize that she wants to be treated like a family member, instead of like an employee, and that formal questioning and interviewing go a bit against that grain. As you say in the book, finding a good match usually requires some compromise. In our case, we never thought we were compromising Tom's care and so we should have relaxed a bit about the other things.

The search process Monny and Marnie experienced reflects so well the struggles most working parents go through to find child care that works for them. Will their jobs allow any parental leave time? Can they afford to take leave without pay? Is center-based or family-based child care best for their child? What can they afford to pay for care? When are child care costs tax deductible? How do they figure out what is available? What is a "resource and referral" agency, and how does it work? Should programs be regulated, and what does that mean? What is "good quality" care? Are we choosing a child care program or is the program choosing us?

Gut feelings and impressions. Compromises. Child care horror stories. *I'm scared! I'm so sad about leaving my baby with someone I hardly know.* *Child Care That Works* addresses all of these questions, feelings, and reactions. We can't find your child care provider for you, but the information, ideas, and guidance provided in our book will take the mystery out of the process and point you in the right direction.

Several important developments have occurred in the child care world since the first edition of *Child Care that Works* was published in 1997. One big change involves the Internet. You can now gather a great deal of information about child care on line; you can even use the web to carry out an initial search for the child care programs available in your area (especially if you live in a big city).

Another welcome development during the past three years has been the steadily increasing (although still inadequate) financial investment in early care and education by the public sector. At the national level we continue to see increases in funding for Head Start, and federal funding for School Age Child Care programs has also grown. As the 2000 presidential campaign warms up, both candidates are promising support for continued expansion of national child care initiatives. The states are also expanding their commitments to early education; 42 states now spend more than 1.5 billion dollars on prekindergarten programs, mostly for four-year-olds and their families.

The past several years have also seen greater use of scientific studies to emphasize the importance of early stimulation for brain development in infants and toddlers, and to demonstrate the ways that good quality child care and early education experiences provide those social and cognitive inputs. We now know more than before about how loving care from knowledgeable adults and well-planned play with both adults and other children lead to happy, healthy, thriving young children.

We also know that high quality child care and early education does not come cheap. Most parents cannot afford the $6-8,000 a year per child that it costs to pay well-trained, highly committed early education teachers and child care providers for the very special skills they bring to caring for and teaching your children. The public and private sectors must continue to expand their investments in high quality early care and education programs, so that you can afford the good child care you so richly deserve and your child care providers can afford to continue to offer those services. Child care that works is a partnership among parents, the communities in which they live, and the states and nation of which those communities are a part. For the past 30 years individual parents have carried more than their fair share of the burden for financing their child care arrangements. It is time now for the rest of us—the general public — to pick up our share of the load through the taxes we pay and the companies we work for. All of us benefit when the preschool children of today become the productive citizens of tomorrow. No investment could be more important; the very future of the United States as a great nation depends on it.

Acknowledgments

This book was written around the edges of two full-time jobs, at the crack of dawn, in the late evenings, on weekends and holidays. We would not have even contemplated the task without the prospect of wonderful assistants, constructive critics, and supporters, all of whom came through with flying colors and then some.

First and foremost, we gratefully acknowledge the superb skills, boundless energy, and great patience shown by our acquisitions editor at Houghton Mifflin, Marnie Patterson Cochran. Marnie saw the need for this book, chivvied us until we agreed to write it, and then shepherded us through the process, bolstering our spirits when we were flagging and singing our praises at just the right moments. For all these things, and many more, we are especially thankful to Marnie.

The Day Care and Child Development Council of Tompkins County was a key source of information, guidance, and support. The director, Sue Dale Hall, gave us unlimited access to all of the information stored in the council files and in the heads of her fine staff. She also read the first draft of the manuscript. Maureen Reedy dug out forms, tracked down addresses, sent away for information, and drafted checklists. Alene Wyatt unearthed key statistics, answered endless questions, debugged our computer, and kept us grounded. Kris Bennett provided us with a treasure trove of information about family child care arrangements, regulations, and providers. Marta Sanders walked us through the discussions that she has with parents when they call with child care needs. Lauren Pecoraro found forms and checklists on the council computers and got them to us on floppy disks. And in a larger sense, as one of the first and finest child care resource and referral agencies in the nation, the council provided us with a terrific model for how information and referral can be a support to families with young children.

We had the benefit of wonderfully talented child care and early childhood education experts as readers of the manuscript. Special thanks to Jennie Birckmayer, one of our idols, who saw gaps and helped us fill them and was always available when we needed an idea or a resource. Susan Griffin, director of the Cortland Area Child Care Council, and Elizabeth Stilwell, director of the Early Childhood Center at Cornell, also provided useful comments and insights. Anne Dickinson, administrative manager of the Department of Human Development at Cornell, read Chapter 11 with care and helped us think through parental leave policies and prospects.

Thanks to Yasmina Vinci, executive director of the National Association of Child Care Resource and Referral Agencies, for allowing us to include the NACCRRA directory of programs in Appendix B, and to Denise Fogarty, program director of the national organization Child Care Aware, for making that data file available on computer disk. Both Yasmina and Denise also read the manuscript and provided helpful comments and corrections related to the work of child care resource and referral organizations.

Geraldine Morse, our copy editor, did an outstanding job of tightening our prose and eliminating inconsistencies. The book is much more readable because of the care and attention she gave to the manuscript.

We are especially thankful to Cindy Lee of *careguide.com* for "discovering" our book, and for referring us to Justin Rood of Robins Lane Press. Justin welcomed us into the Robins Lane "family" and has made this new edition possible. We are very grateful.

Finally, we thank all those dedicated parents and child care professionals who have taught us what we know, and who hold the future of American society in their arms every day.

1

Getting Started

ELCOME TO this guide to finding good child care. We understand and respect your need to be away from your child while you work or go to school, or for some other important reason. Our aim is to help you locate and organize child care arrangements that satisfy you and support the healthy development of your child during your absence. Because most child care providers are women, we refer to them as "she," even though we know that some are men. Indeed, we hope that more men will enter the child care field.

As parent or guardian, you are the most important person in the world of your child, which will continue to be true throughout her growing-up years, even as care providers, teachers, coaches, and friends enter the picture. This makes you very special. You are important in a larger sense as well. Any society is only as good as the upbringing of its children, who become the adults who do its work and shape its future. So American society depends to a very great extent on your success as a parent. Be proud in your parenting role! You deserve respect for your efforts. We hope that this book will give you a strong sense of your own value and more confidence in your ability to make excellent choices for your child.

Being a good parent is hard work. In the past, many parents had someone to lend a helping hand. Grandparents were available, as were helpful, experienced friends in the neighborhood or maybe a sister or an aunt who lived nearby. During the past twenty-five years such help has become less obtainable because such people are in the workforce themselves or live too far away to be helpful on a day-to-day basis. But the need for assistance and encouragement is as great now as ever. If anything, being a parent has become more complicated than it used to be.

There are, however, new sources of assistance and encouragement for today's parents, one such being the person who cares for your child when you are at work or at school. Child care programs are a critical part of the modern family support system. Whether formal or informal, these arrangements can provide nurturing, loving, stimulating care for your loved one while you are absent and can be a valuable source of friendly advice when necessary. We strongly believe that parents deserve this kind of community support.

Some parents feel that by allowing a provider to care for their child they are being irresponsible, that is, shirking a duty which is theirs alone. In fact, the responsibility for your child's care remains completely in your hands when you divide care with another. You are responsible for finding that person and ensuring that she is providing nurturing and stimulating care. Your provider is accountable to you for the care she gives. Although the goal is to build a partnership with someone skilled in early childhood education and care, overall responsibility remains in your hands. Sharing child care does not mean giving up responsibility for child rearing. In the United States your responsibilities as a working parent are greater than they are in countries with more developed child care systems because our national, state, and local governments invest less in program quality than is contributed, say, in France or Sweden or Italy.

It is one thing to accept responsibility for the care of your child and another to have the personal resources to carry out that obligation in a way that satisfies you. One key resource is what we call assertive persistence, by which we mean that finding the care plan that is best for both you and your child requires the confidence to ask the right questions. It means being patient enough to keep looking until you discover a solution that really works for your family. Another resource is money or something you can substitute for money, such as time. Good child care is often quite expensive, because 75 percent of the cost usually comes right out of your pocket. There are ways to recover some of that money at tax time, and some public subsidies are available to low-income parents. We tell you about these ways of saving money and encourage you to use them to the fullest extent.

As workers or students with young children you have a *right* to good child care. Be assertive in claiming that right. Take the initiative in finding — even creating — the kind of care that you want, and take advantage of every possible tax break and subsidy. Don't take no for an answer! This book is filled with information about what to look for, which questions to ask, and how to shape what is available to fit your needs. Your job is to be assertive and persistent in putting the information to work for you and your child.

In the United States we are still inventing our child care system. Much work remains to be done, most of which has to take place in local communities, with support from state governments. To date, the U.S. Congress has not provided much leadership in this arena and is unlikely to do so in the future. We still have a long way to go, both in developing programs and in finding ways to make them affordable for all parents.

This reality has several consequences for you as a consumer. First, you will have to make some compromises. Every type of child care arrangement involves trade-offs. No arrangement is perfect, so you need to know what is most important for you and your child — what you can concede and what is not negotiable. In the chapters that follow we give you our best advice on these matters, based on years of experience and study. Second, the local and incomplete nature of child care systems in this country indicates that there is still lots of room for improvement. Individuals and groups can make a difference in what is available locally. This free enterprise society loves entrepreneurs, so get ready to be creative in designing a child care arrangement that works for you. This book abounds with descriptions of the raw materials available in most American communities and blueprints explaining the use of those resources. But you must be the architects of an arrangement that is the best you can make it, within the limits of community resources and your own creativity.

This guide is divided into six parts: Overview, Types of Care and How to Find Them, Staying in Touch with Your Child and with Yourself, Building Partnerships, Economic Issues, and Advocacy. We have organized the information in a sequence that makes sense to us, but you may want to read the chapters in a different order. Start with Part I, Overview, in which we describe the basic "packaged" child care options available pretty much regardless of where you live. We talk about the look and feel of quality care, whether it is provided in a center, in someone else's home, or in your own house or apartment. In the last chapter of the Overview we explain how to find specific programs or providers once you have made a preliminary decision about the type of care you wish to consider.

In Part II, Types of Care and How to Find Them, you may want to focus on the chapter that fits your situation. If you have decided on the type of setting you want for your child, pick the chapter describing that sort of setting. If your child is in kindergarten or beyond, you will want to proceed directly to the chapter on school-age child care. If you have explored local options and are unhappy with what you have found, we suggest the chapter on creative alternatives and possibilities.

Some of the more emotional issues related to sharing care are the topics of Part III, Staying in Touch with Your Child. If your child is yet to be born or less than a year old, we encourage you to read and consider our thoughts about taking time off around the period of the child's birth. The chapter describing differences in the ways that children react to being in the care of someone else should be useful to any parent about to employ child care for the first time. In that chapter we suggest sensible responses to those very natural feelings and behaviors. Finally, we recognize that some of you will feel guilty or anxious about sharing care. In the chapter on guilt and anxiety we explain the differences between those feelings, encourage you to face them directly, and recommend specific, concrete actions designed to help lessen your guilt or anxiety.

In Part IV, Building Partnerships, we discuss various ways to support and assist your provider in her efforts to do the best possible job of caring for your child. We also focus on the other half of the team, pointing to your provider's useful knowledge about children and child rearing and suggesting ways that you might approach her with questions. All of us have questions and concerns as our children go through the various stages of development. Having an experienced professional who knows your child and can answer your questions is a big help. Thinking through the partnership ahead of time is critical. Enduring a bad child care experience and having to start all over again in a different arrangement is very hard on any child and should be avoided if at all possible.

How to pay for child care and how much your provider needs in order to make a decent living are the topics of Part V, Economic Issues. These chapters explain which kinds of care are more and less expensive and what you get for your money in each kind. While we hope that you will not base your child care choice mainly on cost, we do understand that money is a key issue. We also cover tax refunds and subsidies for eligible families.

We believe that the quality of child care will show little improvement until parents like you understand what comprises quality care, then advocate loudly and impatiently for the investments that can bring about that quality. We hope that you will read Part VI, Advocacy, and join forces with millions of other parents in this country to take action in improving the quality of child care.

This guide includes the likes, dislikes, and biases we have gathered during twenty-five years of work in child care. Don't take our word as gospel! Discuss our ideas and recommendations with relatives and friends and especially with parents who have recently gone through the process of searching for good child care. Get their opinions about what kinds of care are the "best buys" *in your community*. And remember, you yourself must feel comfortable and be happy with the choice you make. Don't choose a program or person based only on someone else's say-so — make a decision that works for *you*.

2

What Are
the Options?

CHILD CARE comes in so many different shapes and sizes, it is easy at first to feel a little overwhelmed. It is natural to ask, "How will I ever be able to decide which option is right for my child and for me?" In this chapter we introduce you to the different kinds of care available in most communities. We hope that these brief descriptions help you to begin the process of selecting the one best suited to your family. Once you have sorted out the various options, you'll want to read on for more in-depth information about each type of care.

Every child is different, as is every family. These variations should be important considerations in making your choice of child care arrangement. One factor is personality: Is your child shy or outgoing? Does she demand attention all the time or find it easy to entertain herself? Is he constantly testing the boundaries of a situation or more likely to approach new experiences cautiously? Does he catch every cold that goes by or seem relatively immune to passing bugs? You know more about your child's characteristics than anyone else, so you should keep them in mind as you choose a child care arrangement.

Another factor to consider is what psychologists call developmental stage. The needs of infants and toddlers differ from those of preschoolers and school-age children. In describing the various options, we try to give you a sense of the kind of care that might provide the best fit from the developmental point of view. You should consider your child's present stage of development and what it will be when you want to start the care.

For instance, we believe that infants and toddlers develop best in small, intimate settings, whereas three- to five-year-olds are often ready to benefit from the social and educational opportunities available in larger groups.

An additional factor of importance to assess is whether your child requires special support. Children with life-threatening illnesses, developmental delays, and physical or mental impairments all need special care. Two federal acts — Individuals with Disabilities Education Act and Americans with Disabilities Act of 1990 — mandate that states and communities develop comprehensive, family-centered, community-based programs for young children who need special support. Many communities have a variety of providers trained to care for children with special needs. Because these are so diverse, a description of specialized programs is beyond the scope of this book. However, Appendix A contains a resource list that supplies examples of national organizations you may call to obtain further information about such services.

Then there are practical questions, such as cost, location, and hours of program operation, that you need to consider. We don't mean to minimize the importance of these realities, for they may determine your final decision, whether or not you want them to. But when you choose a program because it is in your price range or closer than others to your home or workplace, don't compromise on quality.

Full-time versus Part-time Care

To choose an appropriate child care arrangement you must first decide whether you want full-time or part-time care. Full-time care is usually considered to be for 35 hours or more a week, whereas part-time care might be limited to mornings, afternoons, or certain weekdays, typically for 10–25 hours each week. Perhaps you plan to begin with part-time care, then expand the number of hours as your child grows older and more accustomed to the new arrangement.

Like computer technology, home construction, sports, and many other fields, child care has its own specialized language. You have to learn this language to understand the options available to you. The following paragraphs list the most common child care terms you will hear used in your community, organized under the headings of full-time and part-time care.

Full-time Care

In this category you are likely to find *center-based care* for infants (0–18 months), toddlers (18–36 months), and preschoolers (3–5 years), and for children in the primary school grades (from 5 years of age through age 12). Some more specialized centers care for just one or two of these age groups, while others cater to all four.

Family child care homes and *group family child care homes* also offer full-time care for infants, toddlers, preschoolers, and school-age children. Again, there may be some specialization by age, although many family child care providers like to cover a range of ages in what some call cross-age or family groupings.

Another full-time option to consider is *care in your own home*. You can arrange for an *au pair* from a foreign country to stay with you or employ a *nanny* to come in each day to care for your child. Maybe you have a *relative* who is interested in looking after your child or children, either in her own home or in yours. Your parents, a sister, or other relative you like and trust may be available and interested in providing child care. Such an arrangement might meet your child care needs very comfortably.

Part-time Care

Perhaps you want a care arrangement for three days a week or every weekday morning. *Nursery schools* and *preschools* offer part-day programs, as do *parent cooperatives*. Although all *school-age child care* programs are part-time arrangements — because the children are in school the rest of the day — some may offer full-day care on certain school holidays. A public school system may offer *pre-kindergarten* (pre-K) and *kindergarten* programs for four- and five-year-olds that run for anywhere from two and a half to six hours per day during the school year. Because pre-kindergarten and Head Start programs are designed for low-income families, both have income-eligibility requirements.

Part-time care may also be provided in center settings, group family child care homes, and family child care homes that more typically cater to families requiring full-day care. And of course you may be able to find a relative willing to care for your child on less than a full-time basis. Most *Head Start* programs also provide part-time care (either three hours a day, five days a week, or four days a week from 9:00 A.M. to 3:00 P.M.), operating only during the regular public school year.

You may also want to combine two part-time arrangements to create full-day coverage. For instance, your child might attend kindergarten in the morning and go to a family child care provider in your neighborhood for the afternoon. This works well for many families, although we caution against using more than a couple of settings in a given day to reduce the stress on the child who has to readjust constantly to different environments and expectations.

Once you are familiar with the basic vocabulary of child care, you need to understand each type of care in a bit more depth. We have organized these descriptions under three main headings based on the location of the service: center-based care, care in someone else's home, and care in a child's own home.

Center-based Care

Center-based care is housed in a facility that may have been built specifically for child care or converted to that purpose from space originally designed for other uses. Such care is often provided in, for instance, church basements or annexes or in public school buildings. In our hometown, the county jail was converted into a child care facility at one point!

Child Care Centers

Child care centers, also called day care centers, can come in many different shapes and sizes. Small centers enroll anywhere from twelve to thirty-five children, medium-size centers serve thirty-five to sixty children, and large centers may have as many as several hundred children in attendance. All states have specific laws related to the operation of a child care center. Regulations prescribe group sizes, adult-to-child ratios, teacher/caregiver and administrator training, health and sanitary conditions, and so forth. These rules are particularly important for infant and toddler care, which should consist of small groups of children with a child-to-teacher ratio of no more than five children per adult, depending on the age and disposition of each child. (Infants, for example, should really be in groups of no more than three, or at most four, infants per adult caregiver.)

It is most important that the center you consider be regulated, but remember that regulations set only minimum standards. You are seeking high-quality care, which requires much more from center staff than simply complying with the minimal stipulations set by a state agency. (See Chapter 3 for a description of high-quality care.)

Child care centers are especially popular and successful with three-to five-year-old children, who really like to socialize with their peers and benefit from a stimulating child care environment. This is also true for most school-age children who, although they arrive at a center after having been in a classroom full of other students all day, may need the security of their own space and a quiet place in which to just "hang out" for a while.

Child care centers are financed in two ways, depending on whether or not they are established partly to generate profits for their owners.

Nonprofit centers are governed by a board of directors and run by an executive director hired by the board. The budget is designed so that fees cover the expenses of the program, and all money earned is used solely to benefit its children and staff. Nonprofit centers are most common in states whose regulations keep group sizes relatively small and require that caregivers have education and training beyond high school.

Proprietary or for-profit centers represent a fast-growing segment of the American child care system. Proprietary simply means that an owner (or owners) of a program wishes to realize a financial profit from running it. There are small and medium-size proprietary centers — mom-and-pop programs — many of which began as family child care homes. But more commonly proprietary child care refers to large national chains like KinderCare Learning Centers, La Petite Academy, Children's World Learning Centers, and Children's Discovery Centers, which are national corporations involving anywhere from two hundred to twelve hundred centers. Smaller regional chains, which operate anywhere from five to fifty centers, also exist. Some of these chains allow each center a certain amount of flexibility, while others require stricter adherence to company policies.

Church-based Centers

Many U.S. churches provide child care as a means of family support, either by offering child care programs themselves or by allowing nondenominational programs to use their space at a reduced rate or free of charge. These range from part- to full-time programs and care for children of all ages. A church-operated program usually includes religious instruction in its curriculum, whereas nondenominational programs contain no specific religious content. Some states exempt church-affiliated centers from regulations. Be aware of whether this gap exists in your state. Verify that the program you choose is of high quality and adheres to all state-mandated standards even if it is exempt from the licensing law.

Parent Cooperatives

These child care programs are usually referred to as parent cooperatives because they were started by parents who avail themselves of the programs and staff them, sometimes with additional hired personnel. Most parent cooperatives are half-day programs, but some offer full-day care as well. Children of all ages can attend parent cooperatives, but they most commonly include children between the ages of three and five. Because they rely on parents to help with the child care or administration of the program, the cooperatives can keep the costs of running the program somewhat lower than those of other centers. If you do not work outside the home or work only part time or have flexible hours, you might find this an especially appealing option. Because parents have a great deal of control over what goes on in such cooperatives, these programs tend to have a curriculum that is especially responsive to the interests and values of participating families and the local community. You are able to spend time working with your child in the group setting and to help govern the program. Remember, though, that this is a time-consuming option. Not only do you have to help in the classroom and with governance, but most of the time you are also the janitor or one of the maintenance crew!

Head Start

Head Start is a federally funded program for children from income-eligible families. To be income eligible to enroll a child in this program, a family must have an income below a certain level, which varies by state. However, a few places are available in each Head Start program for children with handicapping conditions and children who are not income eligible, so you might want to explore this option in your community.

The program, for which there is no fee, is designed to prepare children for primary school by helping the participants learn to socialize with their peers and increase their language and other school-readiness skills. Parent involvement is strongly encouraged. Although most Head Start programs offer only part-time care, this is soon likely to change to better meet the needs of low-income working parents. A small number of pilot Head Start programs offer care for infants and toddlers, an option that is expected to be available on a broader scale in the not too distant future.

Nursery Schools

In most states, nursery school programs operate for up to three hours per day for two to five mornings or afternoons per week. They are usually unregulated, though some states have voluntary nursery school registration. Like Head Start, nursery schools tend to be geared toward children between the ages of three and five. They are more academically oriented than most child care centers or family child care homes. Some nursery schools have extended day programs, for which most states require that they be licensed as child care centers or group family child care homes. If you choose a nanny or an au pair for your children (see below), you might also want to enroll them in a nursery school for a few mornings a week to accustom them to interacting with other children their own age. You could also combine nursery school with a family child care arrangement (described below) if the other children in your provider's group are not the same age as your child or if you feel that your child would benefit from experience with a more structured program than your regular provider offers.

Kindergarten

The term "kindergarten" generally refers to public or private school programs for five-year-old children. Some are half-day programs of two and a half to three hours each day, while others may run for up to six hours daily. All kindergarten programs follow the public school calendar, taking several week-long breaks during the school year and a couple of months' vacation during the summer. Today many kindergarten curricula have been accelerated to include instruction in reading and writing. Some five-year-old children are ready for this more academic orientation, but others are not. When selecting a kindergarten you must ascertain that the program adjusts to your child's level of development rather than expecting your child to meet an arbitrary standard.

Laboratory Schools

Some colleges and universities have "lab" schools on site. These differ from the on-site, employer-supported child care centers (described below) in that they involve teaching and observational research as well as providing child care. The ratio of adults to children tends to be very high, for many adults are involved in these programs, and many student interns participate for course credit. The curriculum in a lab school may be quite innovative, because new teaching and caregiving techniques are being tested for research purposes.

School-age Child Care (SACC)

Most school-age child care programs serve children between kindergarten and second or third grade age, although some enroll children up to twelve or fourteen years of age. They are usually open for an hour or two in the early mornings, for two to four hours after school, and on all the shorter school holidays. Some programs are set up like clubs, with organized activities in a few specific subjects. Other programs are less structured, but they include activities along with homework help and time to just hang out. School-age children, like children in any other age group, differ in their needs and interests. Some want to be able to choose among many activities and projects; some are heavily into sports; and others might simply want to spend time with friends or by themselves, reading a book. Each of these options should be available in a good SACC program.

Care in Someone Else's Home

Care in someone else's home has existed informally for a very long time. Most states issue regulations that cover this type of care, but much of the family-based child care offered in the United States today is still informal and unregulated. Those rules which are in place are designed to help both a child's family and the provider meet the health, safety, and educational needs of the child. Many states provide start-up money for the regulated family child care provider so that she can bring her home up to code and furnish it with the toys, cribs, and other child-related equipment needed to provide adequate care. Family-based child care providers who agree to meet state regulations in order to improve the quality of their care are able to take advantage of free or subsidized training and support.

Family Child Care: Single Provider

Family child care, or family day care, is one of the most popular options in our local communities. The family child care provider looks after a small number of children in her own home. Such homes are proprietary in the sense that they are small businesses owned and run by the main caregiver, usually for two to six children. Her charges may range in age, or they may all be the same age, depending on her preferences and the needs of the child care marketplace. Most family child care providers are required to meet the necessary criteria for an annual or biannual license or registration. As with centers, it is vital to make sure that family child care homes fulfill, and preferably exceed, these regulations, since they are minimum standards at best. In any state, be certain that your provider has first-aid training, follows basic guidelines for child health and nutrition, has plenty of experience with young children, is knowledgeable about child development, has great references, and cares for children in a safe building with easily accessible exits, guarded windows and stairs, and other safety features (see Chapter 5).

Family child care providers are usually flexible, possibly offering a variety of options for both part- and full-time care. Perhaps you need overnight care or care in the early morning hours; maybe you want an arrangement for every other day of the week or only on alternate weeks; or your work schedule may be such that you need care on weekend days or in the evenings. Family child care providers are more willing and able than centers to meet the demands imposed by odd-hour work schedules.

Some children are especially apt to benefit from being in the smaller, more intimate setting provided by a family child care home. Infants and toddlers, children easily overwhelmed in larger groups, and those especially susceptible to infectious deceases may thrive in an environment that includes only four or five other children. In most states a provider who cares for only one or two unrelated children is exempt from becoming licensed or registered. Again, however, you should seek a provider who voluntarily follows the regulatory standards even though she is not compelled to do so by law.

Group Family Child Care: Two or More Providers

The group family child care home is an option that has developed in many states just within the past five years. Although similar in many ways to family child care, this arrangement involves a larger number of children and more than one caregiver. Group family child care, which is regulated in most states, is more likely to be monitored than the single provider home, because the larger number of children involved makes it more visible.

Care is usually provided for up to twelve children in the main provider's home. She hires one or two assistants to work with her when she has more than six children in her care. Group family child care homes and small owner-run centers are similar in some respects, although regulations tend to be more stringent when a program is designated as a center. Because group family child care is always administered in the caregiver's home, whereas small centers are housed in separate buildings, the former has a more relaxed atmosphere. Group care homes also retain some of the flexibility of single-provider homes, especially in terms of the age range served and the provision of full- or part-time care. Representing a compromise between the small family child care home and the larger center, a good group family child care home offers some of the best of both those worlds.

Relative Care

Having a relative care for your child has traditionally been a common solution to the child care dilemmas faced by many families. In this arrangement a child is cared for by his other parent, grandparents, aunts and uncles, cousins, older siblings, or other relatives while one or both parents are working or at school. Parents who work different shifts can take turns looking after their own children. When both parents work the same or similar hours, they may turn to a relative living in the same community for assistance with child care. In families with several children of different ages, an older sibling might provide for a younger brother or sister after school or during short school holidays. Many parents find it comforting to know that someone in the extended family is taking care of their child while they are away from home. They know what their relatives value, and may have watched them raise their own children. They feel secure in knowing that their relatives are like themselves in important ways.

Care in Your Own Home

Like center-based care, in-home arrangements can take a wide variety of forms. You might want to engage an au pair from abroad to live with your family and provide child care for a year. Another option is a nanny, who can either live with you or come in every day to look after your child or children. Still another possibility, mentioned earlier but not usually included in this category, is the in-home child care provided when parents take turns looking after their children. The mother might work an evening shift as a nurse's aide at a hospital and care for the children during the day, while the father, who works the early afternoon shift as the maintenance person at the local school, is the primary caregiver when his spouse is at work. The relative who comes to your home to help look after your child for all or part of a day or week while you are on the job or asleep after working the night shift is also an in-home provider.

Au Pair

The French au pair (literally "at equal" and popularly translated as "family member") — a foreign student who lives with a family and helps with child care while learning something of its culture and language — has long been a fixture in Europe. This system of acquiring a baby sitter in exchange for room, board, and a small weekly stipend, introduced to the United States in the 1960s, has become a fast-growing business. As parent and employer, you contract with an agency to hire an au pair who lives with you for up to one year. You provide a private bedroom, a work week of forty-five or fewer hours, weekly compensation of $100 to $150, and an opportunity for the young person to take at least two college-level courses.

Infants and toddlers can derive much benefit from the personal attention they might receive from an in-home caregiver. We stress "might" because you can't assume that an au pair will be a skilled caregiver. If you have a number of preschool-age children and a spare bedroom, you might also find that having an au pair stay with your family is less expensive than paying child care center fees for several children. We address all these issues more fully in Chapter 8.

Nanny

When we hear the word *nanny,* most of us think of a Mary Poppins–type figure in a starched white uniform, but in the real world, Mary Poppinses are few and far between. The term "nanny" is currently used to mean a person, usually a woman, who comes to your home to take care of your child or children. Some families offer their nannies room and board as well as weekly wages, while others prefer that she arrive every morning and leave at the end of the day. A nanny expects her main duties to be taking care of the children and doing the light housekeeping related to their care.

An American nanny may or may not have been educated or trained in child development, early childhood education, or child care, although that likelihood is greater than for an au pair. An American Council of Nanny Schools accredits nanny training programs, allowing the administrators to present a professional certificate to the nannies they train. (See Chapter 8 for more information about nannies and nanny schools.)

Other Program Categories

As you begin to talk with child care experts in your local community and read program descriptions, you will run across other labels for programs. For instance, your employer or other employers in your area may be directly involved with child care. The school system may sponsor programs for children younger than kindergarten age. And you will come across preschools, with names like Montessori, Waldorf, or High/Scope, which are organized around a specific educational theory or approach.

Employer-supported or -sponsored Child Care

Some employers accommodate their employees by providing a child care center at the work site. Others provide parents with a voucher to pay for child care elsewhere in the community or pay directly for space in a center or child care home selected by their employees. On-site programs generally offer full-time care for infants and toddlers, because many parents feel that they want to be near their very young child. It is nice to be able to visit your infant during the working day, and the availability of an on-site center may make it possible for a mother to continue nursing her child longer than would otherwise be possible. Most on-site programs also offer full-time care for three- to five-year-old children as well as school-age child care.

If you want your children to be close by so that you can visit them during your lunch hour or break, the on-site or near-site child care option is a great choice. However, if you have a long commute on public transportation or in an unreliable car, or feel more comfortable leaving your child at a neighborhood center or family child care provider, the voucher program will work better for you. Unfortunately, only a small number of employers sponsor child care options, but the available evidence suggests that for those who do, it is a sound business investment.

Pre-kindergarten or Pre-K Programs

The term "pre-K," or "pre-kindergarten," has two well-defined but separate meanings: One pre-K reference is to a part of the public school system, the year or grade before kindergarten. In a growing number of states, the departments of education have initiated pre-kindergarten programs in public schools serving disadvantaged children. Some of those states blend the pre-K programs with the Head Start programs at the local level.

The other pre-K refers to an age range or program in a child care center, ordinarily three-, four-, and five-year-olds as distinguished from infant/toddler groups. The latter include children from just a few weeks old to their third birthday.

High/Scope

When you decide to visit child care centers or preschools, you may hear talk about the High/Scope curriculum. Developed in the 1960s by David Weikart and his colleagues at the Perry Pre-school Program in Ypsilanti, Michigan, it has been continually refined over the past thirty years. Many teachers and caregivers across the country have been trained to use it in their schools and centers. In programs taking the High/Scope approach, you will notice that the rooms are organized with various learning centers. The children are encouraged to plan their activities together with their teachers, who also follow up with each child at the end of an activity. The children in High/Scope-inspired programs go through a process of "plan, do, and review," spending a lot of time interacting with the other children and with the materials around them. One major goal of the program is to enhance the children's critical thinking skills. The High/Scope curriculum, which is aimed at the three- to five-year-old child, is well suited to the developmental stages of that age group.

Montessori School

U.S. Montessori schools vary a great deal depending on the education of their teachers and the adaptations they may have drawn from other educational philosophies. These schools took their names from Maria Montessori, an Italian physician who started working with children from the slums in Rome in the early 1900s. Most Montessori schools have a few distinct elements in common: they use Montessori materials, which are beautifully crafted and self-correcting so that the children know immediately whether they have succeeded with their task; the children work by themselves — or occasionally with a partner — and at their own pace; the materials are displayed on low shelves, making it easy for the children to get their own materials as well as to clean up when they finish an activity; and the teachers guide the children toward the materials that are appropriate for each one's level of development.

Strict Montessori programs have been criticized for not building in enough interaction between the children and between the children and their teachers, which in turn may result in a less than optimal amount of language stimulation. Montessori programs sometimes also lack outdoor curricula, experiences with the creative arts, and block building, all of which are included in most high-quality early childhood programs today. Reserved or shy children may find it difficult to develop relationships with their peers in this type of a program, because there are few natural avenues for interaction. Many Montessori programs have adapted the strict curriculum to compensate for some of these shortcomings.

Waldorf Schools or Programs

The U.S. Waldorf Schools or programs are part of an international Waldorf movement whose curriculum is based on the teachings of Rudolf Steiner, an early 1900s German educator. The curriculum, which emphasizes the creative arts, employs fairy tales as a significant teaching tool, underscores the importance of community, and fosters respect for each person's individual needs. Waldorf teachers tend to stay with the same group of children throughout their early childhood years. Steiner stressed that the child care environment should be an extension of the child's home; uncluttered, aesthetically pleasing, warm and inviting, and filled with objects the children can manipulate and use to create their own pretend family life. Waldorf programs require strong family participation. If you decide to consider one, allow enough time to visit and observe to ensure that you understand and are comfortable with this unique program philosophy.

*   *   *

You can see from these summary descriptions that child care comes in many different shapes and sizes. To choose among the options, you must begin by figuring out whether you require full- or part-time child care. Then decide whether you prefer care in a center or in a home setting, yours or someone else's. The third step is to learn as much as you can about what constitutes quality care so that you can find a child care program that will provide a really beneficial experience for your child. Quality is the topic of Chapter 3.

3

What Is
Quality Care?

NOW THAT YOU HAVE a feel for the kinds of child care available in most communities, you may be eager to get out into your own area and start shopping around. Please read this chapter before taking that next step.

In order to make a wise child care choice, you need a good idea of what comprises quality care, wherever it appears. The basic elements of quality child care are as important for centers and family child care as they are for care provided in your own home.

To introduce quality care, we start you off with a visit to a family child care home owned and run by Mrs. Ann Jones.

You ring the doorbell, a little nervous because this is your first visit to a family child care provider in her home. You talked to Ann Jones over the phone after you got her name from a friend, then made arrangements to take your three-year-old daughter to Ann's house for a visit this morning. You ring the bell again, and again. The door is finally opened by a smiling woman who says, "You must be Mary Peters, and is this little Sarah? Please come in." She explains that she is in the kitchen/dining area helping the children grind flour for the bread they are going to make that morning. Kneeling to Sarah's level as she speaks to you, Ann asks whether Sarah wants to have a look at what they are doing. Sarah hides behind your legs. Ann looks at her, back at you, smiles, and invites both of you into her kitchen, where three children are grinding flour and a fourth is sitting at a table cutting the pages of a magazine into tiny pieces.

Ann tells you to make yourselves comfortable and to feel free to wander around any part of the house that is used for child care. She says that she wants to continue to work on the bread baking and that you can join in any time you want to do so. The kitchen is bright and friendly, with children's pictures hanging on a clothesline across one side of the room. The furniture is a mix of adult-size and child-size chairs and tables. It is clear that this is a room where a family lives, not just a room for child care.

As you first walk around, Sarah is attached to your pants. But slowly she gets used to the environment and begins to show interest in the children's books that she finds in a bookcase. She picks out a book and asks you to read it to her. Ann notices and comments that this is one of her favorite books. Sarah looks at her and then at the book.

After a while it feels perfectly all right to walk around in Ann's house. Sarah is moving closer and closer to where the bread is being kneaded on the low table. Two hours after your arrival, Sarah is covered with flour, playing with the other children. You have watched Ann hug a child who stubbed his toe, read a book to one of the three-year-old boys, and been pleased to see Ann wash her hands after a toilet visit with another child. As you prepare to leave, Ann says, "Please call me tonight so we can talk. I need to give my attention to the children now, but I'll answer any questions you might have when you call later." Sarah reluctantly leaves the table where she has been eating freshly baked buns. Ann kneels to look her in the eyes, and they discuss the possibility of Sarah's coming back for another visit. When you leave, you feel as if you and Sarah have known Ann all your lives and that you'd love to be a part of her "extended family."

Imagine that you have just finished that visit with Ann Jones and the four children in her care. What was it that gave you a positive feeling about the experience? Was it that Ann so obviously cared about children? She immediately got down to Sarah's level and showed her respect for the child as a person with a mind of her own. Maybe you liked the way that she encouraged you to look around and didn't seem to be hiding anything. Perhaps you were attracted by the busyness of the children and the fact that they had the freedom to choose different activities. Clearly Ann took her work as a child care provider very seriously, and the children were her highest priority.

The concept of quality care can be viewed from many different angles. But experts agree that quality is not limited to one particular type of setting or another. Ann was a good provider not because she was providing child care in her own home, but because she interacted with the children and organized her environment to support that interaction. Quality of care is not related to *where* the care is offered, but to *how* it is offered. Of course, high-quality care cannot take place in a dirty environment in which the equipment is in poor repair, toys are scarce, and space is cramped or unsafe. But at the same time, poor-quality care can be, and too often is, delivered in beautifully designed settings with all the toys and materials a child could ever wish for.

Our definition of quality blends what researchers, child care providers, and other parents have learned with a solid dose of common sense drawn from our many years of personal and professional experience related to both child development and child care. Searching for the best way to explain the meaning of "quality," we found ourselves returning to four basic words and phrases: "caring," "tuned-in," "respectful," and "safe." With those ideas in mind, turn on your imagination again and pretend that you and your wife are expecting a baby in a couple of months. The two of you have taken the morning off from work to go to the new child care center downtown. All your friends have urged you to arrange for child care long before your baby is due. So here you are, eight weeks ahead of time, ready to enroll your unborn child!

Last week you called the local child care resource and referral agency after finding its number in the Yellow Pages *under "Day Care: Referrals." The person you talked to said that she'd send you a computer printout of the child care centers in your area that provide care for infants. When you received the list in the mail a couple of days ago, you found that only two centers in your town take care of infants. You also received a pamphlet printed by your state department of social services, which gave you a list of questions to ask a new child care provider, as well as elements to look for in the environment when you visit a center.*

With these lists in hand the two of you find yourselves in the infant room at the ABC Children's Center, where there are two caregivers present. You can see five babies and hear at least two more. Two children are in wind-up swings, two in walkers, and one is having her diaper changed by a caregiver. You guess that at least a couple of babies, whose voices you hear, are in the cribs you see at the other end of the room.

One caregiver comes up to you, introduces herself as Sally, and offers to show you around the room. Sally shows you the charts on which they record the times the children eat and have their diapers changed as well as how long they sleep. As you listen to Sally, the other caregiver finishes diapering one baby and turns to pick up another without first washing her hands. Sally takes you over to the cribs, where you find not two but five more babies, three sleeping and the other two voicing their discontent.

She tells you that the crying babies have been spoiled by their parents and are learning to go to sleep on a schedule. As you walk by the swings she winds both of them up again. A tiny baby is asleep in one swing, and in the other a somewhat older infant is sitting with a blanket and pacifier. This baby reaches up her arms as Sally winds up her swing, but her gesture goes unnoticed. The baby reacts by sucking harder on her pacifier and looking vaguely around at her surroundings.

You spend half an hour in the infant room. During that whole period, Sally spends most of her time following you around, almost too eager to answer your questions. When you leave the center both of you have an uneasy feeling, wondering if this is really the right place for your baby.

You left *this* center feeling uncomfortable and trying to put your finger on just what made you feel that way. After visiting Ann Jones you had a good feeling. What made the difference?

Again, we want to emphasize that the differences in quality between these two settings were not caused by one's being home-based and the other's being in a center. The differences had to do with those key words we flagged earlier: "caring," "tuned-in," "respectful," and "safe." Ten babies with two caregivers, one of whom wasn't paying attention to the children, didn't add up to personalized caring. The adults weren't tuning in to each individual infant — with ten babies to look after they couldn't afford to attend closely to any one of them. Forcing two babies to "learn to go to sleep on a schedule" wasn't respecting each individual child, but instead was making the infants conform to the needs of their caregivers. Ignoring the outstretched arms of a baby who wants to be picked up is not tuning in. Safety was being compromised when a caregiver failed to wash her hands after changing a diaper.

Your intuitive feelings of comfort and discomfort are most important. We want you to listen to what your gut feelings tell you. But our job is also to help you turn those feelings into observable facts, things you can point to and talk about specifically. You need to be able to pinpoint what you like and dislike about the child care providers and programs you visit so that you can make informed choices and advocate for high-quality care.

Caring, tuned-in, respectful, and safe summarize all the little things the two of us look for as we observe a caregiver's interaction with a child. For us, *the caregiver/teacher is the key to the quality of care.* If the caregiver isn't able to convince us that she is a caring person tuned in to each child's needs and desires, if she doesn't show respect toward the children, the parents, and the other adults around her, if she cannot demonstrate that she provides the children with a safe and secure environment, if she doesn't offer interesting play materials and experiences, we conclude that she is not furnishing high-quality child care.

All these concepts are closely related. We find it hard to rate one ahead of the other because all are equally important aspects of quality. Demonstrating each of them requires feelings and instincts as well as learned information about how children grow and develop. In our experience, actions speak louder than words. Sometimes caregivers say one thing while doing something quite different — their habits contradict what they have been taught to say. The caregiver or teacher who says repeatedly that she loves children ("Aren't they all little darlings!"), then pushes a child roughly into her cubby with the announcement that "she is a bad girl and has to stay in there until she can be nice again" is not the person we would recommend to anyone as a child care provider.

Caring and Tuned-In

These two qualities work in harmony with each other. The caring and tuned-in provider is a person who

- is listening to, and aware of, a child's verbal and nonverbal communications;
- watches for clues to how a child feels and picks up on those clues as she interacts with the child;
- really attends to the children constantly without spending time chatting with other adults about last night's TV program.

The tuned-in, caring teacher/provider is not afraid to show physical and verbal affection, but isn't overly effusive about it. With one child in her arms, she listens carefully to a second, who is tugging at her sleeve with a question. At the same time she is watching a third child struggle to put on some dress-up clothes, ready to assist if the task becomes too frustrating. This person doesn't need to tell you she really likes children, because her feelings are reflected in every move. Her warmth is obvious, and she spends most of her time directly interacting with the children in a meaningful way.

Respectful

Many adults do not respect young children. They are not particularly interested in children, which shows in their tendency to ignore the young people's ideas and treat them as mindless objects. Unfortunately, there are people working in the child care profession who fit into this category.

The traditional assumption has been that all women love children and that they all have the "natural" ability to be good child care providers. Neither of these myths is true. Even women and men who do love children may have neither the patience nor the skills to become great early childhood teachers and caregivers. (We two love music, but neither of us is a good musician.) As is true in any profession, some people have much more aptitude than others for work with young children.

The capacity to really listen to very young children and to understand what they are trying to express is central to showing respect for them. Listening and responding sensitively shows consideration for the feelings and needs of children, who feel valued by this kind of undivided attention.

A respectful caregiver values the input of children, is considerate of their feelings, and demonstrates her high regard for them through her warm and affectionate manner. Teachers and caregivers who can appreciate children in these ways often show the same amount of respect toward the parents and coworkers with whom they interact daily.

Safe and Secure

Everyone agrees that safety and security are the foundations of high-quality care. Your child has to *be* safe (physical safety) as well as *feel* safe (emotional safety), both with the caregiver or teacher and in the child care environment.

All rooms must be clean, uncluttered, and free of hazards like uncovered electrical outlets and poisonous chemicals. Furniture, materials, and toys should be age-appropriate. For example, the toys within reach of infants and toddlers, who put everything in their mouths, must be large enough so that the children cannot choke on them.

The outdoor environment has to be inviting and secure as well. This means safe, easily accessible, and age-appropriate outdoor equipment, and lots of space for running and other large motor activities. No broken toys or hazardous trash should be in the play area. In some neighborhoods this requires great vigilance on the part of staff, because bottles, old newspapers, and other debris are tossed into the yard every night. The play area must be enclosed, either by a fence or a natural border of some kind. The outdoor space should be designed so that the supervising teacher or caregiver can observe all the children at all times to make sure they are safe.

Emotional safety is more difficult to observe during a short visit. Emotionally safe children dare to explore and try out new things. They are spontaneously affectionate with their caregivers and each other. If they do something that is forbidden, they don't hesitate to admit it and accept the consequences. In these ways the children show trust and confidence in the fact that the caregivers or teachers are really concerned about them and can help them through the day in a caring, affectionate fashion.

Any discussion of safety as a dimension of quality must include the issue of child abuse and maltreatment. A few highly publicized cases of suspected child abuse in child care settings have inflamed public opinion. The fact is that children are comparatively safe in child care settings. About 90 percent of child maltreatment incidents are caused by parents and other relatives, whereas only about one percent are caused by other caregivers. The best way to protect your child is to make unannounced visits to the program he attends. A high-quality group program encourages unannounced visits at any time. If a child care provider does not agree to your doing so, remove your child from the program. Even if you decide on a care arrangement in your own home, it is wise to drop in unannounced occasionally, just to indicate how important your child's care and welfare are to you. *All* care should be monitored in these ways. In addition, you need to tune in to your child's feelings and moods on the way to and from child care to be as aware as possible of how emotionally safe your child is feeling in the child care arrangement you select. We will return to this issue in later chapters.

Continuity of Care

A high-quality child care program provides your child with the same caregiver over a substantial period of time. You should strive to ensure that your child has the same adult primary caregiver for at least a year at a time. Transitions from one age group to another are normal in a child care center, usually involving a shift from one primary caregiver or teacher to another. These changes can be anticipated, and their impact reduced through good preparation. But abrupt changes owing to resignation or termination of a child care provider are different, and far more disruptive. Ideally, a good center should be able to employ staff who remain with the program for at least a couple of years at a time.

When your child experiences a caring, tuned-in, respectful caregiver, she will form an emotional attachment to that person, which is very healthy, and important for further development. (See Chapter 11 for more discussion of why such "secondary" attachments are good.) Each time an attachment is formed and broken, there is emotional pain and a feeling of loss. This discomfort makes it a little harder for your child to take the risk involved in trusting the next person hired to care for her. So a center where caregivers and teachers continue to work with the program over a number of years provides higher-quality care — *other things being equal* — than one in which teachers seem to be rotating in and out every six months or so.

High turnover is a symptom of underlying stresses and strains. Salaries may be so low that teachers leave the moment a better-paying position opens up elsewhere. The director may be unpleasant to work with, causing teachers to quit. Whatever the cause, high turnover rates signal unpredictable and frequently low-quality care and should prompt you to look for more desirable alternatives.

In the case of family child care providers and those offering care in your own home, primary prevention in the beginning goes far in avoiding turnover later on. The extra time invested in being confident that you have found the right person initially, and receiving assurance that she plans to be a care provider for at least the next year, pays dividends later in continuity and emotional stability for everyone involved.

Minimum Standards: Not Enough!

Most state and local regulations establish a *minimum* standard for full-day centers and family child care homes with more than two children unrelated to the provider. *If* your child is in a state or locally regulated program, those rules address some of the most basic aspects of the issues discussed above. But this minimum standard for child care does not result in quality care as we have defined it. It simply provides a steppingstone in that direction.

Child care provided in your own home is not regulated by any state or local agencies, except in special cases involving an au pair. Most nursery school programs, many church-operated programs, and some school-age child care programs cannot be regulated, even if they want to be. Many states have simply not developed regulations for those groups.

If you have an opportunity to look over the child care regulations in your locale — each licensed program and your local resource and referral agency should have copies — notice that attention is paid primarily to the physical layout of the facility. There is very little in the regulations about program content or teacher and caregiver behavior.

So be careful! Be sure that your program or provider is regulated if that is the law of your state, but remember that this means only minimum standards. Once a program has been licensed, follow-up inspections are rare, sometimes occurring only once every two or three years. In the case of family child care providers, there may well be no follow-up checks at all. So it is up to you, as caring and responsible parents, to support and monitor your child's program and staff and help to make certain that they meet and exceed these minimum standards.

Other Predictors of Quality

In the past ten years, several significant studies have been conducted to better understand what aspects of a child care program lead to the provision of quality care.[1] These studies have identified the threads that hold the tapestry of care together in ways that result in healthy, happy children and families.

The most important quality indicators identified in these studies are related directly to the people who take care of your child. The findings confirm our own experiences, as described earlier. The education and training of staff, the number of children for whom each caregiver is responsible — staff-to-child ratio — the ability of staff to build team relationships with parents, and the capacity of staff members to develop a child-centered program in a stimulating environment are all closely interrelated indicators of quality identified in this research. We discuss each of these factors more fully in the chapters on center and family child care. You will see that we have tried to capture these important dimensions of care in the checklists and interview guides included in later chapters.

An additional quality factor to consider is the total size of a group for which one person or a team of caregivers or teachers is responsible. Very young children don't do well in large groups. They are easily confused by all the different faces and activities and feel lost. The National Association for the Education of Young Children, which works to improve early childhood programs nationwide, recommends that no more than twenty three- to five-year-old children be included in the same group, no matter how many adults are involved. The recommended maximum group size for infants through seventeen months old is six to eight children and for toddlers, eighteen to thirty-six months, it is ten to twelve children.

We believe that the educational level of a teacher or caregiver has been given too little attention in discussions of standards for quality care. Every other profession has set educational criteria for its members, so why shouldn't this be the case with child care and early education? By educational level we don't simply mean the number of years of schooling attended beyond high school. The studies show that more education makes *little difference unless the courses relate to working directly with young children.*

The more child-related knowledge a practitioner has, the better she can perform her job. Experience also plays a role, but it has to be the right kind of practice, that is, carried out under the watchful eye of an experienced mentor or supervisor. The fact that someone has been a wonderful parent to three children, and used to baby-sit the neighbors' kids now and then, doesn't mean that she will be a good child care provider. Taking care of your own children is much different from taking care of other people's children. Baby-sitting occasionally is quite different from running a child care business in your own home or taking care of a group of children in a center setting.

Research shows that caregivers with many years of experience tend to provide less stimulating care if they have not also had specialized education and training. This may be because relatively untrained caregivers, who have been providers for many years, feel that they know all there is to know, so they don't take advantage of new training opportunities. Certainly early childhood educators and caregivers have developed greater professional awareness in the past ten or fifteen years, which probably means that people coming into the field more recently are likely to have taken education and training more seriously.

Early childhood practitioners who make the effort to obtain more education usually do so because they view working with young children as a stimulating and enjoyable occupation. The result is that they are "intentional" about their work, providing stimulating, responsive, positive, and informative care to children. They are not satisfied with simply hugging and holding the children, nor do they feel the need to direct and control them all the time. They are intentional in what they do, planning for the individual needs of children and responding to their expressions of interest and concern.

Caregivers and teachers must have had first-aid training in order to know how to respond to illness or injury. Most communities offer this and many other kinds of instruction through a variety of child care training workshops and vocational or college courses for early childhood professionals. Community colleges across the country are working hard to improve their early childhood degree programs, to meet the growing need for well-educated child care providers and teachers. Teachers attending these workshops and courses tell us how much more fulfilling and fun their job is when they know more about how children grow and develop. This knowledge helps them plan engaging activities and organize a stimulating environment for the children in their care.

Research studies have also found that caregivers and teachers who belong to professional organizations or spend significant amounts of time with others in the early childhood profession tend to provide higher-quality care than those who do not participate in such professional exchanges.[2] Again, this make sense. A provider who makes an extra effort to attend professional meetings and meet with colleagues after working hours is usually open to gaining new knowledge and eager to be seen as a person with high professional standards and goals.

A Quality Environment

When thinking about quality as it relates to the physical environment, the first point we stress is that it is not the amount of space or the number of toys available that matters, though most licensing regulations specify a minimum amount of space per child in a group program. Of most importance is the organization and use of available space and the quality of the toys and materials on hand. A quality environment is a safe environment that is organized into learning areas where the children can occupy themselves for long or short periods of time. Materials should be easily accessible and arranged so that children can return them to their proper place after use. An environment of high-quality materials and decorations offers positive images of different racial and ethnic groups and multifaceted roles for both women and men.

What Is the Curriculum?

You may wonder what child care people mean when they talk about the curriculum. This is a common question, especially from parents with a young infant, who naturally think in terms of finding a warm, caring mother substitute to take charge of their child while they are at work. The word *curriculum* suggests a lesson plan, but of course your baby is neither going to school nor taking lessons in anything. Curriculum is simply an academic term to describe what caregivers and teachers do with children throughout the day. We like the word because it communicates the very important idea that there is more to infant care than changing diapers and feeding and burping babies, and more to child care at any age than providing food and shelter and clean clothes. We now know that children who are responded to and appropriately stimulated as they grow up become curious and engaging adults.

This is the "curriculum" for infants — caregivers who know enough about infant development to attend to a child's intellectual needs as well as to his physical and emotional requirements. The infant curriculum involves talking to, reading to, and singing to a child and taking him on little excursions around the room, the building, and the yard or neighborhood. Skilled caregivers know that an infant needs to be on her stomach on the floor to strengthen her muscles, that she should not sit in an infant seat or swing for long periods of time or be placed in front of a TV set, and that she should be held and cuddled while she is being fed. A good early childhood education or training program will have taught all these things to your caregiver.

Equally important developmental issues most be considered in planning a curriculum for toddlers, preschoolers, and school-age children. At all age levels, the more the caregivers and teachers know about how children grow and develop, the more likely they are to create a program responsive to the needs of the children in their care.

Teachers and caregivers with a solid background in early childhood education commonly wish to share their curriculum ideas and plans with parents. They are quick to notice your child's special interests, and they develop their educational plans around these interests. Caregivers who come into your home should plan their days just as thoughtfully and carefully as those in centers, nursery schools, and family child care homes.

Race, Culture, and Language

In a high-quality child care program you will find providers working with all children in ways that promote positive self-esteem and personal identity. These characteristics are rooted partly in the racial, cultural, and language experiences that surround young children: in your own families, among your relatives, friends, and neighbors — your networks — and in your neighborhoods. Good child care providers appreciate and reflect the wide variety among these racial, cultural, and language experiences, and foster the healthy development of children from many different backgrounds. A study of how child care programs can support and prepare children and families for a diverse society, conducted by an organization called California Tomorrow, identified five basic principles of quality care in a diverse society.

- One: Combat racism and foster positive racial identity in young children.
- Two: Build upon the cultures of families and promote respect and cross-cultural understanding among children.
- Three: Preserve children's family languages and encourage all children to learn a second language.

• Four: Work in partnership with parents to respond to issues of race, language, and culture.
• Five: Engage in dialogue and reflection about race, culture, and language on an ongoing basis.[3]

These principles are ideals that may not be easy to achieve in child care settings, but many of them can be addressed through education and training. Caregivers can learn how to combat racism, foster racial awareness, build upon the cultures represented in the program, and engage in dialogue and reflection about race, culture, and language. Preserving language other than English and teaching a second language requires hiring teachers and caregivers who possess those second language skills and the knowledge to pass them along to young children. A partnership with you, the parent, can be quite valuable in this regard, because you are a potential source of cultural information and language instruction. A child care program of high quality should employ staff who think about these issues and seek ways to address them in practice.

Parents and Providers as Partners

The final indication of a high-quality program is parents and caregivers and teachers working as partners to meet the needs of children.

A partnership is a two-way street that cuts across all types of care. Half the burden for a successful partnership falls on you, a parent who wants the best for your child. Until now we have described your role as primarily one of monitoring and support, assisting your caregiver as she works to create a safe and inspiring environment, takes advantage of educational opportunities, and provides your child with a stimulating curriculum. Here we urge a more active effort — you must go out of your way to know your child's caregiver and to establish a working relationship with her. She should be open to your interest in doing this and help in creating opportunities for relationship building.

A partnership is a relationship of equals — you and your child's caregivers and teachers — all of whom care deeply about your child and want him to have the best possible experiences while growing up. Each of you has a lot at stake, and all bring to the partnership valuable information about how to care for your child in the best possible fashion. The more you support one another in these efforts, the better the results for your child. Home visits by the teacher or caregiver, opportunities for you to observe your child with the caregiver and other children, chances to discuss the child's progress at formal conferences and informal moments at the beginning and end of the day, are the components of a healthy partnership. They result in a continuity of care between you and your caregiver that provides security for your child, helping him to feel comfortable in child care because he can sense that his parent is comfortable with this other important person in his life.

How to Locate Care

T THIS POINT you should have some idea of whether you want full- or part-time care for your child. You probably also have beginning thoughts about whether family child care, center care, or an arrangement in your own home makes the most sense for you. Chapters 5 through 10 provide you with additional detail about what to expect in each of these care categories. But you also need general information about how to search for care providers in your local community, regardless of what kind of care interests you.

Search Strategies

When thinking about finding care, keep in mind that available search strategies range from *very informal* — ask your sister or your neighbor — to *relatively formal* — set up an appointment to consult with a resource and referral counselor at your local child care council. Both approaches are valuable, and we recommend that you use both at the same time. Your goal is to find as many options as possible of the type of care that interests you most — providers in your own home, family child care settings, or center settings — so that you can check them out and choose the one that best meets your needs.

Informal Approaches

The most informal sources of information about possible care settings or providers are your relatives, neighbors, friends, and coworkers. Some of these people might be willing to provide care themselves, either in your home or in theirs. But they are just as important as sources of information about the care provided in the area and the experiences, good and bad, they and others have had with various programs and the people providing that care. The trick is to spread the word that you are searching for care as widely as possible.

If you like the idea of having a relative or friend look after your child, turn to Chapter 10 to read about creative ways to discover that person and get her involved. However, if you simply want to know more about child care programs and providers already available in your local area, here are some simple steps to follow.

1. Make a list of everybody you can think of who might have information about child care possibilities. Start with your relatives. Do your parents live in the area? What about sisters or brothers? How about cousins or aunts and uncles? Have any of these people had experience with child care in the area, *or would they know people who have had such experience?*

   Now go through the same process with your friends. Remember that they don't necessarily have to be *close* friends. Maybe you can think of someone with whom you went to high school who now has young kids and works outside the home. Think about friends at work, people you met at a birthing class, and college roommates. Perhaps you attend a religious institution in the area and have met people there who might have some ideas. Your husband, wife, or partner (if you have one) should join this brainstorming process. Finally, think about the people who live close by. Have you seen other parents with young children? Is there a house in the neighborhood with many playthings in the yard where someone may already be looking after children?

2. Put an asterisk beside the names of those on your list whose judgment you trust the most and a check mark beside those in your area who you think have had the most experience with child care.

3. Telephone the people with either a check mark or an asterisk beside their names. Those with both should be especially useful. Ask them the following questions:

   • What do you think is the best kind of child care in the area for children the age of my child?
   • Can you recommend a particular provider or program? Why do you think it would be a good choice?

• Who else in the area should I talk to about child care possibilities?

This last question is very important because it can lead you to possibilities outside your immediate circle of relatives and friends.

Another way to find out who looks after children in your neighborhood or local area is to keep an eye out for "Will care for children in my home" flyers in a nearby laundromat, grocery store, library, community center, or YWCA — wherever there might be a community bulletin board. Your daily or weekly newspaper is also likely to advertise child care. Recent examples from our daily, listed under "Day Care," included

• IACC is NY's longest operating daycare center. Openings now available. Convenient downtown location. Visitors welcome. Phone [number].

• Little Feet Montessori daycare center. NYS licensed. Near major employers. Now enrolling. Full- and part-time openings. Phone [number].

• Serving children 6 wks–5 yrs since 1979. *Mother* of one & a nurse. I would like to do daycare in my home. Dryden-Freeville area. Phone [number].

Small local advertisement newspapers, with titles like *Pennysaver*, are another possibility. They frequently run ads for under $10, making them affordable to small-scale child care providers. The following appeared in our most recent issue, again listed under "Day Care."

• Kozy Kids Daycare: 1–5 years, after-school openings. Licensed, structured environment, meals, references. Reasonable rates. Phone [number].

• Former Nanny, mother of 2, will babysit in my home, 7 am to 6 pm. $55.00 per week for first child; $12.00 each additional child. Village of Enfield. References. Ask for Marcia. Phone [number].

The ad following those, with no new heading, read "Reasonable roofing: roofing, siding, remodeling, free estimates. Dick Savage. Phone [number]." Sometimes you have to look carefully to pick out the child care providers from the rest of the services offered!

Another source to consult is the *Yellow Pages*. These more expensive listings typically include only child care centers. We let our fingers do the walking to "Child Care Centers," where we found listings for fifteen programs. Most provided full-day services for one- to five-year-olds, but a school-based after-school child care program and a drop-in center were also listed. In addition, there was an 800 number for an au pair agency.

If you want to take matters more directly into your own hands, one possibility is to place an advertisement in the classified section of your local newspaper for the kind of care you have in mind. This makes the most sense if you want someone to provide care in your own home or for family child care in your neighborhood. Make sure that your ad includes information about the age of your child or children, whether you want a live-in provider, background requirements (education, experience), personal characteristics (driver's license? smoker/nonsmoker?), hours of care needed per week, other duties, if any, and hourly pay. If you are looking for a family child care provider in your area, you must be specific about the neighborhood(s) you are interested in. Here are two examples.

- Live-in child care wanted. Full-time for a 1- and a 4-year-old. Valid driver's license required. High school degree plus some child care training and experience with infants. Non-smoker. Must clear background check. Light cook/clean required. References required. $10/hr. Call Mon or Eva at (607) 555-4440.

- Seeking family child care in Northside/Fall Creek neighborhoods. Full-time for infant and 3-year-old. Child care training and experience required. Licensed or certified provider preferred. Smoke-free environment. References required. Call Mon or Eva at (607) 555-9032.

You can shorten your ad with abbreviations. Some common ones include FT and PT for full- and part-time, NS for nonsmoker, hr for hour, back ck for background check, ref reqd for references required, and prev exp for previous experience. *If you advertise for someone to provide care in your home, you are likely to be swamped with calls.* You need an answering machine to help you do telephone screening before setting up any personal interviews. See Chapter 8 for more information on in-home care and the screening process. You may want to post your ad for neighborhood-based child care providers in your local laundromat or even in your church bulletin.

More Formal Approaches

The local phone number for our county's child care resource and referral (CCR and R) agency (it's called a day care and child development council) was also listed under "Child Care" in our *Yellow Pages*. We are huge fans of these private, nonprofit agencies, which often recruit and train providers as well as offer information and referral services to parents. When we designate these organizations as formal, we mean that they are set up specifically to help parents find child care. They are usually current on all the child care possibilities in the community, or at least all the licensed and certified programs. And in this case formal doesn't mean bureaucratic. Child care resource and referral organizations are often run on a very lean budget with a trained referral specialist to answer questions about available options and a few other staff to recruit new caregivers and provide ongoing training designed to improve the quality of care.

There is also a National Association of Child Care Resource and Referral Agencies (NACCRRA), a membership organization that promotes the development, maintenance, and expansion of such resource and referral services. Its members are local child care resource and referral (CCR and R) agencies. NACCRRA works with an organization called Child Care Aware to provide free information to parents about how to contact the child care agencies in their areas. The telephone number is (800) 424-2246. We recommend that you call for this information as one of the first steps in your search for good child care. See Appendix B for the names, addresses, and telephone numbers of the agencies that are NACCRRA members. All fifty states and the District of Columbia are represented. Flip to the appendix to take a look. Californians hit the jackpot — 40 CCR and R agencies spread over the state. North Carolina comes in second with 36. Residents of Alabama, Colorado, Florida, Georgia, Illinois, Indiana, Kansas, Massachusetts, Michigan, Minnesota, New Jersey, New York, Ohio, Texas, Virginia, Washington, and Wisconsin will be happy to learn that 10 or more CCR and R agencies serve parents in those states.

It's possible that the agency serving your county isn't even located in your state! For instance, the Cincinnati agency serves people living in nearby Kentucky and Indiana as well as Ohio. The same is true for the St. Louis agency, which also offers referrals in nine Illinois counties.

If you live in a state where referral services are scarce — Delaware,

Hawaii, Mississippi, Nevada, and Rhode Island have only one — don't despair. In many of them the single CCRR organization operates state-wide, so if you reside in one of those states, give its agency a call. Tell the referral representative where you live and ask whether someone closer to your area has information about child care services in your community. There may well be a referral agency nearby that is not on our list because it is not a member of the NACCRRA.

Suppose you live in Ithaca, New York, and call our county CCRR agency, the Day Care and Child Development Council of Tompkins County, Inc. The phone is answered by a receptionist who asks how she can help. You might say, "Hi. My name is Helen. My husband and I have just moved to Ithaca. We need child care for our two children. I wondered if you could tell us what might be available." The receptionist then connects you with Marta, the referral specialist, who tells you a bit about her referral service. Then she leads you through the following set of questions:

1. How old are your children?
2. Are you looking for full-time or part-time care?
3. What is your home address, and where do you work?
4. Ideally, where would you like your child to be cared for?
5. What kind of care would you prefer (center, family child care, own home)?
6. Do you have any special requirements, such as care at odd hours?

As she asks you these questions, Marta fills you in on basic realities, like the kinds of child care that can be provided legally in your state and a general idea of costs for the different types of arrangement. If you aren't familiar with family child care, for instance, she describes how it works and what it is likely to cost per week. Once you have described your child care needs, Marta can refer you to several programs or providers with services that match your requirements. She can also furnish information designed to help you assess the quality of care offered in those settings. See Chapters 5, 6, and 9 for sample checklists.

Some resource and referral agencies charge you a small amount for this service, while others provide free information and child care counseling. If you receive helpful advice and encouragement from your local CCRR agency, and there is no charge, show your appreciation through a financial contribution. These agencies, which operate on a shoestring, will make very good use of your money.

The child care referral counselor at your agency is usually careful to say that although she can give you the names of programs and providers in your area, she cannot guarantee their quality. This is because *referral agencies must supply the names of all programs and providers that meet minimum state requirements for child care provision. Therefore, you must determine for yourself whether or not a program or provider is delivering high-quality child care.*

In Part II, "Types of Care and How to Find Them," a separate chapter describes each of the major types of child care you should find in your local community. Select the chapter devoted to the kind of care that interests you most, then read about what quality should be in that setting. Finally, use the questions and checklists we include as you explore in detail the providers you are able to identify.

Types of Care and How to Find Them

5

Family and Group Family Child Care

FAMILY CHILD CARE is provided in someone else's home for a small number of children, usually of various ages. This type of care offers several possible benefits to children and to their parents. Children are ordinarily attended to in small groups, making it easier to meet the particular needs of each child. The setting can be warm, intimate, and informal, like part of the extended family, which is particularly attractive for infants and toddlers who need to be held and helped on their personal schedules. Family child care makes it possible to have several children from one family cared for in the same place. Because the groups are small, children who are susceptible to colds and other illness may stay healthier in family settings than in centers. In addition, child care homes often include school-age kids before and after school, which adds to the family atmosphere. Family-based providers may offer more flexible schedules than child care centers, making it easier to arrange care outside the typical 7:30 A.M. to 5:30 P.M. time frame. Finally, family child care is less expensive than center care in many parts of the country, although you may want to pay extra to help your caregiver provide the highest level of care possible. (See Chapters 16 and 17 for comparative costs.)

Yes, family child care also has disadvantages. Most important, states and localities have only the most basic rules for who can look after children at home and how that care is provided. (Actually, several states have virtually no regulations at all!) Rules that do exist are not enforced well and therefore are ignored by many home care providers. You may be the sole judge of the health and safety of a provider's home and how much she knows about tending children. It is also probable that the family child care provider works alone, and if she gets sick, you'll need a backup arrangement. If she decides to go out of business, you have to scramble to work out something else. Also, many of the people who look after children in their own homes have no education or training in child development or child care. This isn't necessarily bad, but we do know that, in general, trained providers are better at what they do than caregivers without educational experience.

The Good Family Child Care Provider

Clearly, family child care, like anything else, has advantages and disadvantages. There are ways, however, that you can maximize the good aspects and protect your child and yourself against possible problems and dangers. First and foremost, you must be confident that the person who cares for your child really views her as a very special little person. Studies have shown that family child care providers who offer sensitive, responsive, and overall better-quality care are more "intentional" than other caregivers. Below are profiles of two family child care providers, one intentional, the other "accidental."

Brenda Jones

Brenda Jones wanted to stay home with her own children during their preschool years. Looking after the children of others had never crossed her mind until her cousin asked whether Brenda would take her five-month-old three days a week. The extra income was nice. Then a neighbor wanted care for her kindergartner after school, and one child just led to another. Brenda liked the business courses she took in high school and plans to continue in the business program at the community college in a couple of years, when her youngest child starts kindergarten.

Several people have mentioned the child care courses at the community college. Brenda has also read about the evening workshops for family child care providers offered by the child care council. But she really doesn't see the need for specialized training because in a couple of years she's going to start something else anyway. It's the same way with getting a county license. "Why bother?" she asks. "I know how to look after my own kids, and I treat the others just like my own. Most days we pretty much play it by ear. A lot of the time they play together or watch TV while I do things around the house."

Brenda doesn't consider what she is doing as a big deal. "It's not like I want to make a career out of this or anything. Some women needed help so they could go to work, and I was at home anyway, so why not look after their kids?"

Carol Smith

Carol Smith also wanted to stay at home with her children when they were young. As a teenager she had loved baby-sitting and after high school had gone on to study child development at the community college. During her second year at college Carol married and started a family. She talked with her husband about adding a family room to their modest, two-bedroom home so they would have more space and she could provide a small child care service. He and a couple of friends did most of the work, and soon she was caring for three other children in addition to their two girls. When she started, the first thing Carol did was hook up with the child care council. The staff helped her get certified by the county and invited her to family child care workshops offered twice a month in the evenings. "The workshops are great!" says Carol. "They help me keep up with the latest information on children and child care, and I get to meet a lot of other nice people who are as interested in children as I am."

Carol considers herself an important member of a very special group of people. "We are really professionals," she says with enthusiasm. "I know a lot about young children, and I work hard to run a top-notch child care home. Each child is special, and I want to give it special care and attention. I look to the parents to work with me, and I work with them. We work together as a team, as best we can."

Carol Smith always intended to work with young children, one way or another, whereas Brenda Jones kind of backed into child care. Mrs. Smith demonstrated her commitment by actively seeking out knowledge. She and her husband added a room onto their home expressly to support her occupational goal. Brenda Jones has no particular interest in children, having started day care as a favor for a friend. Courses and certificates have no interest for her because she thinks of what she is doing simply as an extension of being a mother to her own children. Mrs. Smith expresses pride in being part of the early childhood profession, whereas Mrs. Jones is marking time until she can go on to college in retail and sales.

Really *wanting* to look after children is critical. Many years of experience do not necessarily ensure quality; the key lies in really liking young children and seeking out ways to learn more about them.

Group Size and Age Mix

The biggest asset of family child care is its small size — one caregiver with only a few children. But what is the right number? The first thing to remember is that infants and toddlers need more individual attention than preschoolers. Part of that attention is basic care, like feeding, changing diapers, and holding a tired baby. Part is more focused on development, like playing peekaboo with an eight-month-old or helping a toddler build with blocks. So we don't think that a single family care provider should look after more than four very young children at a time, even when some of those are her own kids. However, if all her charges are at least two years old, a competent provider may be able to manage as many as five or six successfully. Family care providers also look after grade school children after school, so this has to be considered as well. You can quickly see that various combinations are possible: for instance, one or two infants and toddlers, a couple of older preschoolers, and several older children coming by for a few hours after school lets out. Here is a general guide to help you think about group size in relation to the age of the children in the group:

Maximum number	Children under two years	Children two years or older	Children in first grade or above
6	0	0	6
6	0	6	0
6	1	5	0
6	2	3	1
6	3	1	2
4	4	0	0

This table shows only some of the possible combinations of infants and toddlers, preschoolers, and school-age children. But you can see that maximum group size is never more than six children. If all of them are very young, the group should be smaller. School-age kids can actually be helpful to the care provider, adding spice for the other children at the end of the day. But too many of them may add stress to a tired caregiver, distracting her from the needs of the younger children in her care. So think in terms of combinations of children and what mix is best for the needs of your child.

Some parents choose family-based child care because they like the fact that their child gets to know and interact with children of different ages, rather than spending time mostly with children about the same age, as is the case in many child care centers. Mixing children of different ages is part of what gives home-based care that family feeling. But you have to ask yourself how well you think your child will fit in with the particular mix of children that a provider is caring for at the very point when your child would join the group. If he is an infant, will the rest of the group allow the caregiver time to give him specialized attention? If she is three or four years old, are there other preschoolers to play with? Again, a big advantage of choosing a home environment for your child is the feeling of intimacy and personalized attention it can provide, so you want to be certain that the group is small enough and the provider is interested and committed enough to make that happen.

The Environment of the Home

Most parents are attracted to family child care because they want their child to feel "at home" in the place where he will spend many hours. They'd like an informal family atmosphere that doesn't feel institutional. But what are you really looking for when you visit a home to see whether it is right for your child?

In the first place, the space has to be clean and safe. As you look around, apply your own standards of cleanliness. Does the house meet them? Remember, you need to feel good about having your child there. What about light, and ventilation? In terms of safety, think about smoke detectors and fire extinguishers. Are there several exits in case of fire? Is the building in good repair? Are there safety guards on windows that children can reach? Are electric sockets covered? If there are stairs, are there gates? All these questions are included on a handy checklist in Appendix C, which you can use if you decide to evaluate possible homes.

Some family care providers may limit the children to just one room of the house, or they may have different rooms for playtime, naptime, and mealtime. Some providers adapt their living rooms for child care, whereas others create a separate playroom for the children. Either way, caregivers who are really interested in child development will have organized the play area so that it is child friendly — children have easy access to the books, toys, and materials that are right for their age and easy to pick up and put away when they are through with them. So you are looking for a home that is not just homey for adults, but has been adapted to house an early childhood program, which you can see from the way it is organized.

Kitchens and bathrooms are other important parts of homes. Your child will spend time in these spaces, so you must feel good about them. Check them out to make sure they are clean and safe. At its best, the kitchen can add warmth and stimulation to your child's family care experience; at its worst, it can be dangerous and unsanitary.

Outdoor space is also important. Again, safety first. How far is it to the outside play area? How do the children get there and back? If it is a public space, is it fenced? Can the children be seen and monitored easily? Is the ground soft and comfortable? Is all the equipment well maintained? If the provider has her own back yard, is it well protected from driveways and roads? What about other potential hazards, such as swimming pools, ponds, and streams?

The Caregiver

We now come to the crux of the matter. Group size, age of the other children, and quality of space indoors and out are important, but the caregiver pulls these things together and makes them work for *your* child. A family child care provider works alone, which is fine if things go well but a real disadvantage if she isn't right for your child. Your challenge is to choose a provider who can meet *your* child's particular needs.

Part of your decision should be based on personal style. Is this person superneat and organized or relaxed and easygoing? Does she let your child set the pace in the "getting to know you" process or does she want it to happen at her speed? Do you sense that she will be strict or lenient with the children in her care, or somewhere in between? Does she want you or your child to call her by her first name or use Miss or Mrs.? How do you feel about all these things? To the greatest extent possible, you want to find someone whose style works well with your own. You have to work jointly with this person around the needs of your child, which means feeling comfortable enough with her so that you can share triumphs and troubles easily and openly.

Beyond personal style is the curriculum that the provider organizes for the children in her care. We have already pointed out that intentions seem to make a big difference. If a provider thinks of herself as a professional, seeks knowledge about children and child care, and plans activities for "her" children, she is likely to be more sensitive to them and more responsive to their needs than if she sees herself as just a baby-sitter.

You have a right to know how your provider plans the daily routines of the children. Does everyone do everything together, or does she have individual plans for each child? Does the provider seem more excited about one age group than another, for instance, preschoolers rather than infants and toddlers? Does she employ a directive approach or does she offer various options, letting each child choose what he wishes to do? Does she consider herself a specialist in a particular program area, like arts and crafts or storytelling or cooking or gymnastics and dance? Again, you must match this information with your own interests and beliefs about what children want and need. The pleasure and excitement you express about her experiences in child care will help your child enjoy being there. Therefore you have to select a provider whose modus operandi gives you confidence and makes it easy to be excited about her work.

Training for Family Child Care Providers

All care providers, wherever they work, do a better job if they have received training in child development and child care than if they have not had such preparation. Family child care providers are no exception. A study carried out in three different states found that family child care providers who received only eighteen to thirty-six hours of training improved the overall quality of their care significantly, became more committed to their work, and made children feel more secure and comfortable than a similar group of providers that did not participate in the training.[1] Even thirty-six hours of training isn't much, when you come right down to it. So search out a provider who has received some training. If she is in the market for further education related to children, that is even better. Be supportive and enthusiastic about her desire to learn more, even offering to help her pay the cost if you can afford it and she needs the assistance. The long-run benefits for you and your child will be worth the money.

By encouraging education and training we are *not* saying that everyone who has not had special preparation is a poor caregiver. We all know relatives, friends, or neighbors who are "naturals" with children. Our point is that even the naturals can learn more and may well derive the most benefit from training because they love children and get such pleasure out of spending time with them. Caring for other people's children is not the same as caring for your own. As the size of a group increases, more planning is required to keep everyone happy and occupied. Someone else's children are harder to comfort and harder to discipline than your own. Topics covered in most family child care training courses include everything from health, safety, and nutrition to child development and age-appropriate activities, learning environments, guidance and discipline, and how to run a small business. The business aspect is important — like the owner of any other small enterprise, the family child care provider must be able to handle income from parent fees, document expenses, figure in depreciation, and balance the books.

Perhaps you know someone who is really good with kids but hasn't had any formal training. One thing you might do is to check out possible course options in your community and determine whether this person would agree to care for your child and complete the course. Again, you might need to help with the financing, but it would be worth it for your child's sake and your peace of mind.

Family Child Care Regulations

Many states, counties, and cities have instituted basic rules that they expect caregivers who look after other people's children in their own homes to follow. Two different approaches, *licensing* and *registration* or *certification*, are used. Licensing indicates that the provider has received permission to operate a home-based child care program. The home has been inspected by the licensing agency, and health and fire departments have usually checked out the premises for safety. The purpose of the license is to protect you the consumer by maintaining a *minimum* standard for safe service. The license is renewed as long as the basic regulations continue to be met — at least in theory.

Registration and certification are also designed to protect you from unsafe care, but they usually rely on *self-inspection* rather than inspection by outside specialists. Registration standards are written and made available by the appropriate state and local agencies (social services, health, fire). The provider who receives this information looks over her home to determine whether she is meeting the standards. If she concludes that she does, she simply signs a document saying so. No proof of compliance is required, and random inspections are rare.

Please hear us loud and clear! Most family child care homes are unlicensed, unregistered, and uncertified. Even when they have them, those certificates or licenses don't mean much. Family child care regulations set the most minimal standards. They may result in somewhat safer environments, but they provide no guarantee whatsoever of quality.

A study found that 87 percent of regulated family child care homes provided good or adequate quality care, whereas only 50 percent of unregulated providers did; this number dropped to 31 percent if the provider was an adult relative.[2] But we don't think that the license or certificate itself made the difference. Regulated providers were also more likely to have received child care training, to be members of a local family child care association, and to have become providers for "child-centered" reasons, that is, because they really wanted to be with children. So seek out providers who have had some training and are professional enough to meet regularly with other caregivers. If they are licensed or certified, so much the better.

Backup for Provider Illness

Like all human beings, family child care providers get sick, so you need a backup plan when that happens. There are three common alternatives, and we suggest that you avail yourself of all three if possible.

1. Many family care providers arrange with colleagues for backup in times of illness. They may operate with a buddy system, in which one or two other providers take over for the one who is sick in exchange for the same type of support. You should ask a prospective

provider whether she has worked out this type of backup arrangement. If she has, you'll have to check out the alternative provider, using the same criteria as for your primary caregiver.

2. Arrange emergency care with a relative or friend. This can be very convenient and feel nice and safe. But some kind of payback is usually expected, despite protests to the contrary — "Don't mention it! You'd do the same for me if I needed it!" Mutual help among friends and relatives is great, just what a real community is all about. However, if you have limited time and opportunity to return the favor, reserve those folks for real emergencies.

3. Hold some of your vacation time in reserve so that you can stay home when necessary. This is a good strategy should your child become sick, because neither a center nor a family-based provider can afford to care for an infectious child. Vacation time is precious, but keep in mind that nothing is more precious than your child's welfare. We also suggest talking with your employer about the possibility of using some of your own sick days for child care and child health emergencies. Some fringe benefits allow employees to use them either for themselves or for their children. Maybe you can work something out, at least on an informal basis, with your employer. But have that discussion *before* an emergency arises to ensure that it is a realistic backup alternative.

Keeping Your Provider in Business

Perhaps the biggest potential disadvantage to family child care is that your provider may decide to give up the business, leaving you high and dry. Her decision to leave child care would create serious difficulties, both for your child and for you. From your child's perspective, continuity of care is very, very important (see Chapter 3). Your goal should be to maintain the same care arrangement for several years at a time, because more frequent shifts strain the emotional capacity of your child. The demands on you of having to find another good arrangement are also considerable, as you are now learning!

Fortunately, you can have a good deal of influence on your provider's decision to continue in child care or change professions. Before contracting with her, it is fair to ask how long she expects to continue in the profession. It is wise to be constantly thinking about incentives, ways to encourage her to continue providing care for your child. These incentives can range from the amount you pay and the fringe benefits you offer — paid vacation time, sharing cost of new toys, helping with training expenses — to the ways in which you demonstrate appreciation for her devotion toward your child — birthday and holiday cards and presents, invitations to dinner at your home, assistance with the children during a trip to the zoo. We expand on this very important idea of supporting your child care provider in Chapter 14. Give the ideas outlined there serious consideration, and do everything you can to make the care arrangement a long-lasting and satisfying one for everyone involved.

Group Family Child Care

Group family child care is provided in someone else's home by two or more adults, one of whom lives there. Some states have a special licensing category for these group arrangements, while others simply consider them a type of family child care.

The number of children cared for in a group setting is larger than in regular family child care, frequently including as many as twelve children. But even with two caregivers, the ratio of children to adults should remain about the same — no worse than one adult for every six children.

Group family child care homes often function as mini child care centers, with one or more rooms set aside only for child care and environments designed specifically to meet the needs of preschool children with, for example, individual storage cubbies, child-size tables and chairs, designated activity areas. In our experience they are usually run by adults with special training in early childhood education who have a strong professional orientation. These providers generally have a well-thought-out educational philosophy that is clearly expressed in writing and reflected in the way they work with children. The owner of the home usually functions as the head teacher of the child care program with a second adult hired as an assistant.

The licensed group family child care home alternative, a rather new addition to the American child care scene, has benefits to offer families. A well-organized home contains many of the advantages of regular family child care without the disadvantages. Group size is still very manageable, and the adult-to-child ratio is good. The family environment is still easy to maintain, and mixed age groupings — infancy to school age —are possible. Overhead costs are likely to be lower than those of a center, making fees a bit lower. The isolation of caring for children alone is not a problem, and the inconvenience of backup arrangements when a caregiver is sick is reduced. The program is almost certain to be licensed, and the caregivers have received at least some training.

Having said all this, we remind you that these potential advantages don't let you off the hook. Everything we recommend below regarding the search for a family child care provider is equally valid for group family child care. Also, because of the center aspect of this arrangement, we urge you to read Chapter 6 on center care and to use the checklist provided there in addition to the one for family child care included at the end of this chapter.

Visiting and Interviewing Family Child Care Providers

It is a good idea to begin comparing family child care programs well in advance of your child's needing care. Give yourself plenty of lead time, at least three months, and more if you require infant care. The good family child care programs are popular, so you have to reserve space as early as possible.

Five steps are involved in selecting a family child care provider.

1. Telephone screening and reference checks
2. Visits to selected homes
3. Talking with providers
4. Making a choice
5. Getting it in writing

1 Telephone Screening and Reference Checks

There may be a large number of family-based providers in your community. If you are working with a resource and referral agency (see Chapter 4), the referral specialist should have some idea of which providers have openings for a child the age of yours. Try to get as many

Telephone Contact Form — Family Child Care

Name of provider _____ Telephone number _____

Address _____

Space available for child the age of mine when I need it?   ❑ Yes   ❑ No

Number and ages of children cared for now _____

_____

Number of children enrolled full time _____

Licensed or certified?   ❑ Yes   ❑ No   Working toward license? _____

How many years' experience providing care? _____

Fee (hourly, daily, weekly) _____

Names of two references (and phone numbers, if possible) _____

_____

_____

Comments:

_____

_____

names as possible from the agency, through newspaper ads, and via your personal network. Once you have those names and telephone numbers, it is time to do telephone screening. (See the telephone contact form above.)

It is important to remember that the person you are calling is at her place of work, where she is responsible for as many as five or six children. Always ask whether it as a good time for her to talk or whether it would be better if you called back at another time.

Appendix C includes another version of this form, which you can copy for use during the initial telephone interviews. The questions stress issues that affect the quality of care: the number and age of children currently enrolled and how long they are in care each week, whether the program is licensed, and the names of people who are familiar with the care provider. Answers to these questions and contact with references, plus the subjects of fees and more practical issues like location, should allow you to narrow the list to two or three choices.

Reference and background checks are critical. You should talk with parents who have or have had experience with the provider. You do not want character references from people who have not known her as a caregiver.

Questions for References

- How long was or has your child been with (name of provider)?
- How old was your child when she or he started in this care?
- What did you like about the care offered by (provider)?
- Were there aspects of this care that made you unhappy?
- How easy is it to approach (provider) about problems?
- How flexible is (the provider)?
- What words would you use to explain how (provider) deals with children?
- Does (provider) organize activities for children? Please describe some of those activities.
- Does (provider) also care for her own children? How does that work out?
- Knowing what you do now, would you choose (provider) again?

These questions are repeated in Appendix C for easier copying. Each question has a specific purpose. "How long?" is to give you an idea of the length of time the reference has had experience with this provider. "How old?" is to let you know whether the reference was familiar with the provider's work with children your child's age. Answers to "What did you like?" and "What made you unhappy?" should give you some feel for strengths and weakness. But remember that these comments are shaped by the background and previous experience of the reference person, whom you probably don't know. Also assume that the provider gave you the names of parents with the most positive feelings about her abilities as a caregiver.

Child care always has its difficult moments, both for you as a parent and for your provider, so you need to feel good about raising challenging issues with the caregiver. Do you have the feeling that this will be easy to do? Is she flexible enough to adjust her methods to meet the particular needs of your child?

The descriptions of the provider's way with children and the activities she does with them should give you a sense of whether her approach to children matches yours and whether your child will feel both secure and stimulated — happy! — in her care.

Caregivers who look after other children along with their own sometimes favor their own or have a hard time handling their own children's feelings of jealousy. It is important to know whether these problems are issues for the provider.

Use your instincts as you listen to each parent reference talk about her experiences with the provider. Try to read between the lines of what you are hearing. Is the parent excited about and thankful for the experience with the provider, or does she sound unenthusiastic? Is the reference volunteering positive examples or giving you only the information you request? Does the reference sound guarded or protective? What is your gut reaction to what this person is saying?

2 Visits to Selected Homes

Our Family Child Care Checklist, also provided in Appendix C, is organized around the quality dimensions discussed in Chapter 3. Take another look at that chapter if you don't have these concepts of quality clearly in mind.

Family Child Care Checklist

Name of Provider_____

Address_____

Date _____

Yes	No	Basic Information
—	—	Program licensed?
—	—	Hours compatible with work?
—	—	Affordable weekly rate?

Yes No

Health and Safety

— — Is the home secure?

— — Is the home well maintained?

— — Working smoke detectors/fire extinguishers?

— — Electrical outlets covered?

— — Safe windows/gated stairs?

— — Medicines/cleaning agents locked away?

— — Clear emergency exits?

— — Kitchen/bathroom sanitary?

— — Play area clean and uncluttered?

Indoor Play Area

— — Are toys safe and appropriate?

— — Is there adequate space for children to play?

— — Is a variety of toys/materials available?

— — Can children be seen easily?

— — Are lighting/windows/ventilation adequate?

— — Are bathrooms accessible?

— — Is there space for personal belongings?

Outdoor Play Area

— — Is it enclosed and secure?

— — Is it free of hard ground surfaces and rocks?

— — Are climbers, swings, slides, safe and supervised?

— — Can children be seen easily?

— — Is it uncluttered so children can run?

Nap Area

— — Individual cots/cribs?

— — Cots and cribs clean and in good order?

— — Quiet location but can be observed?

— — Evacuation plan clearly posted?

Care Providers

— — Do the children seem happy around the provider?

— — Is the provider in good physical condition and able to keep up with the children?

— — Is the provider warm and affectionate?

— — Is the provider positive and open?

— — Is the provider willing to talk to you?

— — Does the provider invite you to drop in whenever you wish?

Yes No

— — Does the provider seem organized?

— — Does the provider seem genuinely to like children?

— — Does the provider maintain discipline by careful supervision, clear limits, and explanations that the children can understand?

— — Does the provider avoid conflicts between children by listening and watching carefully, then stepping in early to prevent violence?

— — Does the provider use praise and attention to encourage cooperation and helpfulness?

If Working with Infants and Toddlers

— — Does the provider respond quickly to signs of unhappiness or distress?

— — Does the provider hold infants and toddlers often and in caring ways?

— — Are babies who are too young to hold their bottles fed in the arms of the provider?

— — Does the provider talk directly to the infants and toddlers, responding to their sounds and vocalizations?

— — Does the provider set limits consistently and gently?

— — Does the provider allow children to explore and give help when they need it?

— — Are babies allowed to nap when they are tired?

— — Does the provider wash her hands after every diaper change and before feedings?

Program

— — Is there a clear daily schedule?

— — Are activities varied and age-appropriate?

— — Does the provider serve nutritious meals and snacks?

— — Is there a program policy on discipline?

It is best that you make the first visit to your "finalist" homes without taking your child or children along. As you can see from the checklist, there is much to look for and ask about, so you will have enough to do without also having to be concerned about your own child. A get-acquainted visit to see how potential caregiver and child respond to each other will be important once you have found a home that seems like a real possibility.

Visit at least two homes, even if you are lucky enough to find one you like on the first try. You can learn so much, for better or worse, by comparing that first home with another one. Remember, part of this process involves educating yourself. Each visit to an additional home expands your knowledge and sharpens your definition of what you like and dislike about family child care.

Try to visit homes during a time that includes arrivals or departures, so that you can see how the child care provider interacts with parents as well as children. See if you can arrange to visit for at least ninety minutes, say, from 8:00 to 9:30 in the morning or 4:00 to 5:30 in the afternoon.

You will want to interview the provider about what you see and don't see during your visit. That may be difficult if she is busily working with the children. When you set up the visit, ask whether there will be a chance for discussion. If not, arrange to call in the evening following your visit to ask follow-up questions.

Begin by confirming the information that you learned through your telephone interview — whether the home is licensed or certified, if there is space for your child during the hours you need care, and whether the costs will be what you expected.

The section covering safety issues requires that you really poke around in the house, and think about the kinds of things that could go wrong. You may feel somewhat embarrassed at having to be so nosy, but remember that we are talking about the safety of your child. Also keep the team concept in mind — if something needs fixing or replacing, there may be a way for you to help out.

Remember to spend time outdoors, walking around the house and examining the play area. Is it safe? Are there activities to occupy a child the age of yours? If the provider uses the facilities of a nearby park, can the children get there safely? How safe is the playground?

How many children are in the home, and how old are they? In Chapter 3 we discussed limiting the group to no more than six, and even fewer if it includes infants and toddlers. The guidelines offered by the National Association for Family Child Care as *minimum* standards follow.

- A home with one provider should have no more than six children, including the provider's own children. No more than two of these children should be under age two.
- A group home with two or more adult providers should have no

more than twelve children, including those of the providers. No more than four of these children should be under age two.
- A family child care provider should be *at least* eighteen years old.
- The provider must have *at least basic training* in first aid, safety, and child development.[3]

The section on the caregiver and her behavior with children requires that you take time to sit quietly and observe her in action. Try to imagine your child in this situation. Will this person respond quickly and positively to his needs? Do you sense a genuine love for children in what you see?

From a program standpoint, are there enough activities and playthings to keep your child busy and involved? Does the home appear to be child-centered or adult-centered? Is the program organized, or does it seem to operate a bit haphazardly and out of control? The provider should have established routines and planned activities for the children, which should be clear to you from your observation. A good follow-up question for the provider is why she organizes her schedule the way she does.

Notice how the provider receives parents and children when they arrive in the morning and leave at the end of the day. Do the adults seem genuinely to like one another, as friends or friendly neighbors would? As the children arrive, does the provider ask how each one slept the night before and is feeling this morning? At pickup time, does she share information with parents about how the day has gone for their children? Do you have the sense that provider and parents are working together on behalf of the children, or are they ships passing in the night?

What You *Should* See

Caregivers who
- help young children find enjoyable activities.
- talk and play directly with the children.
- respond right away if a child is in difficulty or has a question.
- manage disputes between children fairly and calmly.

A schedule that includes
- active play, such as dancing, building with big blocks, playing outdoors.
- quiet play, such as looking at books, drawing, pasting, playing with small toys.

- a quiet period, including nap or rest depending on the age of the children.
- snacks and meals.

What You *Shouldn't* See

- Children left unsupervised, even for a minute.
- Children running around for no reason.
- Children sitting quietly with nothing to do.
- Children hurting each other, without adult intervention.
- Toys that children can see but can't reach, that are unsafe, or that are not appropriate for the ages of the children.
- Candy, soda, or other sweets as snacks, unless it is a special occasion.
- Food that infants and toddlers can choke on: grapes, peanuts, hot dogs, popcorn, and so forth.
- Physical discipline *of any kind.*
- Children isolated as punishment.
- Any invasion of children's physical privacy.
- Any use of words to shame or embarrass a child or excessive shouting.[4]

In physical discipline we include yanking children by their arms and pushing them around as well as hitting or shaking them. Even if you see a child do something for which you would spank your own child, no one should spank your child. Child care providers must know how to correct behavior in other ways. *If they do not have those skills, don't leave your child in their care.*

We also feel that isolating a child in another room or in a chair facing the wall or standing in a corner is not a good idea. A child who is being disruptive or hurting another child may need to be removed from the group and redirected into another activity. If the child is very upset and unable to control herself, the caregiver may have to stay with her and even hold her until she calms down enough to rejoin the group.

Physical privacy belongs in the "should not see" category because of concerns about inappropriate sexual contact. Young children need and enjoy physical contact with adults, but the children should seek out the contact or demonstrate a need for which contact is appropriate. Caregivers should not continue to hug or kiss a child who shows discomfort or tries to get away.

3 *Talking with Providers*

This interview should come after you've had a good chance to examine a home and observe the provider in action. Don't insist on asking a lot of questions while the caregiver is trying to work with the children; she is too busy to respond in the amount of detail you would like. Catch her after the children have left at the end of the day, or make an appointment to call her in the evening.

Write down your questions in advance of the interview. Work from your checklist and any notes you have written in the margins. Feel free to ask *why* the provider did what you observed. Give her ample opportunity to talk about children and her feelings about them. Here is a sample list of questions to ask the provider. Add others as they occur to you.

Provider Interview Questions

- What is a typical day like at your child care home?

- What kinds of activities are best for a child the age of mine?

- How often do you take the children outdoors? What activities occupy them during outdoor time?

- How do you handle mealtimes? What do you do if a child won't eat what you offer?

- How do you handle naptimes? Do all children have to sleep? How long?

- How do you handle a child who refuses to do what you ask?

- (If you have an infant or toddler) How do you feel about pacifiers?

- How do you feel about security blankets and favorite stuffed animals?

- (If there are children of different ages) How do you meet the various needs of children of different ages? Do you expect the older children to help with the younger ones?

- What are your policies regarding TV watching?

- (If the provider has her own children at home) How do your children feel about the other children who want your time and attention? If they get jealous or upset, how do you handle those situations? Do they have to share their own toys, or do you have day care toys?

- Questions specific to what your child is like (likes, dislikes, habits, needs, personality). Is the provider interested in these things? Do they matter to her? Does she want to learn how you manage them or simply follow her own set way of handling them?

The provider should be able to give you a sense of a daily routine when you ask about a typical day. But she should point out that what happens also depends on what the children, especially the infants and toddlers, want and need.

Regarding what activities are best for your child, the caregiver ought to talk in terms of stages of development. For infants she should provide many chances for face-to-face "talking" and opportunities to touch and handle different kinds of objects. Holding, rocking, and bouncing are also important — it is impossible to spoil a baby with too much holding and carrying. Older infants need opportunities to scoot and crawl with supervision, pull up to a standing position, then practice first steps. Toddlers need chances to practice walking and many blocks and other small — but not small enough to swallow — objects to put into and dump out of cups, baskets, and other containers. The back-and-forth of vocalizing and talking is very important for language development. The child will want to take control of feeding and drinking during this stage. Will the provider allow this to happen despite the resulting mess? Children three and older need more organized activities like art, storybook reading, and music, and free time with dolls, dress-up clothing, puzzles, and building materials. School-age children may need a quiet place in which to do homework, and lots of opportunities for outdoor exercise. A good provider understands these developmental needs and organizes activities to meet them.

Answers to the "refusal" questions regarding eating or other behavior the provider deems unacceptable should give you a feel for her thinking about guidance and discipline. The provider should be able to handle these situations without resorting to physical discipline of any kind (slapping, shaking, spanking), or verbal aggression ("You're a bad boy!"), or punishment through isolation. Although your child may need a chance to cool down, he should always be free to rejoin the group when ready.

As the caregiver answers these questions, she should also be asking what *you* think about these situations, and how *you* handle them. The goal is to establish as much consistency as possible between you and the provider. The provider can't contribute to that consistency if she doesn't know or care about how you organize your child's home life.

TV should not be employed as a baby sitter or entertainment for the provider when she should be engaged in activities with the children. The caregiver should be able to tell you which programs the children watch, if any, and why these shows are good for the children's development. We feel strongly that TV watching should be used as little as possible and not last for more than thirty minutes at a time. A longer video might be allowed as an occasional treat for an older child on a rainy day.

If the provider takes care of her own children as well as yours, she must be extra sensitive to the conflicts that might result. Her children deserve to have their private space and private toys that the child care children cannot touch. These toys should be put away while the child care group is present unless the provider's child wants to share them with the others. Sensitive providers use the same disciplinary techniques with their own children that we recommend for the children in their care. It confuses and upsets all the children when a provider spanks her own child. Providers who show an awareness of this issue in the interview, discussing how they handle situations involving jealousy and competition, are usually equipped to manage such conflicts when they occur.

Once you have found a home that seems quite satisfactory on the basis of the first visit, you should make arrangements to visit again, this time with your child. If possible, pick a different time of day so you can expand your knowledge of the daily routine. Watch closely as the provider approaches your child for the first time. Does she force herself on him or take time to sense the child's comfort level? Does she get down to the child's level and engage in respectful dialogue or talk to you as if he isn't in the room? Does she accept and validate the nonverbal signals and verbal messages he is sending, or "do her thing" regardless of how he feels? How does your child react to the provider? How does he respond to the other children and any other adults in the home?

One other precaution you should take is to make sure the backgrounds of providers you are seriously considering have been checked for possible criminal records or confirmed reports of child maltreatment. If the provider is licensed, certified, or registered, this may or may not have been part of that process. The child care referral counselor at your local or state child care resource and referral agency can tell you whether it was. If no such check has been conducted, contact your local law enforcement agency, regarding criminal background, and social services agency, regarding child maltreatment, for advice on how to obtain this information.

4 Making a Choice

If you have found several family child care providers who meet the general requirements we have outlined, you should feel quite pleased with yourself. When choosing among them, begin by making a list comparing the providers on all the criteria included on the checklist and in the provider interview. Where one provider is clearly better than another on an item, give that person a plus. Then add the pluses to determine which of them comes out on top.

Next, let your feelings and intuition take over. Which caregiver makes the best impression on you? In which home is it easiest to imagine your child while you are at work or school? Remember that you will need to feel comfortable sharing concerns with this person and working through disagreements and misunderstandings when they occur. Do you sense that this will be easier with one provider than with another? Keep in mind that this decision is not carved in stone — you can try an arrangement for a month, then take an honest look at how it is working out. But an initial right decision prevents later discomfort and unhappiness. Both your objective assessment and your feelings should influence your final decision.

5 Getting It in Writing

Once you have accepted a placement in a family child care home, be sure to complete a written agreement that spells out both your expectations and those of your new provider. The days and hours when care is to be provided, the payment plan, illness policies, food arrangements, and notification in case you or she wishes to end the agreement should be described in this contract. Most experienced providers have an agreement form available for use in laying out these details. We have included a sample Parent-Provider Child Care Contract form in Appendix C to give you an idea of what to look for in such an agreement. If the provider you have chosen doesn't have such a form available, make several copies of our sample — at least one for each of you — and fill them out together.

Both of you should also have copies of a child information form containing the names and telephone numbers of the people authorized to pick up your child at the provider's home, whom to contact in case of emergency, the name and number of the child's pediatrician, and any pertinent health information related to the child. You also need to sign a form giving your consent in case your child needs emergency medical treatment. See the samples of such forms in Appendix C. Your provider may already have a similar document for you to fill out. If not, copy these, complete them, and ask your caregiver to post the emergency information form close to the telephone.

Nobody's Perfect

When it comes to child care, America still has a long way to go. Because of this, it is important to be realistic. If you have found a family child care provider who is trustworthy, knows a lot about children, and is open to your own feelings about how best to care for your child, don't worry too much about minor matters. Susan Dynerman put it this way:

> *Say you find a warm, hearty soul who loves children, comes highly recommended, and has three or four kids in her care who are just the right age mix for your own. She gives over her kitchen to mixing dough and finger painting. She has a well-stocked toy shelf and a sprawling backyard full of climbing equipment and swings, and she spends countless hours reading, playing games, and engaging and stimulating her kids. But she gives them lollipops every day after lunch (and you don't like sweets), or they watch a one-hour Barney video every day (and you don't like TV at all), or her grammar is not that great (and you are an English teacher); or*

there are no riding toys (and Janie loves riding toys). You can't have everything.[5]

However, if after many visits and interviews you haven't found a family child care home that makes you happy, we certainly don't want you to make a choice that leaves you feeling bad and puts your child in an unhealthy situation. In that case, would you be willing to consider the possibility of a child care center or someone to provide care in your own home? The information provided in Chapter 6, Center Care, and Chapter 8, Care in Your Own Home, can help you with that decision. Or maybe you'd be interested in joining several other families to hire a child care provider that you'd all share. An even more enterprising solution might be to stay home with your child and become a family child care provider yourself. These two alternatives are discussed in Chapter 10, Creative Alternatives.

6

Center Care

HE TERM "child care center" evokes different images for everyone, depending on background and experience. You may imagine an enormous and rather sterile institution where large, stern, matronly women are watching more than a hundred small children. Or you may think of the mom-and-pop center in the white house at the end of the street, where children are always playing in the fenced-in yard and your teenage daughter hopes to find a part-time job next spring. Or maybe you remember a center written up in a local newspaper whose director talked about how the three-year-olds in her care are all learning to read and how important she feels it is to start academics early.

These and many other images reflect the real world. Child care centers come in a wide variety of shapes and sizes. Don't be confused by this diversity. To make an informed choice, you need to know what features of centers are most important for promoting high-quality care.

The Center Philosophy

At the heart of each child care center is a philosophy for or approach to working with children and parents. In most states the licensing laws require that a written statement of this philosophy be available for parents to read. Three examples of child care center philosophies follow.

Our Goals and Philosophy

Our aim is to provide your child with a fulfilling and rewarding experience each and every day. We encourage each child to explore his/her own individuality and creativity.

We work closely with each child in helping them build a positive self-image. It is very important to our staff that every child know that s/he is loved and is special.

By providing children with a routine in which they can feel secure, we attempt to offer a healthy balance of structure and freedom in our daily activities. Children feel a sense of security in knowing what happens next, and yet they also need a certain amount of flexibility within the boundaries.

Our rules are simple and few. In regard to discipline, the [children are] given choices and taught how to develop their own consequences for negative behavior. Positive reinforcement is the mode in which we operate. Praise and consistency are our tools.

Our hope is that you and your child will find your experience with Happy Day Playschool to be a time of positive growth and development.

Please keep in mind that in order for your child to have the best possible experience, open communication between you and our staff is a must.

We take great joy in knowing [that] your child feels comfortable and content, and we will do everything in our control to provide him/her with an environment that is an enhancement to his/her overall development.

At Happy Day Playschool, we take the responsibility of caring for your child very seriously. We thank you for entrusting us with a very significant period in your child's life.[1]

The next statement, that of a local Head Start center, reflects the goals of that national program.

Head Start Builds Positive Self-development

Our future depends on the development of children who have positive self-image and understanding of personal rights and responsibilities, and a positive outlook on life.

The Head Start Program of Cortland County, a service of the Cortland County Community Action Program, Inc. (CAPCO), is part of the federally funded Head Start Project. The main purpose of Cortland Head Start is to enhance the development of each pre-school child in a positive non-threatening manner through a variety of experiences and activities that will assist the child with his/her transition to public school.

It is the belief of our program that in order to establish success for our children in public school, we must strive to develop their confidence through building their

Self-image — Feeling good about oneself
Self-concept — "If I try, I can do it!"
and
Self-esteem — Pride in oneself

When children see themselves as worthwhile human beings, they can respond to learning in a positive, productive manner.[2]

This example from a not-for-profit center is expressed in terms of mission, values, and vision.

Our Mission

To provide excellent child care for families of diverse backgrounds, and to advocate for children, families, and the child care profession.

Our Values

Ithaca Community Childcare Center provides a *safe, nurturing, and developmentally appropriate program* which fosters: *active learning, support for the whole child, and a child-centered environment.*
We foster innovation.
We embrace teamwork.
We strive for excellence.
We respect and support families.
We commit to service at all levels.
We respect and appreciate diversity.
We actively listen and seek to understand.
We communicate openly and productively.
We use resources creatively and responsibly.
We abide by the NAEYC [National Association for the Education of Young Children] Code of Ethics and Statement of Commitment

Our Vision

To be nationally recognized as an outstanding child care center.[3]

Clearly, each of these centers has a different philosophy, a particular approach to providing child care. Happy Day emphasizes a balance of structure and freedom, positive reinforcement, and open communication between parents and staff. Head Start stresses preparation for public school through the building of positive self-image, self-concept, and self-esteem. The Ithaca Community Childcare Center features active learning, a child-centered environment, and respect for diversity. You'll find that reading a center's philosophy is a good place to start in understanding how it operates and the extent to which that approach meshes with your personal beliefs and values. Certain types of centers have similar philosophies no matter where they are. The national Head Start program falls into this category, as do Montessori and Waldorf schools and the franchised child care chains — Kindercare, La Petit Academy, Bright Horizons, Children's World. The parent happy with the approach of a Head Start program in Alabama is also likely to feel comfortable with what is happening in the local Head Start program in Bangor, Maine. Many independent centers see themselves as unique and take pride in having their own special style and content.

Your personal and family values, ideas, and desires should shape your choice of a child care center. Do you want your child to work with computers? Is ethnic and racial diversity important to you? Do you want your child to have some formal reading and math instruction every day? Do you value sports and outdoor activities? Are you seeking a program with children from the neighborhood so that your child can start public school with preschool friends? The more you think through these priorities and goals the better. By struggling with these questions at this point you can avoid the pain of having to change care arrangements later, a process that can be hard both on your child and on you.

Legal Requirements for Centers

All states have regulations governing the design and operation of child care centers, which are important safeguards for children in such care. Unlike most other countries, the United States has no national child care regulations. In fact, ours is the only nation in the Western world without such standards. What we have is a patchwork of different regulations, all established by a state or local government, which vary greatly from one state to the next and even within a given state.

While these variations can be confusing, the good news is that more and more states are realizing the importance of regulating child care carefully. Remember that these rules set *minimum standards* designed simply to protect the health and safety of the children in center care. Such regulations are only the starting points for development of a good program, not a guarantee of quality. The details of the regulations for centers in your state are available from your local or state child care resource and referral agency or the regulatory agency in charge of child care in your state (see Appendix B for a state-by-state listing of resource and referral agencies).

One of the best national sources for unbiased information about day care center standards is the National Association for the Education of Young Children (NAEYC) or one of its state or local affiliate groups. NAEYC has issued the following recommendations for group size and teacher-to-child ratios in child care centers.

> *Infants:* One caregiver/teacher for every three or four children and a total group size of six to eight children
>
> *Toddlers:* One caregiver/teacher for every four to six children, and a total group size no larger than twelve children
>
> *Three- and four-year-old children:* One caregiver/teacher for every seven to nine children, and a total group size no larger than eighteen children
>
> *Five-year-old children:* One caregiver/teacher for every eight to ten children in a kindergarten program.[4]

Many research studies have shown that both the number of children for whom a caregiver is responsible and the overall size of the group have a major impact on the quality of the child's experience in center care. Put yourself in the caregiver's place for a moment, and you will quickly see why this makes sense. The more children you have to keep an eye on, the less time you have to spend on face-to-face time with any one or two of them. Very large groups make it hard for children, no matter how many adults are available, because the noise and movement of so many children create distraction and confusion. Only two of the fifty states have adult-to-child ratio and group size requirements as strict as those of NAEYC (thirteen other states are close). We remind you once again that state regulations are *minimums* — centers in your state are certainly permitted to maintain smaller caregiver-to-child ratios and group sizes than those required by the state if they wish. Believing that all centers should meet the NAEYC standards, we encourage you to look for centers that offer that level of quality. Although only a small percentage of child care centers have been accredited by NAEYC, more and more of them are striving to meet that standard.

In addition to adult-to-child ratio and group size, the minimum standards in your state also cover the health and safety features of a center's setup and organization. The regulations probably contain standards for fire alarms, exits, and fire walls in buildings housing the centers and the quality of the water piped into them. The rules often include guidelines about the minimum educational qualifications of a center director and staff. Some states require mandatory screening of criminal records for all staff, usually focused on offenses related to abuse and maltreatment. Most states define necessary minimum space as thirty-five square feet per child, not including the kitchen, bathrooms, space used for storage, and areas designed primarily for teachers or parents. Regulations covering outdoor play areas usually specify that they be fenced in or have a natural border.

Even if a child care center in your area has a license, don't assume that the state standards of health and safety match your own. As with everything else you buy, government consumer protection is minimal. It is up to you, the consumer, to make sure that the "product" you buy is of the highest quality. State licensing agencies are notoriously underfunded and rarely have enough staff to inspect even a fraction of all child care centers in their jurisdiction regularly. They depend on you, the parent and consumer, to notify them when you find anything wrong in a center. Some states allow certain kinds of centers to operate without a license — those run by religious institutions or public school systems, for example — which means that many centers across the country have absolutely no regulatory body checking on them. Whether or not the center you are considering is licensed, the only *guarantee* of health, safety, and quality for your child is your vigilance as an informed and knowledgeable parent and child care consumer.

Quality care takes a somewhat different form for infants (zero to eighteen months), toddlers (eighteen to thirty-six months), and preschoolers (three to five years). Such differences include staff qualifications, the design and organization of space, and the daily routines established for the children. Be sure to assess the quality of a center's care as it applies to your child's age. (Care for school-age children is discussed in Chapter 9.)

Infants in Center Care

Enrolling your infant in a center has real advantages both for you and for your baby. From your standpoint, a center is a reliable form of care. Because center directors have well-established routines for hiring substitutes in case of staff illness, you can count on the program's being open on a regular schedule regardless of the health of any particular caregiver. Centers are also likely to be licensed, and have met the minimum state standards. At a center your baby spends time with other children about the same age. Since infants often make friends with other babies in the same room before they are a year old — some even greet each other in the morning! — they can find real pleasure in the company of other infants and toddlers.

> We consider very young children infants until they are able to walk pretty well. Since most children walk without difficulty by the time they are eighteen months old, infant care refers to service for children between birth and eighteen months of age.

There are also disadvantages to center-based care. Some licensing regulations make it hard to create homelike spaces — rules banning soft rugs, comfortable adult-size furniture, curtains, and many breakable decorations or plants, for instance. Some parents don't like the institutional feeling that results from these restrictions. Another disadvantage can be the adult-to-child ratio in a center, which may provide only one caregiver for four or more infants.

Sharing space with many other babies is accompanied by increased risk of colds and ear infections. Infants who are more susceptible to these illnesses than others may have difficulty adjusting to center care.

The Physical Environment

The first thing you'll notice when you visit an infant room is the look of the space and its organization. Between birth and eighteen months children's needs and abilities change dramatically. To support and encourage those changes, the environment in infant care rooms must be flexible and adaptable, a need to which centers respond in different ways. Some place the babies who are not yet mobile in one group, then move them to another group when they become active crawlers and beginning walkers. Others divide infants into age groups. Each group

States with Best Caregiver-to-Infant Ratios (1996)

1 caregiver for 3 infants
  Kansas
  Maryland
  Massachusetts

States with Worst Caregiver-to-Infant Ratios (1996)

1 caregiver for 12 infants
  Idaho
1 caregiver for 6 infants
  Alabama
  Arkansas
  Georgia
  Louisiana
  Nevada
  New Mexico
  South Carolina[5]

stays with the same caregiver for the entire eighteen-month period, but moves with its caregiver from room to room as the babies become more and more mobile. Still others mix children of different ages and developmental levels and design the space to support the different levels of mobility and cognitive growth.

What to Look For: There are many things to observe as you evaluate the physical environment in an infant room. Look for an environment that makes you feel comfortable, remembering that your child could be there for as many as eight or nine hours a day. The room should appear warm and welcoming to your baby, with soft lighting and an inviting, but not garish color scheme. Listen to the sounds around you, which should be muted. If music is playing, it should be soft and soothing. People should be speaking in normal voices, not shouting to one other or at the children.

Appropriate furnishings should include individually marked cribs placed at least three feet apart and away from children who might crawl or walk between and around them. There should be sturdy highchairs and feeding tables and chairs, rocking chairs and other adult-size chairs, and changing tables with individual cubbies near the tables for each infant's diapers and other belongings.

Babies love to watch their own reflection and those of other babies, so low mirrors on the walls are a great addition to an infant room. There should also be wall decorations both at baby level and at a height where babies being carried in a caregiver's arms can see them.

Babies learn from touching and tasting and looking at articles and from listening to their caregivers and all the other sounds in their environment. They exercise their muscles by lying on the floor and kicking or stretching, by reaching for objects, by being up on their hands and knees, rocking back and forth, and by sitting and crawling and walking. Therefore their rooms should contain different textures and ramps, mattresses, boxes, and barrels to climb up on, into, and down from. The ideal place for toys is on low shelves so that the babies can pick their own and, with assistance, put them back after use. Babies cannot see toys that are stored in baskets and spend time aimlessly pouring out all the contents to find a particular object. Low barriers and semiprivate spaces are important features, because they give babies the feeling that they can move around but still have time in their own space.

A quality environment should include a good supply of books written for very young children. Babies love to be read to, and they delight in looking at picture books. We have seen infants as young as eight months engrossed in leafing through a sturdy picture book, carefully looking at each page. Books, as well as other toys, should be in good condition. Sharp edges on broken toys can be unsafe and the toys have to be checked over regularly. Caregivers should encourage the children not to tear or chew their books too much, thus teaching them the importance of looking after their belongings.

Some centers put infants in walkers that allow them to scoot around on wheels or in seats on springs called jumpers. These aren't a good idea for infants in group care or in homes. Children need to be on a floor, stretching their muscles and moving naturally. It is very tempting to leave a child in a walker for too long if he seems happy there. A swing can be used occasionally for a very young infant, but the caregiver should never use it as a substitute for holding a child in her arms or on her lap.

When you visit infant rooms, look around for record-keeping forms and other evidence of the center's sharing information with parents. Your baby can't tell you about her day, so a good system has to be in

> Most very young infants sleep for a large part of the day. As they grow older, they are awake for longer and longer periods. By eighteen months most children are down to one or possibly two naps a day at a center.

place for communication between care providers and parents. Ideally, you should make time in your schedule to chat with your baby's caregiver when you drop off your child in the morning and in the afternoon at pickup time. But the reality is that there will be times when you have to drop off your child in a hurry or pick him up one minute before the center closes, so written records and messages are important backup methods of communication. If the center you choose does not already have such a system, suggest one to those in charge and help them develop a way to share information with you each day. You can find a sample form for this purpose in Appendix D. Remember, events in your home may have an impact on your child's behavior under someone else's care. To this end, notice that our sample has space for parents to provide information about the child's daily eating, toileting, and sleeping patterns and any unusual event that might influence your child's reactions during the day. We also suggest leaving space so you can write an additional message you might want to relay to your child care providers. Of course, your caregivers also need space in which to write about your baby's personal habits and

> Young infants typically eat every three or four hours. However, by the time they approach eighteen months of age, most babies are satisfied with breakfast and a morning snack, lunch, an afternoon snack, and a bottle before each nap. They usually have dinner and a bedtime bottle on their return home.

events of the day that might be relevant to you at home.

Another chart to look for is one on which a baby's sleeping hours, diaper changes, and food consumption are recorded. Quality infant care does not operate on a uniform daily program, for infants have individual schedules. After all, they will not be hungry or ready to play and sleep at the same time other babies are so engaged.

Children of all ages need to spend time outdoors, so outdoor space is an integral part of every child care center. Infant centers should have access to shaded and protected outdoor areas where the children can lie on blankets in the fresh air or crawl around and explore. In order to take babies for walks, center staff need baby carriages or wagons designed to hold more than one infant at a time.

> In Scandinavia, where the population believes that fresh air is healthy for infants, most centers have outdoor areas sheltered from the wind and rain. One often finds babies asleep in their carriages and strollers in those places.

Staff Qualifications and Practices

While the qualifications and practices of child care staff are important for all age groups, nowhere are they more important than in the care of infants. Your infant needs a great deal of love and attention in order to develop optimally. Consistency and emotional support are essential, along with good physical care and a safe, healthy environment. Before you visit the infant room in a center for the first time to observe the caregivers in action, spend some time with the director to learn about her staff's educational backgrounds and how long they have been at the center. The director can also tell you whether they attend workshops and other continuing education opportunities to keep their skills and knowledge up to date. A combination of a solid educational background in early childhood with practical work experience with young children is the ideal background for a caregiver. Providers who work with infants also need specialized knowledge of infant development, health, and nutrition.

What to Look For: The first thing to assess in an infant care provider is her interactions with the babies. Does she respect each infant as a unique person, recognizing that each baby is different from the others? One infant may need to be held quietly, while another really likes to be bounced around, and a third might not want to be touched at all. Does she take time to observe the infants and take her cues from what she sees, or does she simply follow her own adult routines despite the babies' feelings? Is the caregiver in tune with the babies' rhythms? For instance, are staff members listening to a baby vocalizing, responding with a sound or a word, then waiting for the baby to coo or chuckle again? Are they interacting with the quiet babies as well as the noisy attention seekers?

You should never hear a caregiver call a baby bad because of her behavior. Very young children cannot understand the difference between right and wrong or how their behavior affects the adults around them. Therefore, they are unable to be bad on purpose. There may be times when we as parents or caregivers wish they would stop crying or tossing food on the floor or pulling the cat's tail, for example. But babies involved in such behavior neither have us in mind nor do they understand that their actions are wrong. Effective caregivers comfort or distract babies who are doing these things.

Infant caregivers must spend a lot of time on routine tasks like feeding, diapering, and putting babies to sleep. However, they should also play with them in an intentional manner. This should include reading to the infants, playing games like peekaboo and This Little Piggy, exercising each child's arms and legs, singing, offering toys and taking them back, and simply holding children in their laps and conversing *with* — not just talking *to* — them. The caregivers should encourage older babies to move around by organizing the space so that they can safely pull themselves to their feet and walk around holding on to furniture and larger pieces of equipment. Various toys need to be added as the babies grow older, toys that link cause and effect like jack-in-the-boxes and small baskets filled with a few blocks or other items that the children can dump out and put back over and over again! Mobile infants like push-and-pull toys, balls, and large wooden trucks and cars. Child care centers that provide such a range of toys are well prepared to promote the optimal development of your child.

It is also important for you to look at a number of basic care routines as you observe staff in the infant room. Caregivers should be holding the babies and talking softly to them as they give them their bottles. Infants should *not* be drinking from bottles that caregivers prop on pillows. Babies should also be talked to while their diapers are being changed, as they are rocked to sleep — a lullaby or soft humming is appropriate — and when they are lying on the floor on a blanket, exploring a rattle or other toy.

Caregivers should be dressed in comfortable, easy-to-wash clothes, enabling them to spend time on the floor with the babies without worrying about drooling or overflow as they burp them over their shoulders or carry them in their arms. Also check to see whether the caregiver washes her hands and cleans the changing table after each diaper change. High chairs, toys, and other equipment must be cleaned and disinfected regularly. Remember, risk of infection is a significant concern with center-based infant care. One way to reduce that risk is through scrupulous hand washing and the frequent cleaning of everything in the room.

At first, telling the difference between one caregiving style or approach and another may seem difficult. However, as you spend time watching adults with young children, you begin to see who is comfortable and knowledgeable with them and who isn't. Careful observation does take time, however. Plan to set aside at least two hours the first time you visit a center just to observe the work of the caregivers who will be responsible for your child.

Toddlers in Center Care

During the toddler period the advantages of a good center become increasingly obvious. Most important, even eighteen-month-olds can begin to really play with other children. By the time these children are three, various types of play and budding friendships afford them great pleasure and satisfaction. Children this age begin to learn to take turns and to socialize with one another although it is hard for them to cooperate for any length of time. They like playing pretend — seeing all five toddlers in a group being Mommy at the same time is not unusual! As with infants, the reliability provided by having sub-

Children eighteen to thirty-six months old are very active, quite challenging, and loads of fun. The demands they place on their caregivers and on the environment are quite different from those of infants or preschool-age children. Many toddlers are ready to join in a few small group activities. As they grow older, groupwide schedules and routines become more and more possible.

stitutes available for ill caregivers and the added safety provided, in most cases, by state regulations are also pluses for center care.

Again, the lack of a homelike feeling can be one disadvantage to center care. Another may be that center caregivers are being asked to look after more of these active, sometimes stubborn little two-year-olds than they can manage effectively.

The Physical Environment

There are often differences among centers in the ways toddlers are grouped. Some divide the eighteen- to thirty-six-month-old children strictly by age or physical ability, whereas other centers are more fluid and have a larger age span in each room. The latter arrangement is usually best for your child because it allows the group to stay with the same caregiver for a longer time. Although an eighteen-month-old is quite different from a three-year-old, children in this age range can share the same space if their caregivers are willing to be a bit flexible.

As a toddler approaches her second birthday, a little more structure can be added to her life. Most two-year-olds need only one solid nap per day. By this age they can sit down and eat with the caregivers during lunch and snack time, which allows a flexible routine to be developed for the toddler room. This schedule should include much self-directed play, both indoors and out, mealtimes, naptime, and time for diaper changes and toileting. The daily routine should also include a good balance of quiet and active times. Large group activities like circle time, if used at all, should be very short for toddlers, because children this age aren't ready to sit still for any length of time. Transitions are also difficult for toddlers because they don't have a lot of patience and find it hard to anticipate what is coming next. With this in mind, toddler caregivers need to keep the time spent shifting from one activity to another as brief as possible.

Many centers encourage children to pick a little symbol like a teddy bear or a turtle to mark the cubbies in which they store their personal belongings. This helps them to recognize their own space easily while learning to name the toy or creature.

What to Look For: A toddler area should be bright and friendly. Space should be set aside for each child's belongings, clearly marked in a way that helps the child become self-sufficient.

Most of the furniture in the toddler room should be child-size, but there can also be adult-size chairs or a couch for the teachers and visiting parents to use, or on which children can crawl with a good book.

As you walk into the toddler room, you should see space divided into various interest areas. As the children grow older these areas develop into learning centers. Because young children learn through play, these interest areas are where most of the learning takes place in the early childhood environment. They might include a block area, a creative arts area, a dramatic play or "home" area, a manipulative area with puzzles, large Lego pieces, and strings and beads, a music area, a sensory play area with a sand or water table, and a reading and quiet area. Toddler teachers may not have all these interest areas available at all times, but they should strive to include activities related to these areas in the routine of each day.

Colorful and sturdy toys and equipment should be stored on shelves within easy access of the children. Toys and materials may be homemade and simple in design, but they must be in good condition. Books should not be ragged and torn.

Look for washable carpets and cushions that provide soft areas for the children to sit or lie on. Make sure that there is enough separation between areas for noisy and quiet play so that too much sound doesn't spill from one to the other. The children should be able to move around in the room freely, but there should be no large open spaces that allow them to race around so much that they fall and hurt themselves.

Most children become toilet trained during the toddler years. Approaches to toilet training vary from family to family, and children require individual treatment in this endeavor. If you have particular expectations regarding this training, be sure to share them with the toddler staff. When parents and staff agree about how a process should work, life is much easier for the child. As with other aspects of development, the center routine should encourage children to become self-sufficient in this area. The bathrooms must be clean and cheery, with toilets and sinks that the children can eventually learn to use by themselves. If the center supplies potty chairs, be sure they are cleaned and disinfected after each use.

You should certainly ask the toddler caregivers how they approach the issue of toilet training. No pressure should be put on children to begin to use the toilet. It is especially important that no one ever makes them feel bad or ashamed when they have an accident. In many toddler programs a natural process evolves in which the older children serve as models for the younger ones, who can observe them "at work." The result is that the younger children want to use the toilet as soon as they recognize the signals their bodies are sending and have the skills needed to alert their caregivers.

As their rate of growth slows, toddlers may seem to require less food than they did as infants. Mealtime at the center should be relaxed and friendly, a time for socializing around the table with caregivers and friends. When considering a center for your child, try to visit during lunchtime and eat with the children. This is an excellent opportunity to learn more about the atmosphere in the toddler room. Ideally this is when both caregivers and children share information about their lives away from the center in a comfortable, informal atmosphere. As the children get older they should be able to eat family style, passing some of the food around the table themselves and taking as much as they want. They may also have a chance to set the table, help pour the milk from a small pitcher, and serve the dessert. Spills happen with toddlers and teachers should accept these accidents as normal, letting the child or several children help to clean up.

The toddlers in a center should be encouraged to try their food, but not be expected to taste everything or to finish what is on their plates. The food should be nutritious and presented in a way that is appealing to children.

Naptimes vary. Find a chance to talk to the staff about the policy of the program you are considering. Most toddlers need a nap each day, and many bring a special blanket or toy, or both, for comfort when they go to sleep. Make sure they are allowed to have this reminder of home, for naptime is when children tend to feel especially vulnerable. Some toddlers, after resting for half an hour, clearly are unable to sleep. They should be permitted to get up after their rest and play quietly until the other children wake up. No child should be made to stay on his cot for more than half an hour if he is awake.

Occasionally a child might fall asleep early, and accommodations should be made for this as well. The caregiver can put a cot in a quiet corner and when that child wakes up, allow her to play quietly until the rest of the children awaken. Children who are not ready to nap at the set hour should not be made to conform. Ideally they should be allowed to play for a while longer and go to sleep a little later than the others. Parents often have opinions about naptime because it affects the child's evening behavior at home. Some parents want their child to be kept up all day, and others ask that the center put their child to sleep early in the afternoon. A good caregiver puts the child's needs first and cooperates with the parent to determine what works best for child.

Toddlers are on the go much of the time, so their outdoor environment is very important to them. They need soft areas — grass, wood chips — where they can roll and hop and run. Toddlers need swings, slides, and, if possible, a low climbing structure (although this is not always necessary). There should be sandboxes and toys to use in them, balls, tricycles, and other riding toys. The outdoor area must be fenced in or have a natural border because toddlers are explorers. They can wander off to look for a worm or a bird or an airplane, not remembering that they were told to stay on the grass.

A few centers have large indoor areas where the toddlers can play on rainy or cold days. Here you might find a balance beam, riding toys, large balls, push-and-pull toys, low steps or stairs, perhaps even a tunnel. Activities that allow children to use all their energy and muscles indoors are wonderful, but many centers just don't have the space to allow for them. If your child is unusually active, this may be an important consideration in choosing a place for her.

When it comes to telling you what they have been doing all day, toddlers are not the world's best communicators. You will need an easier way to receive information about your child's day. Many centers continue to send home a daily report about each child until the children enter the preschool group at the age of three. Some centers have a bulletin board on which to share information about the children's daily activities with the parents. Watch for these means of communication when you visit the toddler program. If you don't see them, ask how the center addresses parent-caregiver communication.

Staff Qualifications and Practices

A toddler caregiver has to be an exceptional person, because toddler time is such a special period in the life of a child. Toddlers want so badly to be "big" and independent, but so easily crumble and fall apart, needing love and comfort. This is the age when biting and temper tantrums are common, the age when "mine" and "no" are the two most prominent words in a child's vocabulary. Toddlers have little control over their emotions and actions. Although they try hard to follow adults' wishes and instructions, they are often frustrated when they fall short of even their own expectations.

Toddlers grow rapidly in every way. Their bodies are learning to perform so many new actions, like running and hopping and throwing. Their language development is amazing. They add new words every day, yet they often cannot find the ones they need in an emotional moment — suddenly you hear a scream and realize that a child has used her teeth instead of words to make her point.

As they grow and learn, toddlers test everyone and everything. Toddler teachers have to know all this and more to be good caregivers. They have to understand and appreciate the fact that every child goes through this stage. The teachers also need to be able to distinguish between important and unimportant challenges, because toddlers test most of what you do. The solution is not to respond to every one but to guide the children firmly and gently in the right direction, toward increased self-control, competence, and self-sufficiency.

To learn more about the toddler teachers in a center, you must watch them at work. It is a good idea to observe a toddler teacher for at least two hours, and longer if possible. Ask the director about the care-

---

States with Best Caregiver-to-Toddler Ratios (1996)

1 caregiver for 4 toddlers
  Connecticut
  Massachusetts
  Michigan
  Oregon

States with Worst Caregiver-to-Toddler Ratios (1996)

1 caregiver for 13 toddlers
  Texas
1 caregiver for 12 toddlers
  Arkansas
  Idaho
  Louisiana
  Mississippi[6]

givers' educational background and experience. Ideally you want them to have both experience and some theoretical knowledge pertaining to the toddler age. If they have not had specific education or training related to working with children under age three, ask the director whether there is interest in continuing education, and what plans are under way to make this possible.

Center Care for Preschool Children

The U.S. tradition of placing three- to five-year-olds in center-based early childhood programs is at least one hundred years old. These programs have included nursery schools, play groups, day care centers, as they used to be called, and preschools of various kinds. They have served children at all socioeconomic levels and across ethnic groups and religious backgrounds. Because of this long history, most parents feel more comfortable about leaving a preschooler in the care of others than they do an infant or a toddler. Consequently, the range of center-based alternatives in most communities is much wider for preschool-age children than for children under the age of three.

Here we focus on child care centers that serve children on a full-time basis. More specialized, usually part-day preschools, like Head Start, nursery schools, and play groups, are covered in the next chapter.

Preschoolers thrive on the opportunity to spend time with children their own age. They love playing pretend games together, and friendships developed in preschool can often last a lifetime. Most parents see these socializing opportunities as the biggest advantage to be gained from enrolling their children in preschool. Part of that social experience might include the chance to meet people from other cultures and ethnic groups and to learn to appreciate and respect both differences and commonalities. Preschool is also likely to give a child access to a wider variety of toys and equipment than most of us can offer at home.

One disadvantage of center care for preschool-age children can be that their groups are much larger than those for younger children. State regulations usually do not allow full-day child care center programs to have groups of more than seven to nine children per adult, but in some unregulated preschools one teacher can be responsible for as many as twenty children. The capacity to manage comfortably and happily in a group this large varies from child to child. If there is some question in your mind about your child's ability to function well in such a situation, either look for a center that has a low adult-to-child ratio or think seriously of choosing a family child care home (Chapter 5).

Good early childhood professionals understand that preschool children are not simply playing but are learning through play. Caregivers are important in this process because they help children to find and use the materials and toys they need for playing and learning. Caregivers also guide children who don't know what to do next, help them resolve

---

States with Best Caregiver-to-Preschooler Ratios (1996)

1 caregiver for 8 preschoolers
   New York

1 caregiver for 10 preschoolers

Alaska	North Dakota
Connecticut	Oregon
Illinois	Pennsylvania
Maine	Rhode Island
Maryland	South Dakota
Massachusetts	Vermont
Missouri	Washington
Montana	

States with Worst Caregiver-to-Preschooler Ratios (1996)

1 caregiver for 20 preschoolers
   Alabama
   Florida
   North Carolina
   Texas

1 caregiver for 18 preschoolers
   Georgia
   South Carolina

1 caregiver for 16 preschoolers
   Hawaii
   Louisiana
   Mississippi
   Virginia[7]

---

interpersonal conflicts, and teach them how to get along with one another.

The Physical Environment

In a preschool classroom, the environment represents the child's third teacher, after the parents and the caregiver. An effective preschool environment, designed to encourage exploration and initiative, contains areas in which children can work and play in large

> To learn concepts like size, shape, texture, amount, and volume, preschool children must touch and interact directly with materials and learning situations. They construct their own knowledge from what they see, smell, hear, and play with.

groups, in small groups, or by themselves. Toys and materials are readily available, as are many unstructured materials like pens, crayons, paint, paper, scissors, glue, and Play Doh.

What to Look For: The preschool room should be set up with distinct learning centers or interest areas in mind. Staff in different child care centers give various names to these areas, but regardless of the labels, they are all spaces where specific types of activities take place. You are most apt to find separate areas for blocks, creative arts, books and reading, writing, small manipulatives — Lego, Lincoln Logs, puzzles, beads, and so on — house or home or dramatic play, science, and music and dance. Don't panic if all these areas are not present in the child care centers you visit, but do look for the learning areas approach as an important part of the preschool classroom environment. The lack of distinct areas may indicate that the teacher expects children to spend a considerable amount of time in large groups following her instructions. Desks in a preschool classroom suggest that this is likely to be the case. We recommend that you do not enroll your three- to five-year-old child in a program that organizes the pre-

> Early childhood professionals in centers are usually called teachers when they work with two-, three-, and four-year-olds, and caregivers or care providers when they are responsible for children under two.

school environment this way. Preschoolers — and younger primary school-age children — learn best through exploration, hands-on participation, and play.

As you enter the preschool area of a center for the first time, stop for a moment and look around. Listen to the sounds; smell the air. This is where your child will spend most of her waking hours during your work week. You want to be certain that it is a pleasant environment, one you wouldn't mind being in yourself. Look for plenty of light and cheerful colors. Are there attractive and interesting posters on the walls, as well as children's artwork and photographs of the children and their families? Check out the "soft" areas, where there should be pillows or soft chairs for the children, child-size chairs, and soft rugs in a variety of colors and textures. Look for shelves with many books displayed. Soft sounds, including background music, help children relax and feel comfortable. Make sure that there are designated quiet areas with space where a child can have privacy. Are the bathrooms sanitary and clean-smelling, the kitchen attractive and spotless?

Many preschoolers still require an afternoon nap to be able to cope with the rest of the day. Make sure they will be given an opportunity to nap or rest in a quiet, darkened space. Children who have rested on their cots for a while — never longer than half an hour — should be able to play quietly while the others nap. Preschoolers may also need a special comfort toy or piece of blanket that helps them feel at home as they fall asleep.

Outdoors, preschoolers need lots of space to move around, to explore, and to use their imagination. This area should include climbing equipment, swings and slides, and riding toys and tricycles. They also need places, like a sandbox, where they can construct things and ideally, a garden where they can grow their own flowers and vegetables. The space should include both sunny and shady areas and be accessible to water for outdoor water play. A small enclosed structure of some sort, which the children can pretend is a fort or a house (or who knows what else!), is also a welcome addition.

Preschoolers are old enough to begin playing a few noncompetitive group games for which they need balls of all sizes. With the addition of simple hoops and goalposts, children have all they need to imagine themselves as basketball, football, and soccer stars.

Staff Qualifications and Practices

Preschool teachers should have either a degree or considerable training in early childhood education as well as experience working with children this age. Such preparation is important because it provides caregivers with a solid understanding of the capabilities of three- to five-year-olds and why they think and behave as they do. The center director should be able to give you information about the educational backgrounds of the staff and their on-the-job training.

Preschool-age children should be following a predictable daily routine, a written schedule of which should be posted in the classroom to orient you and other visitors. This schedule can offer some flexibility, but children this age like being able to predict what will happen next. Having snacks and meals at a regular time and having a consistent naptime helps them to feel secure in their environment.

What to Look For: When you observe the staff in action in the preschool room, take note of the following.

- How do the teachers and caregivers handle transitions from one activity to another, like getting everyone dressed to go outside during the winter? Children often get antsy and frustrated when they are kept waiting for something to happen. An experienced caregiver anticipates these moments and diffuses the tension with a song or an activity.

- Do the caregivers sit and work with the children as they explore new activities and try out new skills, or do they simply start the children on projects and then stand back and watch? It is important that the adults engage with the children to give them confidence and ease them through frustrations.

- Are the daily routines and activities set up to allow children to make choices? If the room is organized into different activity areas, children should be able to choose among those opportunities during free-play time. Materials and toys stored on shelves that are clearly labeled and easily accessible also help children to choose among various alternatives.

- Are caregivers alert and ready to assist children with personal care routines like eating, going to the bathroom, and dressing themselves when they show a need for help?

- Do you see indications that staff members respect each child's individual needs and characteristics? Caregivers should recognize and respond to the unique personalities and particular habits of all the children, being careful not to play favorites or discriminate against anyone.

- Do the caregivers set appropriate and consistent limits on the children's behavior? Children and caregivers together can establish the rules they all need to follow and list them for all to see. The rules should be stated in positive terms — "We use walking feet inside" or "Inside walking!" Time out should be used only if a child must calm down and collect herself. The caregiver/teacher should remain with the child during this period rather than leaving her in a corner by herself.

- Are all children treated the same regardless of special needs, social class, sex, racial background, or ethnic origin? Check to be sure that they are receiving an equal amount of positive, supportive attention from the caregivers. Is the classroom set up to accommodate children with special needs? Does the staff expect the same behavior from girls as from boys?

- Do the caregivers/teachers greet the children when they arrive in the morning and make an effort to integrate them into the play of those already in the center? This is a difficult transition for some children, who need special attention from the caregiver to adjust smoothly to the new environment each day.

- Watch what happens at snack time and outdoors. Are the teachers actively involved with the children during these times, or do they consider them as time-off periods for themselves?

Good preschool caregivers are explorers. They delight in playing along as the children lead them into worlds of fantasy and imagination and assist in finding new props for the plays the children are creating. The teachers also offer advice when conflicts occur and ask good open-ended questions that help the children expand on their ideas. Look for these kinds of interactions. If you see them, you have found a talented early childhood professional.

Good caregivers are also comfortable expressing warmth and caring toward the children they supervise. They are not afraid to hold or hug or simply touch the children they work with. All human beings require physical contact with others. Ensuring that this need is met for children who spend a large part of their day in a child care setting is especially important. Of course, certain kinds of touching are inappropriate, but preschool children can be taught what kinds of contact are good and what are not right (see Chapter 3). Caregivers should feel comfortable scooping up children in their arms and hugging them. Smiles, soft voices, and sympathetic and encouraging words are also a regular part of the child care environment. As a parent, you may feel jealous at first, knowing that another adult is holding your child's hand and receiving his hugs. It is important for you to work through those feelings and move beyond them to appreciate the wonderful contributions these special people can make to your child's development. Be aware that you are not alone in experiencing jealousy and that you can overcome it (see Chapter 13).

What to Look For Regardless of Child's Age.

Staff turnover, staff schedules, substitute caregivers, and parent involvement with various aspects of a center are additional issues to investigate before making your final selection.

Staff Turnover

Staff turnover is a big problem in many child care centers. Children need to become attached to their caregivers and to feel secure that these special adults will be there for them when they are upset or in crisis. This is especially true for infants and toddlers, but it is a real concern for preschoolers as well (see Chapter 3).

If the staff turnover rate is high at the center you select, take the time to evaluate why this is so. Perhaps you and the other parents can find ways of encouraging caregivers to stay with the center for longer periods of time. Unfortunately, the most common cause of turnover is low pay. Many parents are already too strapped financially to be able to pay the teachers enough to keep them in the child care profession. However, sometimes the problem involves working conditions that can be changed, especially if you are willing to push a little. It is worth your while to find out why caregivers are leaving and think through possible incentives for keeping them involved with your child. For additional ways of making your favorite caregivers feel wanted and important, see Chapter 14.

Staff Schedules

Staff schedules can also present a problem. Getting to know your child's caregivers is important, both to help you feel comfortable away from your child and to ease the process of sharing information about him. It is easier to build a cooperative relationship when the same person is waiting for you each morning when you drop off your child. Because caregivers typically don't work more than an eight-hour day, someone else will probably be with the children when you arrive at the end of the day. The early and late caregivers need to take the time every day to talk with each other about your child, so that they provide consistent care and the afternoon caregiver can pass along anything the morning caregiver wants you to know about your child's day. Ask the center director how the staff address these issues of consistency and continuity.

Substitute Caregivers

To make the best choice for your child's care, you have to learn something about how the center selects its substitute caregivers and what kind of training they have. Most centers have a difficult time keeping well-trained substitutes on call, so the center director may feel a bit defensive on this subject. If there is a child care resource and referral agency in your area, its staff may help local centers recruit and train substitute caregivers. The center may also be able to obtain the names of potential substitutes from local colleges. Students in need of extra money, especially those who want to become teachers or work with children in other capacities, can, with some basic early childhood training, become a great addition to your child's life.

Parent Involvement in the Affairs of a Center

Next to the skills and commitment of the person caring for your child, your involvement in the center is the most important way to guarantee that your child is safe and doing well. You should find out, therefore, how interested a center is in having parents participate, and what kinds of parent involvement are possible.

You can get answers to these questions in various ways. Begin by reading the center's philosophy statement and its parent handbook, if one exists. These documents should give you a sense of how center staff think about parent involvement. Remember, though, that these are just abstract words, so you have to know how to translate the words into interactions and day-to-day activities. The best way to get this information is by talking with other parents and observing them as they interact with the center director and the caregivers. Ask the director for the names and phone numbers of parents whose children are in the program. Choose three names and call each one. Don't limit yourself to parents on the center board of directors; they may not be typical. Ask each parent whether she or he feels welcome in the center and respected as the most important person in the child's life. During your observations, look for signs that parents and caregivers genuinely like and share information openly with one another.

Even when early childhood staff have been well trained in taking care of young children, most do not have much background in working effectively with other adults. Keep that in mind as you begin to develop a working partnership with center staff. Help them understand that you want to be supportive and that you feel responsible for meeting the needs of your child. But also remember that your child's caregiver is concerned about your child and wants to be trusted. Be friendly, be helpful, but don't be too pushy.

Centers vary greatly in their staff's attitude toward and approach to parent involvement. Parent cooperatives (see Chapter 7) require parents to take an active role in running a center and assisting with child care. Some for-profit centers may require virtually no involvement and may even discourage parents from learning too much about how the program is organized and run. Research studies suggest that parent involvement in a child's preschool and later schooling experiences definitely results in better developmental outcomes. Likewise, young children thrive when their parents and their teachers/caregivers are working *together* for them.

Search for a center that lets you participate in its functioning as much as you can. Some centers involve parents in governance, others in repair and maintenance once a year, and still others in chaperoning occasional field trips or contributing special talents and skills (for example, in music, furniture repair, fund-raising, doll making). Workdays at a center, when parents are asked to help with spring cleaning, painting, playground improvement, and the like, are a great way to build a sense of community among parents, caregivers, and other staff. A partnership of care for your child implies agreement about how each partner contributes to it. Check with the director and with other parents on how each center you are considering works with parents.

One thing you want to make sure of is that you can visit your child and the center whenever you want to do so. Parent visits should be encouraged at every age level. A center that doesn't have an open-door policy for parents probably isn't adhering to the licensing law. Parents must be allowed to drop in anytime. This does not mean that you should feel completely free to interrupt your child's day arbitrarily. After all, the caregivers are trying to run a program and your visits can sometimes disrupt their routine. Nevertheless, you should always feel welcome at your child care center.

Choosing a Child Care Center

Once you have decided that center-based care is a good option for your child and your family, it is time to give careful consideration to the centers available in your area. In Chapter 4 we describe two general ways to find the child care resources in your community — talking with relatives, neighbors, and friends about their experiences with centers and contacting your local or state child care resource and referral agency for information about the centers registered with them. It is now time to use those two strategies to create a list of possible centers and to gather opinions about the strengths and weaknesses of each program.

Once you have composed the list, you must figure out which center will best meet your needs. *For an infant or toddler, you should start this process at least six months before you want your child to enter care.*

> For an infant or toddler, you should start the search for a child care center at least six months before you want your child to enter care.

An early start is important because center care for infants and toddlers is scarce, resulting in a great demand for available places. Even programs for three- and four-year-olds have waiting lists, so be sure to start shopping about six to nine months before care is necessary.

Finding the right program involves a four-step procedure:

1. Contacting centers by telephone
2. Visiting centers whose programs meet your basic requirements
3. Talking with center directors
4. Making a choice

1 Contacting Centers by Telephone

A telephone interview is a way of reducing the list of centers to two or three real possibilities without having to spend time visiting each one on your list. Remember that the calls are just to help you decide whether a visit is worthwhile. The following questions can be used as a guide. These and other helpful interview questions, forms, and checklists are reprinted in Appendix D for convenient duplication. Make enough copies of each so that you have one available for each call and visit.

Center Telephone Survey Form

Center name_____ Date of call_____

Location_____ Name of director_____

Ages of children served_____ Hours care provided_____

Is this a year-round program?_____

Will there be an opening when we require care?_____

Is the center licensed?_____ What are the fees?_____

Number of children per adult in our child's age group:_____

Total number of children in our child's age group:_____

Qualifications of caregiving staff_____

_____

When is a good time to visit?_____

You can see that these questions fall into three main categories: logistics (Where is the center? When is it open? Does it have openings?), cost, and quality. At this early stage in your investigation your inquiries about quality can be limited to the number of children for whom each caregiver is responsible — fewer is better! — the number of children in the group, and how much education and training the caregivers have received. You can delve into more specifics when you visit particular centers.

Once you have gathered this information about each center in your area, compare them from your notes and select two or three to visit. *Don't let price determine your choice at this stage!* Cost may make a big difference in your final decision, but allow yourself to visit a more expensive program if it sounds good in other ways. This will give you a standard against which to compare other centers. You might even be able to work a deal on price or a payment schedule that allows you some flexibility.

2 Visiting Centers Whose Programs Meet Your Basic Requirements

The centers you visit will be those which serve children the right age, during the hours you need, at locations convenient to you, with trained caregivers looking after groups of reasonable size (see Quality, Chapter 3). Center directors should be happy to have you visit. It may be difficult for them to accommodate you on a particular day you propose, but in general your request should be welcome. You also should be able to pick the times of the day for your visit — but don't choose naptime. *If you sense resistance to your request to visit at any time besides naptime, be wary.*

When you visit each center for the first time, don't take your child. You need the chance to observe the action closely and ask questions without also having to keep track of him.

It is a good idea to visit during at least two time blocks, each lasting about two hours. One good block to observe is when parents are bringing in their children at the beginning of the day. Plan to arrive between 7:30 and 8:00 A.M., and stay into midmorning. If your child is a preschooler, three to five years old, try to observe during both free-play and teacher-directed activities.

Another valuable observation time comes toward the end of the day, after naptime but before most children are picked up by their parents. Both children and caregivers are tired after six to eight hours together, giving you a chance to see how these providers handle short tempers and low tolerance for frustration.

The following checklist is designed to record all the basic information you need to determine the quality and affordability of the centers that you visit. The checklist distinguishes infant and toddler needs from those of three- and four-year-olds. See Appendix D.

Center Child Care Checklist

Name of center_____

Address _____

Date _____

Yes	No	Basic Information
—	—	Program licensed?
—	—	Hours compatible with work?
—	—	Affordable rates?

Health and Safety

Yes	No	
—	—	Is the facility secure?
—	—	Is the facility well maintained?
—	—	Working smoke detectors/fire extinguishers?
—	—	Electrical outlets covered?
—	—	Safe windows/gated stairs?
—	—	Medicines/cleaning agents locked away?
—	—	Clear emergency exits?
—	—	Kitchen/bathrooms sanitary?
—	—	Indoor and outdoor play areas?
—	—	Play areas clean and uncluttered?

Indoor Play Area

Yes	No	
—	—	Are toys safe and appropriate?
—	—	Is there adequate space for children to play?
—	—	Is a variety of toys/materials available?
—	—	Can children be seen easily?
—	—	Are lighting/windows/ventilation adequate?
—	—	Are bathrooms accessible?
—	—	Is there space for personal belongings?
—	—	Is there room for both active and quiet play?

Yes No

Outdoor Play Area

— — Is it enclosed and secure?
— — Is it free of rocks and other safety hazards?
— — Are climbers, swings, slides, safe and supervised?
— — Are there soft surfaces under outdoor equipment?
— — Can children be seen easily?
— — Uncluttered areas so children can run?
— — Space for quiet and active play?
— — Does the area have regular maintenance inspections?

Nap Area

— — Individual cots/cribs?
— — Cots and cribs clean and in good order?
— — Quiet location but can be observed?
— — Evacuation plan clearly posted?

Caregivers

— — Do the children seem happy around the providers?
— — Are the caregivers in good physical condition and able to keep up with the children?
— — Are the caregivers warm and affectionate?
— — Are the caregivers positive and open?
— — Are the caregivers willing to talk to you?
— — Do the caregivers invite you to drop in?
— — Do the caregivers seem organized?
— — Do the caregivers seem genuinely to like children?
— — Do the caregivers focus on and interact mostly with the children rather than chatting with one another?
— — Is discipline maintained by careful supervision, clear limits, and explanations that the child can understand?
— — Do caregivers avoid conflicts between children by listening and watching carefully, then stepping in early to prevent violence?
— — Do caregivers use praise and attention to encourage cooperation and helpfulness?
— — Do the caregivers work as a team?

If Working with Infants and Toddlers

— — Do caregivers respond quickly to signs of unhappiness or distress?

Yes No

__ __   Do caregivers hold infants and toddlers often and in caring ways?

__ __   Are babies too young to hold their bottles fed in the arms of caregivers?

__ __   Do caregivers talk directly to the infants and toddlers, responding to their sounds and vocalizations?

__ __   Do caregivers set limits consistently and gently?

__ __   Do caregivers allow children to explore and give help when they need it?

__ __   Are babies allowed to nap when they are tired?

__ __   Do caregivers wash their hands after every diaper change and before feedings?

Program and Administrative Structure

__ __   Is there a clear daily schedule?

__ __   Are activities varied and age-appropriate?

__ __   Are the meals and snacks nutritious?

__ __   Is there a program policy on discipline?

__ __   Is there a program philosophy about children?

__ __   Is there an active board of directors with parent representatives?

__ __   Are parents welcome to visit any time they wish?

Based on our definition of quality (see Chapter 3), the checklist places particular emphasis on the person or persons who have direct responsibility for your child. The care provider section lists the kinds of behaviors these key people should display as they work with children of various ages. The best way to tell whether your child will be valued by the person who cares for him is by watching her at work with other children. Place yourself in the room where your child would be based and note *how* care is being provided. Put a check mark by the item on the checklist as you investigate a center.

The physical space in and outside the center is also important. Look carefully at the layout and equipment in the rooms your child would use and take a tour through the entire facility. Then look at the outdoor play space. Check off the items and characteristics that you observe. Ask questions if something important seems to be missing or in poor repair.

Licensing is an important indicator of quality. Make sure it is current.

Finally, there is the question of cost. We recommend that you always pay more if that will result in higher-quality care. Obviously most parents cannot afford to pay more than a certain amount. We urge you to read Chapter 16, Paying for Child Care, before deciding against a program simply because it is too expensive.

3 Talking with Center Directors

The discussion with the director is your chance to follow up on some of the checklist items and acquire more information on policies and procedures. A director is the nerve center of a program. She is responsible for meeting state and local regulations, hiring and firing staff, recruiting participating families, creating and balancing the budget, and ensuring the overall quality of the program. With this obligation and perspective, the person should be able to answer any questions that arose while you were observing caregivers and provide information about policies and procedures set up for the whole center and all participating families. If she is unable to do so, you should view this as a weakness in the program.

It is important to be organized when you first meet with the director so that you come across as knowledgeable and concerned for your child's welfare. We have designed this director interview to help you with that process. (See Appendix D for the expanded version.)

What are the "right" answers to these questions? For the practical items this depends on your schedule and budget. How much can you afford to pay? What times of the day and week do you require care?

On questions of quality, we recommend the adult-to-child ratio and group-size standards of the National Association for the Education of Young Children in the Legal Requirements for Centers section of this chapter.

A caregiver's leaving is a real emotional loss, especially for children six months to two years old. If possible, pick the center with the lowest incidence of staff turnover.

In terms of education and training, specific preparation for working with young children is more important than an unrelated college degree.

Good training is more important than many years of experience without any training.

We believe that policies related to items like favorite stuffed toys or pacifiers, toilet training, and even discipline should be flexible and designed for the individual child. So be concerned if the director says "No pacifiers after the first birthday" or "Children have to keep their stuffed animals in their cubbies" or "Children who don't do what we say spend time in the time-out corner."

Director Interview

What year did the center open for business?

Is your license current? When was the last licensing visit?

How long have your teachers/caregivers been with you? How many have left in the past six months?

What is the calendar for the center — holidays, vacations?

What is your policy regarding sick children?

How many children would be in my child's group? How many adults are with that group?

What is the education and training background of the person who would care for my child?

What about first-aid training, in case of illness or accident?

Do you have specific policies regarding (choose those relevant for your child):

- pacifiers and personal security objects like blankets?
- bottles?
- toilet training?
- discipline?
- bringing toys to the center?

What is the fee for a child the age of mine? What is the payment schedule? Are parents expected to pay any other expenses? May I have a copy of your parent contract?

What are your policies regarding meals and snacks? If meals are served: May I see a weekly menu?

How do you feel about parent-teacher communications? Do you have any policies that encourage communication?

Are there other ways that parents can be involved in the center?

Questions specific to your child's particular needs, for example, food allergies, sleep requirements, personality.

4 Making a Choice

When choosing a program, remember that the most important ingredient is the adult or adults who will be responsible for your child. Obviously, cost is also a critical consideration. Yet if you are trying to decide whether it's worth paying more for better caregivers, and you can afford to do it by giving up something else, *pay more!* This is your child we are talking about! Think back to the caregivers you met — which ones gave you the most comfortable feeling? Have they had some training, so you can be sure that they know what they are doing? If so, they are worth more money.

Another useful way to make a choice is to close your eyes and try to imagine your child in each of the settings you visited. Which one comes out best? At this point you have applied all available objective criteria in comparing programs, so trust your instincts.

Once you select a program, be sure to provide the center staff with the basic information necessary to ensure your child's safety. A sample form, About the Child, appears in Appendix D.

Perhaps you are not happy with any of the centers available in your community. If so, see Chapter 5, Family and Group Family Child Care, Chapter 8, Care in Your Own Home, and Chapter 10, Creative Alternatives, for other possibilities.

7

Part-Day Programs

ART-DAY CHILD CARE programs come in many different shapes and sizes. The types we describe in this chapter — play groups, nursery schools, parent-run cooperatives, and Head Start — are the ones you are most likely to find in your local community. These part-day programs can be combined with other child care options to provide you with full-day coverage. If you work or attend school part time, they offer enough hours of care to meet those needs. For instance, you might use a play group or nursery school as an extension of family child care to give your four-year-old daughter more exposure to children her own age. Parent-run cooperatives are a possibility if you have some flexibility in your work or school schedule, want to have more say in your child's schooling, and can take the time necessary to be directly involved with program operations. The federally funded Head Start program is a great choice for those with a limited income, because it is free to eligible families. Like play groups and nursery schools, Head Start can be combined with other care to provide the child and family with a full-time care option.

Most states do not regulate child care programs that operate for three hours or less a day. Keep this in mind as you consider nursery and cooperative nursery programs, especially if you plan to combine such a program with another option to create full-day care. You must learn enough about the program you choose to be assured that it will provide a healthy environment for your child. Head Start meets a special set of rather strict federal performance standards. Because you attend a play group with your child, you are able to monitor that experience directly.

Play Groups

Play groups typically run for only a few hours each morning, one or two mornings a week. Mornings are chosen because parents want their preschoolers at home for afternoon naptime. Many play groups operate in churches, human service agency buildings, community buildings, family resource centers, and agencies like the YWCA or YMCA. Play groups consist of parents or family child care providers and their children who get together in a space large enough to hold fifteen to twenty people. They bring toys and some play equipment, which the children share as they play together in the presence of the adults.

Some play groups plan a special program for the parents or family child care providers while the children play. These adults take turns monitoring the children and participating in the special program. Other play group meetings are completely social occasions in which the adults interact informally with one another and with the children as the morning progresses.

Although created originally for stay-at-home parents who are looking after their children, play groups can also be used to reduce the social isolation experienced by a family child care provider, nanny, or au pair. Most American neighborhoods have become lonely places for both children and adults during the typical working day. Under those conditions, the opportunity to interact with other children and adults for a couple of mornings a week can be a wonderful change of scenery. If your home-based child care provider is not already a member of a play group, you might want to help her check out the possibilities in her neighborhood or community.

Nursery Schools

A forerunner of our kindergartens, the traditional nursery school has been a part of the American child care scene for more than a hundred years. Although those of us over forty probably weren't in full-time child care, many of us had some experience with nursery school when we were three, four, or five years old.

Three- to five-year-old children usually attend nursery school for two, three, or five half days per week, either mornings or afternoons. Because the younger preschoolers tend to need at least one nap a day, which they typically take in the afternoon, many nursery schools operate only during the morning. Some run an afternoon program for older preschoolers who can make it through the day with just a quiet time in the afternoon. Because nursery schools don't normally have the facilities for changing diapers, most require that your child be toilet trained to be eligible for enrollment.

Nursery schools are quite different from child care centers in several important ways. First, the ratio of adults to children is generally much lower in nursery schools than in full-day child care programs. It is not unusual to find a teacher working with fifteen to twenty-five children. Sometimes she is helped by a parent or another adult, but her assistant doesn't ordinarily have much formal training. A second difference is that nursery school teachers often have a four-year college degree and some background in early childhood education. Some also have elementary school teaching certificates. By contrast, most staff in child care centers have trained on the job, and only a few have four-year degrees with early childhood courses.

Many nursery schools also offer a more academic program than one finds in a typical child care center, partly because their teachers tend to have academic backgrounds. However, another reason is that these teachers don't have to worry about the basic care — meals, naps — or long-term emotional support of the children. Their time can be focused, instead, on helping the children work on their cognitive, physical, language, and social skills.

Because nursery schools provide care for only three hours a day, they are especially useful to parents who work or attend school part time. But like play groups, they can be combined with full-time home-based care arrangements as a way of providing playmates for a child who may not have access to children his own age. Family child care providers, nannies, and au pairs often bring the children in their care to a nursery school for the extra educational stimulation and opportunity to play with age-mates. This type of arrangement has the added advantage of allowing a child to get to know and become attached to a wider range of caring adults than might otherwise be available to her. Many children live so far from their grandparents, aunts, and uncles that they need other, more accessible ways to get to know and trust caring adults besides their parents. Availing yourself of a nursery school program may also make it possible for your regular child care provider to devote some time exclusively to a young child — if she cares for other children — or to attend school, as au pairs do, or simply to have time off.

Some nursery schools also have extended-day programs, which allow some of the children to stay for more than three hours per day. Such an extended program usually has to be licensed as a child care center and abide by the same rules and regulations. If you are interested in a nursery school with an extended-day program, make sure that you evaluate it using our center guidelines and checklists (see Chapter 6).

Parent-Run Cooperatives

Many parents assume that they cannot take advantage of a parent-run cooperative child care center because they have an inflexible work or class schedule. While it is true that these programs require parent participation in center-related activities for a certain number of hours per week or per month, you may find that a co-op program suits you very well if you have *some* flexibility in your schedule and are willing to be a bit creative. The following history is an example of what a group of parents can accomplish when they decide to try something a little different.

The Bank Street Co-op

In the early 1970s, the staff of Bank Street College in New York City created a co-op program that began as an arrangement for just five to eight families. These family members got together to design a center that looked a lot like an apartment, with a living room, a bedroom, and a kitchen. Because each of the founding families included at least one full-time working parent, they soon decided that it would not be possible to take on the primary responsibility of teaching the children themselves. They hired two full-time teachers to provide the day-to-day caregiving for the children and made themselves available to provide emergency care as needed. Some children attended full time, others part time. Each family set its own schedule, notifying the teachers well in advance for planning purposes.

The center offered care for children from newborns to the age of three. Most parents were able to drop in several times a day to spend time with their children. Many also took their child out for lunch during the week or to their office for a visit. There was no director — the center was run by a steering committee made up of the two teachers and two or three parents. The committee had weekly meetings, open to all parents, at which they made the decisions related to running the center. Many parents contributed to curriculum planning through informal discussions with the teachers at lunchtime meetings held once or twice a week. Staff and parents also worked together on a journal of each child's experience. In this way every family received a unique record of their child's development at the end of each year.

The parent fees covered all teacher salaries, supplies, and materials, and space was donated by Bank Street College. The parent group sponsored a number of fund-raising activities to raise money for extra equipment and supplies. They became adept at procuring furniture and other articles donated to the center, much of which they repaired and refurbished themselves. All this work helped to build the cooperative spirit of the group.

The parents and staff of the co-op had equal power in managing the center. Five committees were set up to administer the various aspects of center operations — educational, fiscal, parent involvement, and so forth, and two parents served on each committee. To maintain continuity and pass along the experience of the founding parents as their children left the center, care was taken to ensure that there was always a "new" parent and an "old" parent on the steering committee. Parents and teachers also had a monthly evening meeting to discuss whatever might be on anyone's mind relative to the center and the children. Everyone involved enjoyed the sense that they were helping one another through the child-rearing process. This was especially important for the families whose relatives did not live nearby.[1]

The Bank Street Co-op has served as a model for many of the cooperative nursery programs that have been developed since then. You can see that a primary focus of this center was on the partnership among the parents, the children, and the teachers. The parents wanted to minimize the conflict between career and family by having a facility near their workplaces and to have a lot of say in running the program. They liked the family feeling that resulted from keeping the program small and saved money by taking on much of the responsibility for equipping and running the center.

Parent-Run Cooperatives in the 1990s

Many present-day parent-run cooperatives operate on schedules similar to those of nursery schools. They are part-day programs that enroll each child for two to five mornings or afternoons a week and adhere to the regular public school calendar. The school is staffed by teachers hired by the parents.

Parents in a typical co-op program must commit themselves to helping in the classroom at least once a month. They are also expected to be present at monthly meetings, serve on a board committee, attend biannual work parties to help maintain school property, and help set up and dismantle the program at the beginning and end of each school year. Parents usually receive instruction in how to assist in the classroom and interact with the children. Parent helpers may also often be responsible for supplying the children's snack for the days they are on duty.

Because most part-day programs are unregulated, no minimum requirements are set for teacher education, and teacher qualifications can vary a great deal. Given a choice, parents involved in hiring usually seek out the most qualified people available, so that co-op centers are typically staffed with well-trained, experienced teachers. And because they need fewer paid staff members, the cost for parent co-op programs is usually somewhat less than for a regular nursery school.

Some parent co-ops offer extended-day programs, which, in most states, must meet the licensing requirements of child care centers. If you are considering this option, make sure that the adult-to-child ratio and other aspects of the program meet the standards required for quality care in a full-day child care center (see Chapter 6).

Head Start Programs

The federally funded Head Start program is the most comprehensive part-day child development program in the country. Head Start, which began in the mid-sixties, is so named because its goal is to provide children from low-income families with a head start in preparation for public school. Although most Head Start programs are run by a local community action program agency, some are operated by school districts, some by local child care resource and referral agencies, and some as independent organizations.

The overall object of Head Start is to promote the social competence of the children in its programs, each of which is guided by national performance standards that are revised and updated regularly. The programs offer their participants a wide range of services in addition to preschool education, including health screening, parent involvement and education, social services, disability services, and a supportive and nurturing relationship with all staff members.

If your child is three or four years old, and you think that your family may fall within the Head Start eligibility guidelines — a 1996 income below $15,600 for a family of four — call your local Head Start office to learn more about the program. Your local child care resource and referral organization (see Appendix B), school district, library, and phone book should be able to supply the phone number.

If you are working or going to school full time and wonder whether a part-day Head Start class can meet your needs, don't write off the program just for that reason. More and more parents are facing the need to be employed or seeking further education while their children are still preschoolers. Many Head Start programs try to meet the child care needs of working parents either through extended-day programs or by busing children to family child care providers when the program ends for the day. Head Start is also beginning to operate programs for infants and toddlers, so call the program nearest you even if your child is very young.

One obvious advantage to Head Start is that it is free. A second strength to the program is the additional services it offers you and your family; for example, a medical and a dental screening for each child with follow-up visits if necessary. The program also has a social services coordinator who can help you gain access to other community services and an education coordinator whose job it is to be sure that the educational quality of the program meets the standard set by the national Head Start organization.

Another important element of the program is its emphasis on parent involvement. The Head Start philosophy is that the family, the neighborhood, and the community are all important factors in a child's life, and all need to become actively involved in the child's learning. Program staff begin by making getting-acquainted home visits before each child enters Head Start. They also encourage parents to attend evening parent meetings and to visit the classroom during the school day if at all possible. Parents not employed outside the home who are interested in and capable of caring for young children are encouraged to become volunteers in the classroom and can gradually move into positions as paid classroom aides. After further education — training as a Child Development Associate or the equivalent — they can become classroom teachers in Head Start classrooms or Head Start Home Visitors calling on Head Start families in their homes on a regular schedule, bringing toys and information about educational activities.

Head Start, a federally financed program, depends on action by

Congress for funding. Currently Congress provides only enough money to serve about half the eligible families. Hiring well-qualified staff is also a problem in some areas because of the generally low salaries offered to child care professionals, a situation not limited to Head Start! Training staff is a high priority for Head Start. The Child Development Associate credential is the minimum requirement for a Head Start teacher, and Head Start provides money to each program for continual in-service training for the teachers and all other personnel.

Part-Day Programs – Avoiding the Patchwork

If you are working or going to school full time, part-time programs can be wonderful complements to other arrangements that you make for your child. Our one caution is that you avoid the danger of piecing together too many different programs and caregivers for any given day or week. Children do best in a consistent, predictable set of daily routines, surrounded by a small number of warm, caring, and stimulating adults and a manageable number of familiar children.

Of course, emergencies do arise, and most parents have to patch together care alternatives now and then. Keep in mind, however, that these can be exhausting and disorienting for a child who is constantly moving from one setting to another, always having to start over again with new faces and demands and never being able to just relax and feel safe. Family child care or in-home care can be combined with any of the part-day options as long as they remain regular and predictable. Extended-day programs can be great, but only if they meet licensing standards, provide a reasonable ratio of children to adults, and include a well-thought-out afternoon curriculum. Head Start programs are lifesavers for some working families, presenting comprehensive child development programs without charging the participants a penny. But don't ask your child to manage more than two care arrangements in any given day, and do your best to keep them consistent from day to day.

Choosing a Part-Day Program

When choosing a part-day program you must consider your child's personality and disposition, your family's characteristics and needs, and how the program will mesh with your other child care arrangements.

In general, part-day programs advertise in local newspapers or the *Yellow Pages*, and are usually listed with your local child care resource and referral agency. See Chapter 4 for more information on how to locate programs through these channels.

Play Groups

Picking a play group is a relatively simple process, partly because you usually attend the program yourself and can support your child in building friendships with other children. Your primary goal should be to find a group that includes children of approximately your child's age. Ideally you will also want to find a group of adults whose company you or your family child care provider or in-home caregiver can enjoy for a few hours each week.

Nursery Schools

When seeking a nursery school, take the time to read the literature each provides and to visit first without and then with your child. Most nursery schools have handouts describing their philosophy. If you are interested in an academic program or one designed to bring out your child's creative abilities, look for these kinds of emphasis in the descriptions of the programs and during your visits. Its geographic location can be important in determining your choice of nursery school, especially if you must depend on a family child care provider to transport your child to and from the program. Even when your nanny or family child care provider is the primary contact with the nursery school, remember that you must stay in touch with the program as well. When all the key adults in the child's life talk to one another and work together, the result is a level of consistency and continuity that provides maximum opportunity for healthy development. Reread the indicators for a quality program described in Chapter 3 and use them in reaching your decision. See Appendix E for a nursery school assessment sheet you can use as a guide in comparing the programs in your area.

Parent Cooperatives

You choose a parent-run cooperative because you want to be more involved in your child's education and care than is possible with other care options. But parent-run co-ops also have different philosophies regarding the extent of your involvement and how it is accomplished. Be sure you understand and are comfortable with this philosophy, and *like* the people with whom you will have to share many hours. You should spend time with the other parents and in the classroom with and without your child to be certain that you understand and like the program. Learn as much as you can about the teacher. What is her background, her education and experience, her interest in continuing education, and her ability to work with parents? Take another look at the characteristics of a good program described in Chapter 3. They apply to co-op programs as well as to other child care arrangements. Do you find most of those characteristics in the program you are considering? Can you compromise somewhat and still be happy with the program in general? Watch your child in action in the classroom during a visit, and use that as one of the guidelines for your decision.

Head Start

It is not as easy to "shop around" for a Head Start program as for other child care programs. Most of the community programs have only a few classes at each geographic location. However, you still need to be an informed and savvy "consumer" when you enroll your child. The more you can learn about the program the better. Some Head Start groups have several classrooms, and you may feel that one will suit your child and you better than the others. Talk to the Head Start director or the site coordinator about visiting the various classrooms. When you visit, ask how the teacher will work with your child and what your role in the program will be. The quality guidelines in Chapter 3 can help you think about some of the features you'd like to see in the classrooms you visit. In Head Start you can also become involved in a parent board, giving you the opportunity to help in making decisions about ways to improve the program.

As you explore the part-day child care choices in your community, you may hear conflicting opinions about the quality of the Head Start experience as compared with the alternatives. Staff and parents involved with Head Start are likely to speak highly of their program, pointing out the services it provides and the strong performance standards that shape its educational approach. People interested in nursery schools, regulated child care centers, and family child care homes, who are likely to point with pride to improvements in the quality of their programs, may suggest that Head Start is a "poor people's" program. The truth is that Head Start and other child care programs can be equally good and equally bad. Good child care centers offer all the educational and social benefits associated with Head Start, but they don't include the comprehensive medical and dental supports, and they're not free. Good Head Start programs provide extraordinary opportunities not only for children, but also for their parents and other family members. Poor Head Start programs, like poor nursery schools, child care centers, and family child care providers, may actually interfere with the healthy development of young children. Your task as a parent is to take the time to figure out which of the programs in your local community offer experiences that will both enhance your child's development and meet your own needs as a worker or student.

8

Care in Your Own Home

CHILD CARE in your own home can take a number of different forms. You may arrange your schedules so that you and your spouse or partner work different shifts and share the care of your child or children. You can also arrange to have a relative or a nanny come into your home to care for your child while you are at work or school. Or a relative, nanny, or au pair can live in your home and care for your children in exchange for room, board, and a stipend. Because the nanny and au pair arrangements require the most care and planning, these options are the focus of this chapter.

Imagine that it is 6:45 on a dark, snowy November morning. You are struggling to awaken a two-year-old and a four-year-old and to get them dressed and fed so that you can rush them off in your car, on slippery roads, to two different child care facilities in time to make it to work for your 8:00 A.M. meeting. Help!

Now imagine instead that you have an in-home child care provider. In one scenario this "angel of mercy" shows up on your doorstep every workday morning at least fifteen minutes before you have to leave for work. You don't have to dress or feed the children if you don't have the time, because Nanny will be happy to do that as soon as she arrives. You go off to work knowing that your children are in good hands for the rest of the day. When you get home after a long day at work, the nanny has fed your children their supper. They are ready to join you for some quality time, after which you'll read them their bedtime story and put them to bed.

Another scenario has the nanny or au pair living in your home, responsible for taking care of all your children's needs while you are at work or school. No handing them over to a stranger at a center the morning the child care teacher has the day off or is sick, no long drives back and forth to day care, no hurried breakfast, and no after-work trip to the grocery store with a crying child. Nanny has everything under control.

At first glance, Mary Poppins sounds like the perfect child care provider. But she and her friends come with drawbacks as well, the first and most obvious being cost. As in-home child care has become more and more professional, costs have been rising. The in-home caregiver is no longer the girl who lives around the corner and baby-sits for $2.50 an hour.

In the past, only wealthy American families could afford a live-in child care provider. But two changes have altered this picture somewhat. First, an expanded au pair system has developed over the past ten years, which makes it possible for young people from foreign countries to reside with an American host family while participating directly in the home life of the family and providing limited child care services. This choice is not cheap, as you will see, but it may make financial sense for a large family. The second change involves the growing number of two-income couples who can afford the added expense of in-home care and feel that the convenience and security of the arrangement are worth the money. In fact, if you have two or more young children under the age of three, you might end up spending less money on a nanny or an au pair than for a child care center or a family child care provider. For instance, high-quality center-based infant care costs up to $180 per child per week in the United States. Multiply that amount for three children, and you are spending $540 weekly. You can hire a nanny or an au pair for anywhere between $175 and $600 per week, depending on location, additional benefits, and whether you offer a live-in or live-out position.

But beyond cost there may be other disadvantages to these types of in-home arrangements. You'll have no backup when your nanny gets sick, goes on vacation, or has an emergency and has to leave town for a few days. If she is stuck in heavy traffic while trying to get to your house on time, you are likely to be late to work. Another possible drawback is that the children will not have the chance to interact and socialize with other children, as they would in group child care. Preschool-age children benefit from opportunities to interact with children outside their own families and expand their social skills before entering kindergarten and elementary school. (See Chapter 7 for ways to combine in-home care with part-time group programs.)

There has been much press coverage about the problems parents have encountered in trying to monitor what goes on at home when their children are in the care of a nanny. Some parents have secretly videotaped their home caregivers, learning that the children were being neglected and mistreated while they were away. The American Civil Liberties Union, a group that tries to safeguard the privacy of all U.S. citizens, has deemed it illegal to tape someone's conversations secretly and frowns on the idea of videotaping people without their permission. However, parents who take such steps argue that the safety of their children must be considered ahead of anyone else's rights. Indeed, there are organizations that rent cameras to parents who wish to spy on their children's nannies! Surely the mistrust created by such behavior poisons a relationship with a caregiver, and the spillover is bad for a child's sense of well-being. As an informed employer you can institute a selection process that is personal and thorough enough to weed out any candidate whose qualifications or commitment is at all questionable.

Whether you want to hire an au pair, a baby sitter, a mother's helper, or a nanny, you will expect that person to possess certain personal qualities. The good child care provider is a concerned, tuned-in person, someone who respects your children and will strive to make them feel safe and secure in her care. This individual should have some knowledge of child development and young children. She, or perhaps he, should have drive and initiative. Remember that she will be alone with one or more children every day. She has to be enterprising and resourceful to make those days stimulating and fulfilling, both for your children and for herself. If you have not already done so, review the description of quality care provided in Chapter 3, and keep it in mind as you consider the various in-home options and go through the caregiver selection process outlined below.

Baby Sitters and Mother's Helpers

A baby sitter is someone who does not live with you and whom you call on irregularly to provide care for your children on a full- or part-time basis. Baby sitters, who are paid an hourly rate, ordinarily have no special training.

A parent or mother's helper may come in during the day or live in your home. She provides full- or part-time child care and domestic help under your direction and supervision. You are normally at home during her working hours, but may leave her in charge of the children for brief periods. Mother's helpers, who are usually paid by the hour, have no special child care training.

If you employ teenagers as baby sitters, learn as much as you can about local baby sitter training opportunities, and encourage your sitters to take advantage of them. Many communities have baby-sitting courses at a local YMCA/YWCA, Red Cross program, or Cooperative Extension Center. These courses are helpful in teaching basic baby-sitting skills, and they provide inexperienced young people with information and training in how to handle emergency situations.

You also play an important part in keeping your child safe and happy in a sitter's care by being sure to give your sitter a great deal of information about your child's habits, routines, and preferences. In order to be effective, your baby sitter has to know your child's likes and dislikes, where you can be reached, and how to get hold of a doctor or an ambulance if an emergency arises.

Nannies

The American Council of Nanny Schools (ACNS) distinguishes between two general classifications of nannies: those who are *experienced but not certified nannies* and those who are *professional certified nannies.* Both types may live in or away from your home, and both generally work without supervision. A nanny who has not been trained in a certified nanny school, may be expected to do domestic work as well as child care. A certified nanny limits her work to the care of your children and the promotion of their emotional, social, and cognitive development. She has prepared for her work, which she views as a profession, by completing course and practicum requirements at a school accredited by the ACNS. In addition to her salary she expects such benefits as paid vacation and sick days.

A Nanny's Duties

The duties of live-in and daytime nannies are quite similar, although those who live in tend to work somewhat longer hours, and receive room and board plus a salary in exchange for their services. Nannies perform a wide variety of duties related to the care of your children. First and foremost, they tend to all the children's needs throughout the day. They change diapers if necessary, provide meals, ensure that the children get their rest, and create a safe and secure environment for them. A nanny also cooks their food, cares for their clothes, and transports them to doctors' appointments or sports practice as required.

This wide-ranging list of tasks reflects the kinds of skills a good nanny must possess. She needs to know something about child health and nutrition. She may well need a valid driver's license. She must have some background in child development and be able to plan an interesting and stimulating day for your child. She should be able to bring structure to your child's day and serve as a good role model for the children in her care. Your nanny should take the children outdoors at least once a day, weather permitting, and be sure that they get plenty of exercise even on days when they cannot go out. In addition, you may wish to have your nanny join you on vacation trips — not to play but to work! — and to be available on occasional evenings — for extra pay.

A nanny can help you understand how she and the children spend their day by keeping a record — in the form of a diary or a log — of daily activities and concerns. She can also help by keeping a written record of her expenses. The diary provides you with a report of what went on during the day — the food your children ate, whether a child felt sick or upset, how often they left the house and where they went, and any interesting activities they engaged in at home while you were at work. The expense record helps keep all of your monetary dealings aboveboard. There will never be a question of how much the nanny paid and for what when she shops for the child or how much she paid for gas when she took him out for a ride in the car.

There should also be a set time every week when you and your nanny get together to check in with each other and compare notes, when you share the good times as well as the frustrations and challenges. Like the parent-teacher conference in a child care center, the weekly meeting is a time to communicate with your nanny about your children and to hear what she has to say about how they are doing.

Hours of Work and Rate of Pay

Most nannies work about thirty to sixty hours a week. They tend to have long workdays, weekends and holidays off, as well as an average of six to eight paid legal holidays per year. In addition, a paid vacation of at least two weeks is generally part of the package. Many nannies have the use of a family car and gas during workdays.

What you pay your nanny depends on where you live, the number of hours she works, whether room and board is part of her arrangement with you, and what other benefits are included. Rates can vary from $175 to as much as $600 per week. Nannies must be paid at least minimum wage, and any hours worked beyond full time — a maximum of forty-five hours per week — should be figured at one and a half times the hourly rate.

As an employer you have to pay your nanny's Social Security taxes quarterly, filing IRS Form 942. Although you do not have to withhold federal income tax, you must provide your employee with a W-2 form describing her earnings and send a W-3 form with the same information to the Internal Revenue Service. You also must obtain an employer ID number. In some states you are required to withhold city and/or state taxes from the nanny's paycheck. For more assistance call your local IRS office and ask for all the available information relative to employing household help. Other employment-related expenses to consider include the following:

- Certain states require employers to pay workers' compensation insurance. You can find out about these requirements and costs from the company that carries your renters or homeowners insurance.
- Ask your insurance agent whether you have to adjust your car insurance because your nanny will be driving your car.
- Some states require employers to pay an unemployment tax. For advice on this issue, contact your state unemployment office. The federal unemployment tax must be paid quarterly and reported to the IRS annually on Form 940.
- Some parents offer their nannies paid health insurance. Others provide them with a certain number of paid sick days a year — usually six for a full-time employee.
- Room and board is valued between $60 and $100 per week, depending on where you live. Figure it in as you decide on the weekly salary of a live-in nanny.

Education, Training, and Experience

At least two national organizations set standards for nannies and their education in the United States. American Council of Nanny Schools, which accredits nanny institutions, has developed guidelines for training nannies. The International Association of Nannies is an organization that promotes the education and training of nannies through professional membership. Accredited nanny schools offer a number of college-level courses related to the development and care of young children. Most require a minimum of two hundred hours of classroom work — equivalent to twelve-plus college credits — and an additional hundred hours of fieldwork in child care — six college credits. Some classroom-based courses are directly related to in-home care, covering subjects such as professional conduct, grooming, and time management, and others are more broadly related to children, for example, children's literature.

There are also nannies who have a lot of experience but not much formal education. If the nanny you choose fits into this category, you might suggest that she enroll in child care–related workshops and college courses offered in your local community. The nearest child care resource and referral agency or community college can help you locate such courses and workshops. Just as in centers and in family child care, the ideal provider combines warmth and caring with hands-on experience and some education related to children and child care.

Finding and Hiring a Nanny

A number of special agencies offer their assistance to parents who are seeking a nanny. Look for a nanny placement agency advertisement in the classified section of your local newspaper or a paper from the nearest larger city. Be careful to check out the standards of the placement agency you choose. Ask about the training its nannies receive, how it recruits its nannies, and what recourse you have if you are not happy with its referral after you have paid its fee.

There are a number of other ways to find a nanny. Go to your closest public library to look up the listing of the nearest nanny school. Then give it a call and ask whether the school can recommend any recent graduates. Your local child care resource and referral agency may also have information about nannies, although it concentrates primarily on connecting families with child care centers and family child care providers. (See Chapter 4 and Appendix B for information about these agencies.) Check the classified section of the newspaper for nannies who are advertising for a position or place your own advertisement for a nanny. Information on advertising for an in-home care provider can be found in Chapter 4.

Word of mouth is another effective way to make contacts with potential nannies. Check with everyone you know. Sometimes a nanny in a family you know has a friend who is just beginning to look for work as a nanny, or a friend may have a relative who is on the lookout for just such a position.

Interviewing and hiring a qualified nanny takes awhile, so be prepared to start several months ahead of the time you would like the nanny to start. Your best bet is always to interview the nanny yourself and to check her references personally and carefully. You'll also want to hire the nanny for a trial period to discover whether your child — and you! —and the nanny hit it off. Appendix F contains sample forms to guide you through the hiring procedure. If the nanny is a recent graduate of one of the nanny schools, you may also be able to get references from her instructors.

The first step is to write down your expectations and requirements for the person you are seeking. Think about these carefully. Could you compromise on some requirements if you find someone who fits all your other criteria? Perhaps you can help a nanny acquire the skills she lacks if she has most of the other qualities you're looking for.

When your list of expectations and requirements is ready, do some preliminary telephone screening of applicants to avoid spending valuable interview time with people who are obviously uninterested or unsuitable. You may find the sample telephone contact form in Appendix F useful for this purpose. When you call, give a brief description of the position to the prospective nanny and be up front about hours and salary. If the applicant continues to show interest, ask about her qualifications and training as well as previous experience. Also ask why she left her latest position and what her plans are for the future. Your children need the stability of having a nanny who will be with them for a long time and with whom they can form a solid emotional attachment.

When you have narrowed the list to three to five candidates, the next step is to set up a visit to your home so that you and the nanny have a chance to see each other and talk and she has a chance to see your home. Both of you will have questions for each other. Be sure to leave plenty of time for this interview, so that you both can learn as much as possible about each other. If you require a live-in nanny, it is essential to ensure that you will feel comfortable having this person residing in your home. Even if her living quarters are somewhat separate, you are likely to share common spaces and will often interact with each other. If you can't be comfortable with her in a common area, you may not want her to care for your children.

Also be quite clear about your expectations with regard to the nanny's living quarters. Will you allow her to have overnight guests? What areas beyond her room can she use? Appendix F includes a sample list of questions for use as a guide to the interview process.

Before you make a final choice, it is extremely important that the nanny candidate and your child have a chance to spend time together. Some people can paint a glowing picture of themselves but simply cannot develop an easy rapport with children. Others connect quickly and easily with children but are not very good at describing their own virtues and capabilities. Suggest to the prospective nanny that she spend half a day with your children — for pay — while you remain at home to observe their interactions. This should give you enough time to judge how your children react to her and her approach to learning about and working with them. She should present clear evidence that she respects them, has a warm and caring attitude, and is able to engage them in a range of stimulating activities. Because many children are especially difficult to work with when their parents are in the background observing, you will be putting the applicant through one of the more challenging tests she will face.

The Hiring Process

Once you have made up your mind that you have found the best person available to care for your children, it is time to negotiate a fair contract with her. Spell out in writing every detail of what you have discussed so that later on neither of you feels that the other one wasn't clear or totally honest. This is an important point in the process. Your future relationship depends on building a solid base at the beginning so that you both start off in a positive, optimistic frame of mind. The more you can demonstrate how much you value the expertise and compassion of the nanny, the more likely she is to do everything she can to live up to your expectations.

If you are able to spend time with your children and the nanny during the first week of her employment, do so. This is a big change for your children, who need to feel that you are comfortable with the nanny and that they have your "permission" to become comfortable with her. Young babies also need time to become familiar with a new caregiver.

Older children can tell you about their day with the nanny, and you can question them about their activities. With infants and toddlers you need to be sensitive to any change in mood or behavior which might indicate that they are not comfortable with the nanny. As time goes by, make unscheduled visits to your home. Tell the nanny that your work schedule is flexible, allowing you to drop in at home unexpectedly and that you like to come home when you can. Yes, you are checking up on her, but that is your right and your responsibility. The nanny would probably do the same if these were her children. You have no other way of knowing that all is well, so be honest about the fact that you will pop in once in a while to see how things are going.

Au Pairs

An au pair (pronounced "oh pear") is a young foreigner between the ages of eighteen and twenty-five who lives in the United States for up to one year as part of a cultural educational exchange program. The first U.S. au pair placement agencies are almost thirty years old, and growth in the au pair system has been especially rapid in the past decade.

When the au pair system started in Europe, it was designed as an inexpensive way for young people to visit another country and learn a bit about the language and culture. In exchange for room and board and a small weekly stipend, these young people provided forty to fifty hours of baby-sitting services per week. From the host family's point of view, it was a fairly inexpensive way to have someone look after their child. As an added benefit the family had an opportunity to get to know a person from another culture. The au pair was always considered to be a family member — au pair is French for "on even terms" or "equal" — who was not treated as an employee but as a guest who contributed to the common good of the family. The system was unregulated, and most au pair students spent only a summer in the host country.

Seven agencies are authorized to bring au pair students to the United States. They operate exchange visitor programs, regulated by the U.S. Information Agency (USIA), which allow the au pair a special one-year visa. If you want to hire a "real" au pair, you are required to work with one of these agencies.

There are also American-born baby sitters and nannies who call themselves au pairs. Although this may not be illegal, it is certainly false and misleading. Other foreign citizens also use the term "au pair." These people, lacking a work permit or the appropriate visa, provide child care illegally. We advise you to stay within the law. Hire only a legal au pair through an agency authorized by the USIA to bring exchange visitors to the United States.

Au Pair Rules and Regulations

The au pair system in this country is highly regulated. It is controlled both by the U.S. government and by the seven legitimate au pair agencies listed in Appendix F. To quote the federal regulations,

> *Au Pair programs permit foreign nationals to enter the United States for a period of one year for the purpose of residing with an American host family while participating directly in the home life of the family and providing limited child care services. The foreign national also attends a United States accredited postsecondary educational institution.*[1]

The USIA regulations, published in the *Federal Register,* are designed to safeguard both the au pair and the American host family. Each au pair placement agency has also established its own regulations for the protection of the au pair, the host family, and itself.

To give you a sense of what is involved in setting up an arrangement with an au pair, consider the experience of the Holland family.

The Hollands, who live in Cambridge, Massachusetts, need help with child care. There are three preschool children in the family, and both parents work outside the home. Reading the local newspaper, Claire Holland sees an article about a family that employs a French au pair, which catches her attention. She looks in the Yellow Pages *for the name of an agency she can call for more information. Under "Child Care" she finds "Au Pair," calls the number listed, and reaches a local au pair coordinator for one of the seven national placement agencies. Ann, the coordinator, sends Claire information about the au pair system and sets up an appointment for a home visit.*

When Ann visits the Holland home, she brings along many application forms and additional information. She interviews the family and walks through their house to check out the living conditions for the au pair. The Hollands fill out personal information forms, provide several references, and pay an application fee to get the process started. Ann explains that their au pair must have her own bedroom and preferably her own bathroom. She also tells them a little about other requirements that the USIA and her own agency have established to make sure that this becomes a good experience for both the host family and the au pair. Ann explains that the au pair should be treated more as a family member than as an employee.

In exchange for room, board, and a stipend of a minimum of $125 per week, the au pair is to provide child care and help with other child-related activities, cooking for the children, washing their clothes, and cleaning up after them. The au pair is to work no more than forty-five hours per week. Claire is worried. Even though she works only four days a week, both she and her husband are away for ten hours a day, Mondays through Thursdays. Ann assures her that this will not be a problem, as long as they do not exceed the forty-five-hour-a-week limit. The au pair must also be given the opportunity to attend educational classes — college courses preferred — at least three hours a week for two semesters. This sounds possible to the Hollands.

Claire asks about the age and training of the prospective au pair. The Hollands have a three-month-old baby, a two-year-old, and a four-year-old. They are concerned that the au pair have some background in infant care. Ann reassures her, pointing out that an au pair expected to look after an infant must be older than twenty-one — her agency's requirement — and demonstrate a minimum of six months of prior experience in infant care.

Ann tells the Hollands that as many as ten thousand au pairs arrive in the United States every year on what is called a J visa. Federal law allows these visitors to stay only one year. Claire wonders how good it can be to change caregivers every year. Ann tells Claire that her concern is legitimate, but points out that centers and family child care settings also experience high turnover. Ann then describes cases in which friendships established between au pairs and host families have lasted a lifetime.

Ann informs the Hollands that they will be able to select the au pair they like most from the names given them by her agency and to interview the candidates by telephone before making a final choice. The Hollands tell Ann to go ahead and sign them up.

Au pair field coordinators like Ann play a key role in helping prospective host families to think through the idea of employing an au pair to meet their child care needs. The coordinators for au pair placement agencies also monitor ten to fifteen au pairs in their geographic area of responsibility, a valuable function both for you and for the au pair. It is a way to be sure that you are satisfied with your au pair's performance and that your au pair is receiving the benefits to which she is entitled — weekly days off, vacation, enrollment in college courses.

Background and Training

Au pair applicants, both men and women, must be between the ages of eighteen and twenty-five. Before the au pairs leave their home country, they must have had a physical checkup, and a criminal background check of some sort must have been performed. Each country handles these differently, but the au pair placement agency sorts out these details. Once the au pair arrives in the United States, he or she usually goes through a three- to four-day training session with placement agency staff. The au pairs are required to have had no less than eight hours of child safety training and at least twenty-four hours of basic child development instruction.

The U.S. regulations governing au pairs stress over and over again that this is a cultural exchange program, not employment of a domestic servant. The au pair is to be treated as a family member, receiving room and board, some tuition money, a small weekly stipend, and paid time off — one and a half days a week plus two weeks' vacation — in exchange for child care. The coordinators check in regularly with both the host family and the au pair and arrange monthly get-togethers so that all the local au pairs can talk about their experiences with people in similar situations. If necessary, the coordinators help to mediate conflicts between au pairs and their host families.

Locating an Au Pair Placement Agency

The Hollands found, in the *Yellow Pages* under Child Care, a Boston area agency that could provide the information they needed to arrange for an au pair. These agencies operate in many major American cities. Other sources of information about arranging for an au pair are your local child care resource and referral agency (see Chapter 4 and Appendix B), major newspapers, and word of mouth.

Au Pair Screening

In addition to the placement coordinator's recommendation, it is most important that you yourself screen the au pair applicant as carefully as possible by telephone. The purpose is to acquire detailed descriptions of her or his family background, experiences living away from home, knowledge of children, and child care experience. This screening should be just as thorough as for an American employee you might hire to look after your children in your own home. Use the questions for nanny interviews provided in Appendix F to guide you in your choice. Also try to follow up on written references with a phone call to learn more about the reliability and personality of the applicant. Remember, you will be leaving your children alone with this young person, so make sure that you can be confident that he or she is fully capable of meeting all their needs and can provide them with a warm, caring, and stimulating environment.

Once the au pair has joined you, the more support and assistance you can provide the better, especially during the settling-in stage. Help him or her find opportunities for further education and training related to the development and care of young children. Do what you can to see that this young person meets and make friends with Americans of the same age. Everyone will benefit from a happy au pair who feels like a welcome member of your family.

The Costs of an Au Pair Arrangement

Arranging for and "employing" an au pair is not as inexpensive as many parents believe. Most placement agencies charge between $3,000 and $4,000 for their services, which usually include the au pair's transportation to the United States, the coordinator's salary, and other placement expenses. In addition to providing room and board, valued at about $60 to $100 per week, you must also expect to pay, directly to the au pair, a stipend of about $125 per week for fifty-two weeks. Other costs generally include an application or registration fee payable to the placement agency and up to $500 per year for the au pair's college tuition fees. Most placement agencies figure that it will cost you $10,500–$12,000, excluding room and board, to engage an au pair for one year, about the same amount as the minimum wage you would pay an in-home provider who does not live with you. Since wages for nannies vary greatly depending on where you live, your nanny's salary, plus the benefits you offer, especially if you include room and board, can run as high as $30,000 a year.

Of course, if you have three preschool-age children, or work unusual hours, the cost of an au pair may be a bargain. You would pay an average of $150 per week per child to have your three children in good center care, which would work out to an annual expense of about $23,400. And centers, which operate during normal working hours, are no help if you work evenings or on weekends.

Remember, too, that by including an au pair in your home you get much more than just someone to look after the children while you work or go to school. You are participating in a cultural exchange program through which you may well get to know people in another country who will enrich your international understanding and become your lifelong friends, and your children will form a strong bond with a young adult who can introduce them to some of the customs and traditions of another culture.

9

School-Age Child Care

The years of childhood between the ages of six and twelve are . . . wedged between the rapid growth of the preschool years and the dramatic experience of early adolescence. . . . These years are rich with possibilities. They are the time when the critical foundation is laid for adolescence and beyond. During these years children learn to interpret the world. When children reach the age of six they are receptive; their eagerness and ability to learn are at a high level. But the clock is ticking.

— Joan M. Bergstrom, School's Out — Now What?

CHILD CARE for school-age children takes many different forms: after-school care, before-and-after-school care, care for latch-key kids, after-school clubs or sports programs, and summer camps are some examples. We have chosen to group these programs together as School-Age Child Care, known in the child care profession as SACC. Although our emphasis is on SACC programs for children in kindergarten through third grade (ages five through eight), we also consider the needs of older children. After presenting general information about legal requirements, staff qualifications, and parent involvement, we provide ideas and guidelines tailored more specifically to specific types of school-age child care settings.

School-age programs are found in a variety of settings: 35 percent in child care centers, 28 percent in public schools, 14 percent in religious institutions, 23 percent in other locations — community centers, work sites, private schools, colleges, and municipal buildings.

Anticipating the Need for SACC

Most parents feel relieved when they send their child off to kindergarten, thinking, *Finally! Those nasty child care bills are behind me!* They believe that their public school system, funded by their taxes, will provide them with safe and inexpensive child care. Unfortunately this is only partly true. Yes, many school districts offer full-day kindergarten programs to all the five-year-old children in their areas. But consider the number of hours each day that your child is actually in school. Then there are the holidays, spring and summer vacations, and times you must be at work even though your child cannot attend school. Some parents let their children stay at home alone after school hours, but we don't think that is a great idea.

- More than 2 million children aged six through sixteen attend school-age child care programs.
- The vast majority of children attending school-age child care programs are in their early elementary years.
- The largest providers of after-school care are YMCAs and YWCAs, which serve school-age children in nearly 2,800 locations.

Source: "Who's Who in School-age Care," *Child Care Information Exchange*, no. 110 (July/August 1996): 12.

When is school not in session while you are at work? Check with your school district well ahead of the date your child will enter school to determine the hours your child's class will meet. The annual school calendar is available months before school opens, so you can use it to plan the upcoming year. Knowing when school vacations and other days off occur helps you to plan your own schedule.

In school districts that transport children by bus, the earlier bus runs usually carry the older children, with the later ones reserved for the kindergartners, who may not start school until 9:00 A.M. Your having to be at work or in class by seven-thirty or eight in the morning can create a hardship for you and your child, leading to the need for alternative care before school opens, or the schedule may be one that necessitates care only after school.

> In the middle childhood years, almost 80 percent of a child's waking hours are spent outside school.

If you work part time, your child care needs might be limited to vacations and holidays. If you work irregular hours, an after-school club flexible enough to allow your child to attend occasionally might best suit your needs. These are all factors to consider as you search for an arrangement that covers the hours you cannot be home while your child is not in school.

Legal Requirements

Most SACC programs located in or run by child care centers and family child care homes are regulated by the state in which you live. These minimal requirements are designed only to ensure the safety of your child. They specify adult-to-child ratios and group sizes, which are generally 1 to 10 for four- to ten-year-old children, with a maximum group of 20, and 1 to 15 for ten- to fourteen-year-old children, with a maximum group of 30.

Regulations also exist to ensure safety against fire and to promote health standards, the appropriate education and training of staff and director, and adequate space. For instance, most states require thirty-five square feet of space per child, with one toilet and washbasin available per twenty children.

> The National Association for the Education of Young Children recommends adult-to-child ratios of 1 to 10 for four- and five-year-olds, with a maximum group of twenty, and 1 to 10–12 for six-, seven-, and eight-year-olds, with a maximum group of twenty-four and a second adult present.
>
> Source: Sue Bredekamp, ed., Accreditation Criteria and Guidelines of the National Academy of Early Childhood Programs (Washington, D.C.: National Association for the Education of Young Children, 1984), Table 2, 24.

Independent school-age child care programs and residential and summer camps are often regulated by different organizations or agencies from those which regulate child care centers and family child care programs, *if they are regulated at all.* Check with your local child care resource and referral agency (Chapter 4 and Appendix B) to learn whether the program you are considering must be licensed. If this is a requirement, ask the program director to show you the license, and ascertain that it is up to date. Remember, a license tells you only that the organization met the minimum requirements on the books at the time it was issued. You must check out the program yourself to make sure not only that it exceeds minimum requirements, but also that it addresses the particular personality, interests, and needs of your child.

Staff Qualifications and Practices

Staff qualifications for SACC programs and camps vary widely from one type of program to another. In states where programs are licensed, staff must usually be at least eighteen years old or a high school graduate. Some states check staff applicants through the state register of child abuse and maltreatment and require a minimum of twelve hours of in-service training. The licensing rules frequently state that smaller programs — fewer than forty-five children — must have at least one person with an associate degree in a "child-related area" or two years of college with a minimum of twelve credits in child-related courses or two years of direct experience working with children. In a program with more than forty-five children, the lead person must also have previous administrative experience. To head a group of twenty to thirty children, a SACC teacher needs only a high school degree and one year of experience or has to be older than eighteen and have a year of experience in a child care–related area. An assistant teacher generally has to be only sixteen years old, have some experience, and be in good health.

These minimal requirements are not enough to ensure quality care for your child. It is important that adults working with school-age children have both experience and education or training related to this age group. Training in educational methods, recreation, psychology, and social work is helpful. Staff should be familiar with the developmental stages of five- to twelve-year-olds, have good conflict resolution skills, and be able to apply problem-solving approaches appropriate to this age group. They should be relaxed with school-age children, and enjoy interacting with and listening to them. They must be comfortable talking about hurt feelings and broken friendships and able to guide children through the difficult task of developing lasting relationships with peers and adults. Staff should involve the students in the planning and operation of a program — especially for the nine- to twelve-year-olds — but also allow them time just to hang out without having to be engaged in meaningful activities every minute of the day. The program should include a planned approach to staffing, with each new staff member receiving written policies describing work expectations. Ask to see these guidelines, for they can tell you a good deal about how the program is organized.

The organization of the environment contributes greatly to how the children function within a program. Learning centers work well with most ages. Field trips and guests should also be part of the agenda. Outdoor space should reflect the activity levels of older children. Ideally it should include large open areas, for soccer, baseball, and other games, plus areas for more intimate play, like building a tree house, and undeveloped land for exploration and discovery. The nature of an environment communicates the appropriate behavior to children — open spaces tempt them to run, intimate spaces inspire quiet play, a stage might stimulate play production, and unusual and interesting materials encourage exploration. Staff should have a variety of developmentally appropriate activities planned for the students as they arrive from school each day, balancing active and restful projects.

Many group SACC programs borrow space in a cafeteria or gym. A major challenge for staff is how to make this type of room an attractive, interesting environment each day prior to the children's arrival. The better the relationship between the site and the SACC program, the easier it is for staff to rearrange the space to their own liking.

Development in Middle Childhood

Adults besides their parents or guardians assume increasing importance in the development of a school-age child. Children between the ages of five and twelve need to connect with adults who support them in beginning the extended process of separating from their immediate families.

Five- to eight-year-old children model themselves after favorite adults, often turning to them for help. These children are busy working on their social skills, so peers are important to them. Although they like to be with older children — remember your tagalong brother or sister? — the older kids tend to stay with their own age-mates.

Eight- to ten-year-olds, who like to spend time with children of their own sex, often hang out in small "gangs." Their conflict resolution skills are immature, but they are trying them out. Groups of children this age wear similar clothes, like to see the same movies, and frequently reject the opposite sex, but this last characteristic begins to change as they move into early adolescence.

Eleven- to thirteen-year-olds begin to form close individual friendships and develop cross-sex interests. Children this age take on particular roles in the group to which they belong — for instance, clown, jock, intellectual, cheerleader, "substitute parent." Although they test the rules, they can also control their behavior, and their social skills are much further developed than they were at younger ages.

Parent Involvement

Like all child care arrangements, SACC programs and summer camps exhibit varying attitudes toward parent involvement. Some programs welcome parents, while others may be less enthusiastic about their interest or even discourage it. Your ability to have regular, daily contact with the staff of the program or the camp might depend on the nature of the transportation to and from the setting that you choose for your child. If she goes to the program directly from school and returns home in a car pool that you drive only every third day, face-to-face opportunities for discussion with the staff will be rare.

Despite these potential obstacles, thinking of this care arrangement as an ongoing partnership is important. Every adult with whom your child comes in regular contact as part of the program should have been introduced to you through information sent home. Because you are the expert on the characteristics, interests, and needs of your child, program staff should provide you with ways to share this vital information with them. At the start of the program, you should receive a parent handbook outlining the ways in which you can help your child succeed in it and opportunities for your involvement in it. Information about program activities may reach you via a newsletter or be posted on a bulletin board you can read when you pick up your child at the end of the day.

There should also be opportunities for conferences and parent education workshops. Most programs can benefit from periodic work parties made up of parents, participating children, and staff. Perhaps you can provide leadership in organizing such community-building events if staff is not already doing this. If you have a specific interest or talent that might appeal to the children in the program, find the time to come in to share this resource with them and their caregivers.

SACC in a Family Child Care Home

In the past, informal, family-based options have been the primary source of child care for school-age children. Many parents still ask a neighbor, a friend, or the parent of one of his schoolmates to look after their child when school is out and they are at work. But as more parents have entered the workforce, increasingly formal family child care arrangements for school-age children have become more popular. Most states have regulations allowing licensed or certified family child care providers to look after a few school-age children in addition to the maximum number of preschool children they are allowed to care for each day.

Family child care offers many advantages for you and your school-age children. Because many family child care providers open for business at six in the morning, they are often willing to serve your child breakfast and see that he gets on the school bus. You can usually arrange with the school district to have your child picked up at the child care home in the morning and dropped off there after school. The smaller, more intimate nature of a home setting is well suited to the relaxation and unwinding that children need so badly after school, before they are ready to shift gears and become involved in new activities. Especially if he is only five or six years old, your child may benefit from close contact with a caring adult who is able to offer him laptime after his busy day at school. If the provider lives in your neighborhood, the familiar surroundings may also comfort your child, who might even have access to playmates who live close to your home. Some family child care providers can also arrange to look after your child during summer vacations, school holidays, teacher in-service education days, and on occasions, such as snow days, when school is not in session.

A disadvantage to family child care could be that few children your child's age are available as playmates. Some home-based providers depend quite heavily on television to entertain the older children after school. Although family child care providers frequently have training in the care and development of preschoolers, they may know little about caring for and stimulating a school-age child. Because your family child care provider operates alone, you need to have backup assistance if she is unable to provide care for one reason or another.

If you decide to consider a regulated family child care home for your school-age child seriously, check your state regulations to make sure that your provider follows its guidelines for basic health and safety. Again, remember that these guidelines are only minimums. It is up to you to question the provider about daily routines and activities and to walk through the house to be certain it meets your standards. For more information on family child care homes, including key questions and checklists, see Chapter 5 and Appendix C.

SACC in a Center or School Setting

The past ten to fifteen years have seen phenomenal growth in the development of SACC programs. Many child care centers have added an on-site school-age component or run such a program at another location. Some centers sponsor SACC programs in the public schools. Occasionally, public schools sponsor their own SACC programs. Some nonprofit agencies like the YMCA or the local youth bureau run school-based programs.

Many center-based SACC programs serve only children under the age of eight or nine, whereas programs run in school buildings are more likely to accept children up to middle school age — a few programs even take children up through the eighth grade. The reason is that child care centers are not designed to care for older children. Center staff who can make adjustments to accommodate five- to eight-year-olds have a harder time developing activities suitable for children nine or ten years of age.

The number of children for whom each adult is responsible is much higher in SACC programs than in those for children younger than five. If your state regulates SACC programs, check to learn the legal ratio and to ascertain that your program is following these minimum guidelines. Some states also regulate the training and experience needed by SACC program staff. Where regulations are weak or nonexistent, staff may consist primarily of teenagers with a great deal of enthusiasm but almost no training. At the other extreme you may find a program staffed with highly trained professionals who have spent years learning how to work with and stimulate this age group.

SACC group programs usually offer a variety of activities for the children they serve. Most include opportunities for children to relax in quiet surroundings and to engage in noisy games and physical activities. Certain times are set aside for homework, snacks, and outdoor play. Art, drama, music, and sports activities are common. Sometimes staff organize smaller clubs within the large program. Children usually have the opportunity to choose carefully each day from a variety of offerings.

Some group SACC programs run year round, offering care whenever school is not in session. Others operate only during the school year but include the school holidays. Still others provide care only on days that school is in session. Study the program schedule carefully in the fall so that later in the year you are not caught without child care for a national holiday or a teacher in-service day.

Advantages to SACC programs run at a public elementary school include the fact that transportation is not a problem and that your children remain in a familiar environment with children they know well. A disadvantage involves the continuous noise generated by a large group of children all operating within the same large space. Some children find it hard to unwind and relax in such a group setting where few adults are available to respond to their individual needs.

SACC Programs in Community Centers and Other Nonprofit Settings

In many communities, churches, Big Brothers/Big Sister programs, the Ys, Jewish community centers, youth bureaus, and similar organizations sponsor SACC programs, many of them similar to those operated by child care centers and school districts. Some may have a religious component or other dimension designed to meet the special requirements of the sponsor. Others may focus on one or more sports — soccer, basketball, tennis — or emphasize one or more specific intellectual pursuits — computers, history, geography, for example. Some SACC programs are devoted exclusively to music and drama, and others concentrate completely on the visual arts. The advantages of these specialized programs center on the opportunities they provide to develop specific interests, skills, and talents that you may have identified as important for your child or your family. Narrow specialization can also be a disadvantage, however, if it deprives your child of an opportunity to develop a wider range of interests. Many such specialized programs don't run for enough hours per week to meet the child care needs of full-time working parents, necessitating your making still another arrangement for the period the special program is not in session. The transportation demands involved with juggling several after-school arrangements can become difficult to manage reliably.

SACC in Your Own Home

You can arrange to have a nanny, an au pair, or a baby sitter come to your home to take care of your child before and after school and when school is not in session. An au pair arrangement might work out especially well, because au pairs are expected to attend college courses during their U.S. stays, which they could accomplish while your child is in school. A big advantage to a nanny or au pair is having someone right in your home who can make sure that your child gets on the bus in the morning and welcome her back home when school is out. A potential disadvantage can be missed opportunities to play with age-mates after school and to participate in the various projects that are part of good SACC group programs. You can probably have your in-home provider transport your children to particular group activities several times a week, so they get the best of two worlds. Of course, the nanny/au pair option is expensive, so you must balance that cost against the convenience of the arrangement. See Chapter 8 for more information on nannies and au pairs.

Baby sitters — usually neighborhood teenagers who occasionally care for your children in your home — are sometimes considered an inexpensive alternative to a nanny or au pair. Baby sitters rarely have any formal knowledge or training in child care. Although they may be useful as an emergency backup, baby sitters should not be hired for regular after-school care. After school your child needs the kinds of attention and stimulation that an untrained baby sitter is unlikely to provide.

Self-Care or Latchkey Children

Despite the tremendous expansion of school-age child care options during the past ten years, about 15 percent of all five- to twelve-year-old

U.S. children are left alone at home, to fend for themselves, every after-noon after school lets out. Some people call this self-care, while others refer to the latchkey phenomenon.

Experts agree that children under the age of twelve should not rou-tinely be left alone. Although children develop at different rates and there are probably eleven- and twelve-year-olds who can look after themselves for short periods, most children this age and younger cannot manage crisis situations. Children younger than twelve are unable to evaluate all possible alternative courses of action in an emergency and select the one most appropriate for solving the problem. What might seem like a minor occurrence to adults can become a major catastrophe for a young child home alone. The howling wind, a clap of thunder, or the pounding rain that accompanies a weather change can add a scary dimension to the life of an unaccompanied child. The telephone caller who hangs up without speaking or the stranger ringing the doorbell can severely challenge the self-confidence of a child with no one to turn to for reassurance. Children often worry excessively over seemingly minor accidents — spilling milk on the couch, breaking a glass, or burning food while trying to fix a snack.

Don't leave your under-twelve child at home alone. If you are think-ing of having your teenager provide after-school care for your younger children, wait until the youngest is eleven or twelve. This is a lot to ask, especially in a family with limited resources whose children claim that they can look after themselves. However, think of the worst-case sce-nario — Are your children mature enough to anticipate and avoid dan-gerous situations, or respond to them intelligently should they occur?

If your child must be left at home alone, think of the arrangement as a job that requires him to be formally prepared and trained. Think of everything that happens daily in your home and try to anticipate the unexpected. What should he do if the electricity goes out? What if some-one rings the doorbell? What if someone gets hurt? Suppose the cat runs out the door and won't come back? Discuss all these possibilities with your child and establish clear guidelines for how to handle them. Write out the guidelines and post them on your refrigerator. During the last couple of weeks before school starts, describe such situations to your child and ask her how she would handle them.

Another important support for the child who is home alone after school is a well-established routine for how to use the time until you return from work. Try to have him perform simple chores. If your employer allows it, set a regular time for telephone contact with your child. Maybe there is an adult relative or friend he can call as well. Also try to arrange for a "safe house" where he can check in before or after school if necessary. Perhaps a neighbor is at home during the day or you have a friend who doesn't live too far away. Some communities have established "phone friend" telephone help lines for children who are home alone, either as a community service or a service available to paid subscribers. Children who call this number can speak with an adult trained as a counselor about any worries they have or simply to hear a friendly, reassuring voice when they have been by themselves for several hours and may feel lonely or scared.

Never leave a young child at home alone. If you can arrange nothing else, try to find a college student or a retired person who is willing to provide regular help for a modest fee. Perhaps a relative can come to your home for a couple of hours a day for a small amount of money. Some area family child care providers offer their homes as safe houses for children who are old enough that they don't need constant supervision. To explore these and other options further, check with your local child care resource and referral agency (Chapter 4 and Appendix B). Other places to seek information and ideas are a school newsletter, neighborhood newsletters, and bulletin boards at local libraries and food markets. The PTA organization at your child's school might also have useful suggestions for you.

Ultimately, the success of an after-school program depends on the particular characteristics and needs of your child and your family. Here are some questions to help you think about her strengths and needs:

1. How would you describe your child's temperament?
2. What are her strengths?
3. What activities does your child enjoy most?
4. What are the low points in the day and in the year for him? Why do these occur?
5. Was anything in the last year a negative or painful experience for your child? What can you learn from that experience?
6. In what area do you think your child needs the most help? Can an after-school program be helpful in that area?
7. Has your child become involved in something because of a friend? Has that been a good experience?

Child Care in Summer Months

Mid-June has arrived, the weather is wonderfully warm and sunny, the local public swimming pool has just opened, and your children are looking forward to two glorious months of summer vacation, but you must spend most of that time at work. What are your child care options?

If you've had a family child care provider for after-school care, she can probably accommodate your child full time during the summer months. Some group after-school programs organize themselves as day camps in the summer. Residential summer camps are a more challenging, and expensive, possibility.

Day Camps

Churches and temples, the local YMCA and YWCA, child care centers and nursery schools, country clubs and yacht clubs, the city youth bureau, or another community group may operate day camps in your area. When selecting a summer camp, as with an after-school program, your child's level of development, her interests, and how much money you can afford to spend should be the key factors shaping your decision. Some programs are focused, while others offer a general menu of activities. Some concentrate on academics — science, languages, computers — some on sports — soccer, baseball, swimming, sailing — and others on a broader range of subjects and skills — scout and Y camps. The camp may or may not provide transportation. Many day camps are based in local parks or community recreational facilities. Prices vary tremendously, ranging anywhere from $10 per day for a community program to $50 to $80 per day for a private tennis camp or a camp at a local yacht club.

Residential Camps

The Guide to Accredited Camps is a nationwide directory of 2,100 residential camps.[1] Call (800) 428-2267 to request a copy of this guide, which will give you a good idea of the possibilities. Some camps have weekly sessions, others have programs ranging from two to eight weeks in length. Like day camps, they may design residential programs around a specific activity, for example, music, soccer, or computers, or offer a broader range of social and recreational activities. Residential camps operate both as profit-making and as nonprofit organizations.

Private camps are more expensive than those run on a break-even basis. You should expect to pay anywhere from $35 to $100 per day for a private camp and $15 to $55 per day for a nonprofit alternative.

Going to a residential camp is much more socially and emotionally challenging than attending a day camp. Is your child experienced and self-confident enough to handle the experience? Has she already been to day camp and had a successful experience there? Has he slept over at other people's houses? What is his reaction to new people and places? Might he become homesick? Every child is different, even within the same family. Your first child may be outgoing and love spending time away from home, while your second is unhappy spending the night at Grandma's house, even though he loves Grandma. When exploring possible residential options, learn what you can about each camp's policies regarding telephone calls home. Your child might feel secure enough knowing that you are only a phone call away. Be sure to involve him in selecting a camp so that he feels he's a participant in the decision-making process and has plenty of time to become mentally prepared for the experience.

Choosing an SACC Program or Camp

Finding the right school-age child care program or summer camp is a four-step procedure:

1. Contacting programs by telephone
2. Visiting programs that meet your basic requirements
3. Talking with program directors
4. Making a choice

1 Telephone Contact

Because some of these programs only operate during the summer months, it is wise to gather information *a year before* your child needs this care so that you can observe the programs in action before enrolling her. Check with your local child care resource and referral agency for the school-age child care programs in your area. Also ask relatives, friends, and neighbors for ideas and possibilities. When you have a good sense of the alternatives, pick two or three that seem to meet your most basic requirements. Give each of these programs a call, using the questions provided on the SACC telephone survey form. See Appendix G for an expanded version.

SACC Telephone Survey Form

SACC program name_____Date of call_____

Location_____Name of director_____

Ages of children served_____Hours of care provided_____

Days program does *not* operate_____

Do you provide transportation from my child's school to program?_____

Will there be an opening when we require care?_____

What are the fees?_____

Is the program licensed/registered?_____

Ages of children in my child's group?_____

Number of children per staff in my child's group?_____

Total number of children in my child's group?_____

Qualifications of program staff?_____

_____

_____

When is a good time to visit?_____

If you are considering a day or residential camp as a way of meeting your summer child care needs, adjust this form to gather initial information about the camps that you are considering.

2 Visiting SACC Programs and Summer Camps

Think about the following key factors as you visit potential school-age child care programs and camps.

- How does the program match up with your child's personality, interests, and likes and dislikes?

- What is the underlying program philosophy? Is the emphasis on cooperative play or primarily competitive games, or a balance of the two approaches?

- Does the staff show respect for the children? In what way?

- What is the approach to discipline? Are the children allowed to help set the rules for individual and group behavior?

- What is the physical layout of the program? Is it open and flexible? Is it designed to keep the children stimulated and occupied? Are there spaces for retiring with a good book and relaxing? Is there a place to do homework undisturbed? Is there space in which to run around and get rid of extra energy?

- What types of food are served? Are nutritious meals and snacks planned that are appropriate for children of this age group?

- Are the activities geared toward the differing developmental levels of the children in the group?

- Are the materials and equipment available for self-selection? Are they safe and of interest to children the age of your child?

- If your child has special needs, can the program accommodate them?

Be sure to check all the standard health and safety issues — cleanliness of bathrooms and kitchen, health policies, staff training in CPR (cardiopulmonary resuscitation) and first aid, fire drill practice, and so forth. Appendix G provides a checklist to help you remember all these questions.

When visiting a residential camp and interviewing the camp director, you need to ask additional questions. What is the camp's overall philosophy? What are the educational backgrounds of the director and the staff? How old are the counselors, and what kinds of special training in the care of school-age children have they received? What is the ratio of adults to children? What about special safety issues, such as medical staff on call, lifeguards on duty at the waterfront, and nighttime supervision of the children? What kinds of vehicles are used for transportation, and what is their condition? What happens during a typical day at camp?

Always obtain the names of three families whose children attended the program or camp during the previous year or summer, including, if at all possible, at least one family *whose name you obtained on your own.* Call these references right away, and include their thoughts to help shape the questions you ask when you visit and interview the program director. Speak to the parents and, if possible, to the children who participated in the program or camp. What did the parents and children like most about it? What did they like least? Would they recommend the program to friends?

3 Talking with Program or Camp Directors

If you are unable to visit the program or camp while it is in operation, you will have to rely heavily on what you can learn from the program director. Remember that this person, who has a vested interest in convincing you to enroll your child in the program, unless it has a long waiting list, will portray it in the best possible light. Use the questions outlined above. The director will have played the major role in hiring the staff who will work directly with your child, so ask questions about their qualifications and experiences, whether their backgrounds have been checked to make sure they have not previously been involved in abusive situations, and how they are supervised and evaluated. Ask about the program approach to parent involvement and staff-parent communications. Balance what the director tells you with what you learn from families whose children were in the program or camp in the recent past.

4 *Making a Choice*

When you are choosing an after-school child care program, practical matters like location, transportation, and cost will influence your final decision the most, but don't lose track of the interests and needs of your child! In the long run, convenience does not make up for a child who is miserable and whose unhappiness makes you miserable.

When you are choosing a summer camp, your child will benefit from having had a successful day camp experience before graduating to a residential arrangement. When you are choosing a residential camp, remember that your child's happiness will depend at least as much on living arrangements and social activities as on sports and educational activities. Select a camp whose counselors understand the social dynamics of cabin life and are prepared to intervene if children are being singled out at all negatively. If your child can attend camp with a friend, that relationship can provide emotional security in times of social stress and uncertainty.

When you are choosing a program for your school-age child, the most important ingredient is the adults who will have responsibility for her. Think back to the directors and staff you met or talked to — which ones made you feel most comfortable? Have they had some training, so you can be confident that they know what they are doing?

Another useful way to make a choice is to close your eyes and try to imagine your child in each setting you visited. Which impressed you most? At this point you have applied all available objective criteria in comparing programs and camps. Now trust your instincts.

School-Age Child Care/Camp Checklist

Name of program _____

Address _____

Date _____

Yes	No	Basic Information
—	—	Program licensed?
—	—	Hours compatible with work?
—	—	Affordable rates?
—	—	Transportation available, safe, and convenient?

Yes No

Health and Safety

— — Is the facility secure?

— — Is the facility well maintained?

— — Working smoke detectors/fire extinguishers?

— — Electrical outlets covered?

— — Safe windows and stairs?

— — Medicines/cleaning agents locked away?

— — Clear emergency exists?

— — Kitchen/bathroom sanitary?

— — Play area clean and uncluttered?

— — Staff trained in first aid and CPR?

— — Are fire drills held regularly?

Outdoor Play Area

— — Is it enclosed and secure?

— — Is it free of hard ground surfaces and rocks?

— — Are climbers, swings, slides, safe and supervised?

— — Can children be seen easily?

— — Uncluttered so children can run?

— — Are there large open areas for ball games, etc.?

— — Is there an undeveloped area for exploration and discovery?

Indoor Play Area

— — Are toys and materials safe and appropriate?

— — Is there adequate space for children to play?

— — Is a variety of toys/materials available?

— — Are activities progressive according to age?

— — Can children be seen easily?

— — Is there adequate lighting/windows/ventilation?

— — Are bathrooms accessible?

— — Is there space for personal belongings?

— — Is an area designed for doing homework?

School-Age Program Staff

— — Do the children seem happy around the staff?

— — Are the staff members in good physical condition and able to keep up with the children?

— — Are the staff members warm and affectionate?

— — Are the staff members positive and open?

— — Is the staff willing to talk to you?

— —   Does the staff invite you to drop in whenever you like?

— —   Does the staff seem organized?

— —   Do the staff members seem genuinely to like children?

— —   Do staff members avoid conflicts between children by listening and watching carefully, then stepping in early to prevent violence?

— —   Do staff members use praise and attention to encourage cooperation and helpfulness?

— —   Does the staff work well as a team?

— —   Have you checked the age and training of staff members?

Program and Administrative Structure

— —   Is there a clear daily schedule?

— —   Are activities varied and age-appropriate?

— —   Does the program offer a variety of field trips?

— —   Are nutritious meals and snacks offered?

— —   Is there a discipline policy?

— —   Are children allowed to help set rules for individual and group behavior?

— —   Is there a program philosophy about children?

— —   Does the program encourage active parent involvement?

— —   Does the program have a specific focus? If so, what is it?

Additional Questions for Camp

— —   Are lifeguards on duty at the waterfront?

— —   Is there adequate nighttime supervision of the children?

— —   Is your transportation safe and reliable?

10

Creative Alternatives

AMERICANS FORM a do-it-yourself society. We admire a person who builds her own house or starts his own business. If you have that kind of energy and self-confidence and don't mind being a little different, this is your opportunity to create a tailor-made child care arrangement for your child and yourself.

American child care is still being invented. There is an obvious downside to that undeveloped state — many communities without enough affordable child care choices, teachers and caregivers with too little training, and too few employers who understand and appreciate their employees' child care needs. But the upside is that very little is carved in stone. By taking the initiative, you can create your own child care arrangement from scratch, so to speak.

You need raw materials in order to develop a good child care arrangement. First, you must find an adult who loves young children, has time to spend with them, and is willing to learn more about them. Nowadays such a person is likely to be a parent with preschool children — usually a woman, but this is changing — who wishes to remain outside the regular workforce so that she can stay home with her children. Or maybe you know people in your community who have already raised their own kids and might be interested in running a small child care business from their homes.

The second raw material is space. You are looking for someone who has the indoor space required to provide a mini–child care environment for a small number of children, as well as safe access to outdoor play space. Or possibly you have space in your own home and would consider having a caregiver come to you, perhaps bringing her own children. But you may not want to reshape your home that much or deal with the resulting wear and tear.

Once you have the basic materials, you need a third ingredient: the guidelines within which this person will operate as she cares for your child. You need a consultant to help you and your provider meet the local building code regulations and pull together the knowledge, skills, and equipment necessary to promote health and happiness in your child. The person you are seeking must be able to help you shape those materials — a willing and competent caregiver, the necessary space — to meet your particular needs.

Where do you find such an adviser? Start with your local or regional child care resource and referral agency. In your community this organization may be called a day/child care council, a child care coordinating council or an information and referral agency; there are more than 400 nationwide. A call to your local public library or nearby child care center will help you find this organization, if there is one in your local area. You can also call the Child Care Aware national toll-free parent information line — (800) 424-2246 — to be connected with your local child care resource and referral program. Appendix B contains the names, addresses, and telephone numbers of most of the local and statewide networks. (See also Chapter 4.) The resource and referral staff have a fund of knowledge and experience and are happy to provide you with good advice.

Other potential sources of child care expertise are your local community college and the nearest office of your state's University Extension Service. If the community college has an early childhood program or offers child care training of any kind, the person in charge of those programs may be able to help you. An Extension Service is the outreach arm of a state university. Most people think that Extension personnel simply help farmers or run 4H clubs, but county or regional Extension programs also include home economists and human development specialists who are familiar with child care. For the names of Cooperative Extension staff in your county or region, contact the Extension office at your state university or look for Cooperative Extension in your local telephone directory.

Once you have identified her, the child care expert can help your chosen caregiver learn what she must know in order to provide high-quality child care. The expert can tell you about child care courses that may be given at the community college and whether the nearby information and referral organization sponsors training sessions for new providers. She can also recommend good reading materials on how to provide a safe, stimulating child care environment at home. Our suggested reading list is in Appendix H.

We believe that education and training, combined with much parent involvement and oversight, are the best ways to produce competent caregiving. But most states also have regulations about how many children of different ages one person can care for at one time and what kind of space one requires to provide that care. Your local child care specialist is familiar with those rules and can help you interpret them. For instance, a person who cares for only one or two children unrelated to her may not need a license or certificate, but in most states she has to be registered to care for more than two. Then again, registration may not be a big deal, and it could even lead to access to extra goodies like a toy-lending library or partial reimbursement for food costs. Your consultant can inform you about all these aspects.

By now it must be clear that creating this child care arrangement will take time. This is especially true if your caregiver needs eight to twelve weeks of training to be ready to supervise your children when you return to work or school. *So start this process early!* Give yourself time to get organized, at least six months if possible.

Of the materials required to create a satisfactory child care arrangement — the right person, her educational preparation, and the necessary space — the most important is the person. This special adult must, first, love children and want to spend long periods of time with them. Second, her life circumstances must be such that this is a good time for her to take on such work. You certainly want the arrangement to last for at least a year, so the time dimension makes a difference as well. You are searching for someone who is already trained to care for children (unlikely) or is willing to gather that knowledge (take a course, do some reading). When you find such a person, you are well on your way to meeting your child care needs.

We suggest three possible strategies for locating someone who will join forces with you in meeting your child care needs. They are not the only alternatives, and you may well think of other avenues to pursue. But we hope that by considering these, you will at least get a good sense of what is involved in creating a personal child care solution.

Relatives, Friends, and Neighbors

A good place to start the search for the right person is through your personal network — relatives, friends, and neighbors. Be systematic. The question is, Whom do I know around here whom I trust, who loves young children and might be willing to look after mine? Here is an example.

Our friend Carol adopted Patrick, a baby boy, just ten days after his birth. Planning to return to work part time three months later, she began to look around for an informal child care arrangement a month after the adoption. In thinking about who might provide good care, Carol remembered Pam, a neighborhood friend with a ten-month-old baby, who had stopped work as a public health nurse temporarily to stay home with her child. Carol wasn't on best-friend terms with Pam but liked the idea of her nursing background, and the two had friends in common. So she called Pam and asked whether she would consider looking after another infant for about twenty hours each week. Pam agreed to think about it, and they met at her house to discuss possibilities. Pam approached the meeting being pretty doubtful about the idea, but she fell in love with Patrick on the spot, and Carol was eager to be helpful, sharing a couple of good books on child care. They met again several times to talk about Patrick's routines and the games Carol played with her baby to stimulate his senses and encourage new skills. Pam visited Carol's home to learn about Patrick's routine and how he lived.

In the two weeks before returning to work, Carol began to leave Patrick with Pam, first for an hour, then for two, and finally for the full four-hour period she would be away on the job. The transition went well, and Patrick stayed with Pam until he was sixteen months old. Later that year, when Pam decided to return to nursing, Carol began to interview registered family child care providers on her side of town. After several tries she found a woman with two of her own children, ages seven and five, who had completed a two-year program in early childhood development at the local community college and had been caring for two other children during the past couple of years. Again Carol brought Patrick through the transition gradually, making the shift over a three-week period. After some initial uncertainty Patrick adjusted well. When he turned three, Carol began to think about combining the family child care with nursery school three days a week.

This real-life example is helpful in a number of ways. First, it underscores the importance of early planning. Carol started seeking the right person several months before she needed her. Second, it provides an idea of what to look for, at least as a starting point. Although she didn't know Pam very well, Carol was attracted by her nursing background. In addition, Carol had close friends who vouched for Pam, which was reassuring. Third, Carol understood that the idea of looking after Patrick would come as a surprise to Pam, so she thought of ways to make the proposal attractive and worked hard to arrange a relatively easy transition.

Is there someone in your network who might work out as well for you and your child as Pam did for Carol and Patrick? Here is a way to find out. Make two lists, the first for the names of possible caregivers, people you trust and think might consider the idea of child care. On the second, write the names of people who might *know someone else* with caregiving potential. Again, you have to trust the judgment and instincts of the people on the second list in order to have confidence in those they suggest.

Now consider the possibilities. Start with relatives. Do your parents live in the area? What about sisters or brothers? How about cousins or aunts and uncles? If any of them lives nearby, and you have good feelings toward them, think about which list to put them on. Are they in a position to provide child care themselves? If yes, they go on list number one. If not, put their names on list number two.

Next, go through the same process with your friends. Remember that they don't necessarily have to be *close* friends. Maybe you can think of a high school classmate who liked young kids and lives in the area. Think about friends at work, people you might have met at a birthing class, and college roommates. Perhaps you attend a church in the area where you've met people who may have suggestions. Your husband, wife, or partner should join this brainstorming process. Finally, think about the people who live close by. Have you seen other parents with young children? Do you have a neighbor whose yard is filled with playthings and who may already be caring for children?

If you have few names on list one after all your thinking, don't be discouraged. That was just the first step in the creative process. Step two is to get in touch with everyone on list two. Because these are all people whose judgment you trust, ask them to suggest people who might be interested in providing child care. As they make recommendations, add those names to list one.

At this point you have cast a pretty wide net. You've thought about your relatives, friends, and neighbors, then gone on to friends of friends. The time has come to start talking to the list-one candidates. Think carefully about each person before you make contact. What is her current situation? What can you do or provide that might make your proposal attractive? Try to create an opportunity to discuss possibilities face to face.

If making the first contact by telephone, you might want to begin with something like, "Hi! This is Sally Hamilton. I'm trying to set up a child care arrangement for my daughter Julie. I was thinking of people who may have some good ideas, and thought of you." Or "My friend/aunt/cousin Connie suggested that you might have some good ideas. Is there a time when we could get together to talk about possibilities?" When the two of you meet, remember that there are still two alternatives. Start by being up front with the person. Ask whether she would be willing to *consider* caring for your child while you are at work or school. At this point you are not asking that she agree to provide care, but that she be willing to *think about* it. Remember that many details have to be worked out before the two of you decide to go ahead and that you are simply agreeing to examine those practical questions.

If this friend or friend of a friend says no, proceed to your backup question, that old standby, "Do you know of someone who might be interested in providing care?" Take down the name and address of anyone she suggests and hold on to the information for possible future use.

Suppose one of your list-one people says, "Yes, I'm willing to think about the idea." Be appreciative of that positive response. At the same time, remember that there are still crucial practical issues to be worked out, and most of them have to do with the question of quality that we discussed in Chapter 3. Will this person treat your child the way you want her to be treated? Do you agree on how children should be disciplined? Will she be positive and warmhearted with your child, or are there negative sides to her personality? If she has children, how will they handle the arrival of a newcomer? Are there rules about TV watching, and if not, can you agree on some? Is the space in her home safe and large enough for an additional child? What about naptimes? Is she willing to stick with your child for a long time? Remember that stability and continuity are important and may be hard to achieve with caregivers who don't view themselves as being in it for the long haul. Then, of course, you have to sort out the question of cost. How much should you pay? These kinds of questions should be the topics of conversation at your next meeting. Make sure that you set it up before ending the first one, and try to schedule it in the next couple of days, while the feeling of excitement and possibility is still strong.

As you plan for your second meeting, think about incentives you could offer to make it easier (1) for your prospective caregiver to take the job, and (2) for you to feel secure and happy about the arrangement. For instance, would it help if you provided extra toys, a crib, or a changing table? If changes are needed to make the house safer — gates at staircases, covers for electrical sockets, fire extinguisher — could you cover the cost of those modifications or at least split the expense? If you sense hesitation stemming from lack of knowledge or training, could you help by providing good reading material or paying the fee for a local training program offered by the community college, child care council, or family child care association? Here again is a chance for you to be creative — figure out how to build a partnership with this person whom you want to make a part of your extended family.

As to how much to pay, it is important to know the going rate in your area, or at least have a salary range based on educational background and experience. Your local child care expert has that information. Then encourage your prospective provider to make the first proposal. If that offer is lower than you expected, *don't* jump at the chance to save a few bucks! You are not buying a used refrigerator; this is about someone who will care for the most precious person in your life. Instead, offer to pay a somewhat higher rate as a way of saying how important her care is to you. If the first offer is much higher than the going rate, explain what you understand about how much other people are paying and try to make an offer in the upper half of the range.

Relatives, friends, and neighbors are our most important safety net. We turn to them in times of sorrow as well as times of joy, when we need advice or to borrow necessities in all the areas of our lives. Do be careful not to use up these resources with your child care needs only to find that they are not available in times of crisis. Suppose you approach your cousin about child care, and she says, "Sure, I'll look after your Jimmy." Then when you offer to pay she says, "Hey, don't worry about it. Blood is thicker than water." Be careful! It is only fair to give her equal support in return. Money for service is clear and easy to understand. Unspecified future expectations based on "Blood is thicker than water" or "That's what friendship is all about" may turn out to be tough to fulfill and lead to hurt feelings.

The Three-Family System

So far we have discussed finding the right caregiver as the primary step in creating your own child care arrangement. Now let's talk about a different approach. Instead of beginning the search with a *caregiver*, you could start the process by seeking out *other families* with preschool children who are also in the market for a child care arrangement. Perhaps you met the mothers at a birthing class, when you were all pregnant. Or maybe your sister has also just had a baby or is unhappy with the current arrangement for her three-year-old. The idea is to recruit a couple of other families, meet with those parents, and dream up a child care arrangement that works for all of you.

This idea did not spring full-blown into our fertile imaginations. The so-called three-family system has been a formal part of the Swedish national child care program for about twenty-five years. Here is how three-family collaboration, Swedish style, works.

In this arrangement, the parents provide the space for child care and the local community child care agency provides a trained caregiver. Two to four families with children, living in the same neighborhood, join to file a request with the agency for an available provider. At least two homes must meet agency requirements for safe and adequate space to accommodate the number of children projected for the group.

Once the application is approved, the caregiver looks after their children in the homes of those families, usually rotating from one home to the next weekly. The provider has several years of training as a "children's nurse," through which she acquired specialized knowledge about the development and care of preschool children, especially infants and toddlers. The parents pay the agency rather than the provider.

The cost is the same as for center or family child care, about 9 percent of the families' income, no matter how much the amount. The agency pays the caregiver a salary about equal to that of family child care providers in her local area. In fact, Swedes consider this three-family system a variation of family child care, in which children are cared for in their own homes every third week instead of in the family provider's house. Regulations are about the same as those for family child care: three to six children between the ages of eighteen months and twelve years, with no more than two of those children under age three.

No one in a local U.S. community is about to organize a three-family child care arrangement for you, so you must do the work yourself. One reason to make the effort is the sense of security your child receives from being cared for in his own home every third week. Another advantage of this arrangement is that you share the cost of your provider, a kind of group nanny, with several other families. Indeed, the nanny channels would be one place to seek the person you and your companion families require — see Chapter 8 for ideas on recruiting nannies.

From a licensing standpoint, the provider of child care in your homes falls into the category of an au pair or a nanny and is therefore not likely to be covered by state or local regulations. *This is not to suggest that you can forget about quality standards.* We agree with the Swedes, who apply the same high standards to three-family providers that they do to family child care providers. The key features of quality family child care are outlined in Chapter 5: a trained provider who views herself as a professional, plans her daily program, tunes in to the unique needs of each child, consults with parents as partners, and operates in a safe, stimulating environment — or environments, in this case.

You and your parent colleagues have to sit down and reach a consensus on the kind of provider you require. At first, the need to talk through good caregiving with other parents, and maybe having to compromise a bit to reach agreement, may strike you as burdensome. But look at it the other way round — the group is your sounding board when you have questions and doubts, and a resource for information to which you may not have access. Another advantage to working with other parents is that each has networks different from yours. When you have decided what type of person you wish to employ, your combined network of relatives, friends, and neighbors who might be potential providers, or contacts for provider names, is much larger than yours alone.

Obviously, one or more of your homes must have adequate space to serve the needs of all the children in the group and it must be child-proofed to make it safe. Think about what it will mean for you and your child to have two or three other children occupying your home for five days every third week. (The parent group is free to choose a different schedule.) This sort of arrangement is likely to work best for infants and toddlers, partly because their physical capabilities don't demand too much running and jumping space and partly because they are not old enough to become jealous about sharing space and playthings, although competition over toys and other objects can begin as early as twelve months.

Establishing Your Own Child Care Service

A third alternative to accessing the child care "out there" is to start your own child care business. A surprising number of parents — usually mothers — make this choice. Many of the family child care homes in your community were started by women who wanted to care for their own children at home while earning some income.

Looking after the children of others is serious business. Each of the children you serve is entitled to personalized care. The parents require respect, reassurance, and understanding. Your family must be able to adapt to constant involvement with other children and their parents. The following are key questions to ask yourself before taking the next step:

- Do I enjoy working with children? Feeling enjoyment is a key to success. If the answer is no, please don't become a child care provider. If you don't know, volunteer to spend a few mornings or afternoons looking after a couple of your friends' preschoolers. Ask yourself honestly whether the children interest you and if you can become excited by their interests and needs.

- Can I care for other children and still have the time and energy I need for my own family?

- How do I feel about parents who leave their children with someone else while they work? Can I respect their decision even though it is not my choice?

- Am I prepared to rearrange my home to meet the needs of other children?

- Are the other members of my family willing to share their space and belongings and my attention?

These are just examples of the questions you should ask yourself and the other members of your family before deciding to go further with the idea of starting your own child care business. A more extensive list of questions, in Appendix I, is not meant to be discouraging but to help you look before you leap into this new venture.

Let's assume that you have given these questions a great deal of thought and decided to go ahead. This is the time to connect with the consultant or adviser we mentioned at the beginning of the chapter. Your goal is to find out what is involved in setting up a family child care home in your state and how to provide good care for children of different ages. Each state has its own rules about how many unrelated children of diverse ages you are allowed to care for at one time, so you have to learn what they are. For instance, most states do not require a certificate or license if you look after fewer then three children who are not related to you. The local expert can give you the information and plug you into a formal process for learning all the necessary details. Many communities offer regular classes at which you can learn how to set up and run your own child care business, how to arrange your home so that it works well as a child care environment, and how to plan and carry out the daily routines of family child care. On the business end there are regulations, parent fees, taxes, record keeping, and insurance to consider. The child care environment includes spaces for various kinds of play, naps, eating, and storage. Children need playthings, materials for projects and other activities, and child-size tables and chairs. The daily routine must meet the learning and security needs of children of assorted ages and personalities. Your local consultant knows how you can learn more about these topics through local orientation sessions, workshops, and classes.

Another way to think about the care you wish to provide is to view it through the eyes of the parents whose children you will serve. In Chapter 5 we offer parents various ways to think about family child care and advice on what to look for and what to avoid. Read that chapter as if we were talking about you and your child care home. Survey your community for the kinds of assistance that will help you meet those quality standards.

Other family child care providers comprise another wonderful resource. If you are lucky, you will find a family child care provider association in your area, where you can meet other providers and learn from them what works best and how to solve problems. If no association exists, find out whether the staff at your local child care referral agency can recommend an experienced provider who would be willing to host a friendly visit. However, be aware that she is trying to run a successful business and may feel threatened if her own home is not filled to capacity.

In this chapter we have tried to open your mind to new possibilities. All our examples demand more of you than simply exploring existing options and enrolling your child in one. To create a new arrangement requires energy, confidence, a do-it-yourself attitude, and perhaps a strong feeling of dissatisfaction with existing possibilities. It is more work than using an established center or family child care home — if you assume that there are shortcuts, you'll be disappointed. But it is also a way to have more control over the results and perhaps a happier outcome, especially if you have surveyed long-standing programs and found them wanting. We know of many parents who have taken child care into their own hands in these ways and been satisfied with the result. If you feel ready to make this kind of investment in time and energy, don't delay. Get out and find those raw materials — the right person, the space, the expert consultant. Use them to build your personalized child care arrangement. Remember that the bottom line is a caregiver you can trust, who has the skills and commitment to support and enhance your child's development.

Staying in Touch with Your Child and with Yourself

11

Time Off after the Birth of Your Child

THE ARRIVAL of a new baby — especially a first baby — is one of the most powerful events in the life of a family. As the mother, you feel the impact most immediately. You must recover from the physical demands of delivery. At the same time, you need to sort out the many unfamiliar emotions connected with this lively little person, newly arrived after growing inside your body for nine long months. And so many other things change once the baby is born: no more spontaneous decisions to take in a movie or go out to visit friends; even a trip to the mall or a walk around the block becomes a major outing.

Then there are the new expectations. Everyone expects the mother to *be a mother*, but no one is clear about what being a mother entails. As you are figuring out what is involved in being a parent, you usually also have to keep track of a relationship with a spouse or partner. Spouses and partners may feel left out when all the attention is focused on mother and baby. No matter what the relationship was before the birth, it changes with the arrival of your baby. Perhaps you had agreed to a fifty-fifty split in the housework, which worked well over the past year or two. Suddenly your baby appears, and one of you, her mother, is home for at least six weeks. Will you still split the housework fifty-fifty, even though you can do more after the first couple of weeks? Or will you slip into a more traditional pattern, with the father at work all day and the mother at home taking care of the baby and all the household chores? These are hard decisions that take time to sort out. You are both trying to cope with this new arrival, to figure out where you fit into a set of family dynamics that have suddenly become a good deal more complicated. If you both want an equal part in caring for the baby, what does that call for and how can it be organized? If you are content to carry most of the burden, how will that affect each parent's relationship with the baby? Relatives and friends may have opinions about what you should do or not do, but their beliefs may be in conflict with yours and with each other's. Employers probably don't want to provide much time off or rearrange schedules to make it easier for your spouse or partner to help out during this readjustment process.

All these disruptions and changes are complicated by the need for single mothers or parents to return to work or school and to determine when to make that transition. Once the mother has recovered her strength after giving birth, the safety, security, and developmental needs of the baby should be the primary concern in making that decision. Unfortunately, American society is not organized well enough to grant the time parents need to assess a baby's readiness for child care.

This chapter suggests a number of ways to find that time. The first step is to figure out how much you might need. To do that, you have to know some basic facts about how your baby develops a strong emotional tie with you, the parent, and with a few other special adults.

Building an Emotional Base

Building a secure emotional connection between you and your child is essential both for the child's development and for your happiness and peace of mind. The trust that comes from knowing that at least one adult can be counted on to relieve distress and provide comfort allows your child to feel safe enough to explore his surroundings, which leads to physical, mental, and social growth and development. Your child's expression of this connection, by sadness at separation and joy at reunion, also signifies that you are loved and are doing a good job of meeting your child's needs, that you are good parents.

Until quite recently most people believed that only mothers could form the intense emotional relationship needed to provide a child with a secure base from which to explore and grow. We now know that infants can, and quite often do, connect in the same way with their fathers and with other significant people in their lives. The most notable ingredients in determining who is important to a child seem to be that the significant person is available or on call regularly, cares about the child, and is sensitive to the child's feelings and needs. Think of the babies adopted at birth by strangers. Despite lacking a biological link, such infants form deep emotional attachments with their parents, because these special adults care so much and are so responsive to the babies' physical and emotional needs.

Forging an emotional attachment with your child begins at birth. The entire first year of a baby's life is an important time in the building process. Your baby comes into the world ready to connect, wired to receive and respond to the signals you send. Your care and constant presence say, "I'm here! You can count on me. I am aware of your sounds and movements. I am looking for ways to make you comfortable and happy." We are not suggesting that all is lost if secure attachments are not completely formed in the first twelve months. Trust relationships can be developed later on as well, but they may be harder to establish, especially if a child has already experienced adults who are unresponsive or react to her signals in uncaring and unpredictable ways.

Key Phases in Your Infant's Development

During their first couple of years, most children go through a series of predictable stages in their physical and mental growth. These changes affect their ability, first, to recognize their parents and other significant people, and then to be aware that when those special people leave, they will return.

During the first four or five months your child is busy learning to focus on faces and recognize voices. The increasingly familiar combination of your voice, face, touch, and movement becomes a pattern increasingly fixed in your baby's mind. But the ability to recognize one face as strange and another as familiar, and remember that information, usually isn't complete until your infant is about six months old.

Once your baby is able to remember your face, other faces will seem strange. The ability to distinguish one face from another generally emerges between the fifth and the seventh month. Several faces may become familiar because your baby has consistently received care from several adults. But unfamiliar adults will seem strange because your child can recognize that their faces, voices, and gestures are different. By eight or nine months your baby is likely to cling to you when strangers approach, because their unknown faces are startling and a little scary. This reaction is known as *stranger anxiety*. Some babies don't respond as strongly as others, perhaps because they have regularly experienced three or four caring adults during their first six months of life.

At about this time your baby is likely to start crying when you leave the room. He can remember your face, but not yet whether you will return. This is called *separation anxiety*, and like stranger anxiety, it is perfectly normal. Concern at your departure usually becomes less intense once your toddler is eighteen months to two years old, because by then she has learned that when you leave you always come back. At eighteen months your child can actually *imagine* what you look like, holding on to you as a mental image even though you are not physically present.

Time and Energy as Resources

To start the attachment process you must have three prerequisites: to care deeply for your infant, to be available on a regular basis, and to learn to respond sensitively to your child's feelings and needs.

Deeply irrational caring — what we call love — is the precious gift that you bring to the relationship, your promise to be there always no matter what happens. It takes time and patience to learn to show that love in ways that benefit your child.

You can also work hard to make sure that you are regularly available to your child. But competing demands of job or schooling will probably limit the amount of time you can be present each day. Those demands will spill over into the time you have with your child, causing fatigue and distraction that reduce your ability to focus on child-rearing activities.

For most of us, learning to respond sensitively does not come naturally, as some people still believe it does. It takes practice. You need time to practice and enough energy to be able to keep from getting frustrated and discouraged when your child won't settle down no matter what you do.

Sensitivity involves tuning in to the feelings and abilities of your child. Your goal is to develop rhythms, to synchronize your initiatives and responses with his. Some of these rhythms require only a brief period of time. When your baby is only a few months old, he coos; you coo back and pause; then he coos again. You wait a couple of seconds and coo back once more. Your baby coos one more time, then is distracted by a shadow or his own little hand. When you hear the coo, pause, and coo in response, you establish a rhythm that lasts only a few moments but can be repeated many times. Other rhythms may extend over a full day or even a week. With a toddler you establish a daily pattern of feeding, playing, and sleeping that becomes predictable over time. When you return to work or school you create a predictable weekly rhythm of child care arrangements. Your child learns to anticipate those patterns and feels secure when the predictions come true. But establishing such rhythms takes time and energy, two resources that may be hard to come by.

How Much Time Is Enough?

Our best estimate is that after giving birth you will want and need at least three or four months with your baby before initiating a supplementary child care arrangement. In addition to the mother, our "you" includes a father or other partner, if one is available.

Time for the Mother: Mothers need time to recover from the birthing process. Most doctors agree that this takes a good three to six weeks following a normal delivery and longer if there have been complications. But six weeks may not be enough time to sort out all the new feelings, thoughts, and concerns that come with having a newborn, especially a first child. It also takes longer than six weeks to establish the rhythms described earlier, partly because they depend on your baby's capacity to receive your signals and to respond in ways you can recognize. So you should grab every chance for face-to-face play time with your infant — early morning, evening, weekends — even if you have returned to work or school right after your maternity leave has run out.

Time for the Baby: From the moment of birth your child is developing a rhythm of sleeping, feeding, and wakeful attention to nearby sights and sounds. Months will pass before that rhythm begins to fit with yours, namely, when your baby sleeps through most of the night. (Many babies can sleep through with only one awakening when they are four to five months old.) During those early months, other important developments are also taking place, all of which make it easier to connect with your child. She will begin to smile when she is about eight weeks old. At the same time her eyes are maturing, allowing her to focus at different distances so that she can spot you both close up and far away.

Seeing you more easily means that your baby is likely to smile more often at your increasingly familiar face. His smiles elicit happy responses from you, which lead to more smiles. Soon cooing and gurgling accompany the smiles, letting you know when to respond and what to look for when you try to relieve distress and help your baby find comfort. By four months he can express himself in ways that are not only fun for you to experience but also help you to establish routines and rhythms. Attachments are reflected clearly in his responses to your comings and, a bit later on, to your goings.

Time for the Father or Partner: Fathers and partners are critical to the child-rearing process from the very beginning. This is true in any family, but especially when the mother plans to return to work or school during the first year of the child's life. It is unreasonable to expect her to manage both the demands she will face outside the household and the hard work involved in caring for a young child.

The term "partner" can apply to many different people. If you are a single mother, raising or planning to raise your child on your own, invite a trusted family member or friend to be with you during the birth and act as a special support person during your child's early years. This person can give you a break when you feel stressed, provide another point of view when you need advice, and be another adult your child can trust and count on. Such a partnership can make a huge difference in your struggle to find a balance between work and family life.

If you are the partner in this effort, whether father, friend, or trusted relative, it is important and helpful for you to experience some of the same feelings and be able to manage the same tasks and responsibilities that the newborn's mother is learning. The baby will help you in this endeavor because he will be happy to attach to you and to several other special adults. But to qualify for this status you must have the three essential resources — love, availability, and sensitivity.

Deep feelings of caring or love and the ability to respond tenderly to the child depends to some extent on availability. These emotions and skills can develop only if you give them a chance, if you are around at the right, sometimes long, periods of time. Several things can get in the way of being there, one being your job. Plan for time off from work beginning when the mother is about to give birth — more on that shortly.

Males may face another difficulty. Many people believe that babies are not a "guy" thing. Some may feel that you can't understand a baby, or that you will drop the newborn, or that you don't have the patience to tune in to an infant's needs. That is simply not true; more and more men are demonstrating all the affection and skills needed to play a central role in bringing up children. But if you are aware that one of the key people in your life — the baby's mother, your mother, or your mother-in-law — may want to keep you in the background, out of the way, you had better plan to push yourself into the center of the arena. If necessary, demand plenty of chances to learn what you need to know in order to be an effective partner.

It is important for the father or partner to be present when the baby is born, if at all possible. This is a very special time, when emotions that have built up over a long period are released in a flood of relief mixed with joy and sometimes sadness. Sharing these emotions connects you with their cause — the new baby — in a very special way. Hold the newborn, taking time to sense this tiny bundle of energy and life. Anticipate this opportunity and talk with the mother about your desire to hold the baby so that she can help to make it happen when the time comes.

As soon as you can, get involved with the basic care activities — changing, dressing and undressing, holding and carrying, and even feeding the baby. Take your turn with the late-night feedings when you can, and try to be available when the baby needs attention in the wee hours of the morning. Although your efforts may seem clumsy and awkward to you at first, expertise will develop. You will gradually learn to "read" the baby's needs and be rewarded with calm and growing expressions of pleasure. But all this requires time.

There are certain situations in which adjusting to new routines and building of early bonds between mother, or father, and child takes more time than expected. If your baby is unusually restless in the first few months and finds it difficult to relax and be comfortable with you, it may take longer for her to settle into predictable cycles and rhythms. Illness during the early days and weeks can also slow this process. A child born with special needs requires more than average time and attention. The same thing is true for you as a parent — your illness or highly stressful life may interfere somewhat with your ability to tune in to the baby and lengthen the amount of time you need to secure that relationship.

How to Build the Necessary Time

Three or four months is the ideal length of time for family members to devote to recovering from the stresses of a birth, adjusting to the new demands and expectations associated with parenthood, and settling into stable rhythms and routines. This may seem unrealistic and impossible to achieve, and the fact that our society does not make this time available for all parents is discouraging. It is a much shorter period than the paid parental leave other Western industrialized countries offer (see table on facing page). Even our Canadian neighbors can combine maternity leave, insurance, and sick-leave guarantees to produce six months' leave with job protection and some pay. Most of us in the United States have to beg, borrow, and sometimes steal time that parents in other countries receive as a right that is provided by law and protected by the courts.

While we are behind the times, there *are* five major ways that American parents can scrape together the necessary time to recover from childbirth and to get to know a new baby.

The Family and Medical Leave Act: Your employer is required to give you up to twelve weeks of unpaid leave if

- the company employs at least fifty people at one site or at several locations within seventy-five miles; and

- you have worked for that company for at least twelve months and at least 1,250 hours during the last twelve months.

If you take this leave, your employer is required to reassign you to your original job or an equivalent position when you return. Only about 40 percent of employed parents work for companies large enough to be covered by this federal law. However, a few progressive states have established parental leave laws that apply to companies with fewer than fifty employees — Maine (20), Minnesota (21), Rhode Island (30), and Vermont (10).

If you are eligible for this leave and can afford it, take it all. If both mother and father work for employers required to provide this leave, each can take up to twelve weeks, giving you twenty-four unpaid weeks to be with your newborn. The problem of course, will be paying your bills with less than a full income.

Disability Insurance: If your employer provides disability insurance, you, as the prospective mother, are eligible for disability payments once your doctor decides that you can no longer work because of your pregnancy. Normally you receive this insurance for six weeks after the child's birth. The amount you are paid depends on your salary, because

Parental Leave Policies
Other Countries with High Living Standards

Australia	One-year unpaid leave, with job protected. Right to work part time until child is two years old.
Denmark	Job-protected, paid leave one month before and six months after birth. Father given extra two weeks while mother recovers.
Finland	Nine-month, job-protected paid leave. Fathers given one to two extra weeks at birth of child. Right to part-time work until child starts school.
France	Paid, job-protected leave for two and a half months, with additional thirty-three unpaid, job-protected months.
Germany	Paid, job-protected leave for twenty-four months.
Italy	Paid, job-protected leave for nine months.
Norway	Paid, job-protected leave for nine months.
Sweden	Paid, job-protected leave for twelve months. Fathers given two extra weeks at time of birth, to support mother and care for other children.

Source: Adapted from Moncrieff Cochran, ed., *The International Handbook of Child Care Policies and Programs* (Westport, Conn.: Greenwood Press, 1993), Appendix, 1, 660–661.

Note: Except in France and Italy, these rights are available to both mother and father.

disability insurance covers a percentage of what you were being paid weekly at the time your child was born. However, most employers allow you to supplement the insurance with sick or vacation leave to obtain the full 100 percent.

Vacation Time: Most jobs provide at least a week of paid vacation time each year. This is another source of paid time off that can be used to expand the period between your child's birth and the beginning of a supplementary child care arrangement. Don't think of it as a waste of your valuable vacation time. An extended adjustment period after your baby arrives is far more valuable than a vacation at another time. Think of it as an investment in the health and happiness of your baby, the most important investment you can make. If the husband, partner, or close friend of a new mother also has vacation time available, that too can be invested in caring for the baby.

Sick Time: Most jobs allow a certain number of paid days off in the case of illness. You may have to use a few of these days right after your child is born, during the waiting period before disability insurance payments begin.

Part-Time Work or Schooling: Another way to find the time to invest in being with and caring for your child is to reduce the number of hours that you work or attend school outside the home. Of course, fewer hours on the job means less pay. (It may also result in job reassignment in some cases, and even loss of promotion, so be careful.) But it also means less money spent on supplementary child care, which is particularly expensive for infants and toddlers. An advantage of reducing your work hours is that you are likely to feel less stressed working part time and have more energy for child care. If both mother and father or partner can arrange part-time work and one works while the other is at home, you might be able to delay placing your baby in a supplementary arrangement until he is in his second year.

Setting up a part-time work arrangement usually requires a considerable amount of discussion and negotiation with your employer. If this option interests you, begin to explore the possibilities with your employer well before your baby is due so that she has time to decide how to cover the duties of your job for which you will not be responsible during your part-time employment.

The Cost of Leave

The dollar cost of taking time off following childbirth is quite a bit higher for American parents than for those in Germany, France, Italy, and the Scandinavian countries. But the expense may be a good investment if it buys you and your baby time to settle down and get off to a good start and you have enough income with which to pay the bills. An

	Mother	Father
Month 1	At home, with disability insurance.	One week of vacation, three weeks of full-time employment.
Month 2	At home, two weeks' insurance, two weeks' vacation.	Full-time employment.
Month 3	At home, unpaid leave.	Full-time employment.
Month 4	Half-time employment.	One week paid vacation, three weeks' half-time employment.
Month 5	Half-time employment.	Half-time employment.
Month 6	Half-time employment.	Half-time employment.
Month 7	Half-time employment.	Full-time employment.
Month 8	Half-time employment.	Full-time employment.
Month 9	Half-time employment.	Full-time employment.

example of how to put together a leave package and to estimate the costs involved appears above. In this two-parent family, the father takes home $1,500 and the mother $1,200 per month. Both parents work for large organizations that come under the jurisdiction of the Family and Medical Leave Act.

In this plan the baby is at home with one parent or the other for the first six months, then spends three months in a part-time child care arrangement before entering full-time care. The mother is able to stay home for her full twelve-week family leave, then returns to part-time work for another six months. The father is fully available as a helper during the week following the birth, provides a week of full-time care when the mother reenters the workforce, then shares care equally with the mother during the fourth, fifth, and sixth months, taking his legally available family leave.

This plan takes advantage of four different options: disability insurance, unpaid family leave, paid vacation, and part-time work. You have a legal right to the first three of these benefits if they are included in your contract with your employer. Part-time work is normally an arrangement that you have to negotiate with your employer on a case-by-case basis. If, however, you have a right to family leave, your employer might prefer to allow you to work part time rather than have you totally absent for as many as twelve weeks. The plan also includes part-time child care for your infant for the last three months. Such care is difficult to arrange with a center, which must ordinarily enroll children full time in order to pay its bills. Family child care and in-home care are more likely alternatives in this situation (see Chapters 5 and 8).

To figure the dollar cost of this plan, begin by totaling the income lost owing to (1) the difference between disability insurance payment and full salary (mother) and (2) the time at home on unpaid leave (both mother and father). In this case that total is about $7,600. Subtract from that amount the cost of child care you would have used if you had been working full time instead of staying home with your infant, which you can estimate at $150 per week. If the baby had started full-day care at three months rather than at six months and continued full time rather than part day during the seventh, eighth, and ninth months, the parents would have spent approximately an additional $2,800 on child care. By providing that care themselves, they saved money. Subtracting that saving from the loss in salary income, they are left with a total cost of $4,800.

Under this plan, the couple invested roughly $5,000 to get the family off to a healthy, physically and emotionally manageable start with their baby. This $5,000 purchased:

1. *For the child:* six months at home with a parent followed by three months of gentle entry into child care for twenty hours a week.

2. *For the mother:* three months at home with the baby followed by six months of part-time work, allowing a mix of child time with work involvement.

3. *For the father:* significant involvement with the child, including three months of part-time child care experience without excessive loss of income over the nine-month period.

On an annual basis this works out to $27,000 instead of $32,000 in family income, a reduction of about 16 percent. The big question for you, again, is whether you can pay your bills with such a reduction in income. If you can cover your housing, food, transportation, and other expenses despite the loss in income, the trade-off in the physical and mental health of both baby and parents adds up to a very good deal.

There is nothing magical about the particular combination of disability payments, leave, and part-time work shown above. Other combinations could work for you. For instance, you could save money by having the mother resume full-time work earlier. But this would add more child care costs to the equation, so the saving isn't as great as it might appear at first. You could also try to find infant care for less than $150 a week. However, in most cases you get what you pay for, so make sure that you are buying good-quality care before deciding that it's a bargain (see the guidelines in Chapters 3–6).

The Right Time to Begin Supplementary Child Care

Stranger anxiety and separation anxiety are real experiences during the first fifteen to eighteen months of a child's life. Fear of strangers can begin when your baby is only five or six months old. Anxiety at your departure can start as early as seven months of age. Both reactions are likely to be most intense between the ninth and the twelfth month, tapering off gradually until the baby is about eighteen months old, when they are pretty much a thing of the past.

The particular month in which a baby enters child care during the first year doesn't seem to make any difference in her long-term development. Infants who begin supplementary care during their first year of life do fine later on as long as two things are true: (1) the quality of the child care arrangement is satisfactory; and (2) there are not a lot of other problems affecting the family situation, for example, a stressful job, a major illness, marital tension.

Since, with such acceptable conditions, the long-term development of your child is not a major concern, it makes sense to consider addi-

When a Swedish child enters a center or family child care home, Sweden's social policy allows the parents up to two weeks of leave to ease the transition. First the center teacher or family care provider makes a home visit to get to know the family better. Then the parent and child go to child care together, where they spend time getting acquainted with the new environment and people. The transition to full-time care is gradual. After a few days together, the parent begins to leave the child alone at the facility for short periods of time. As the two weeks unfold, the child becomes more and more used to longer periods without the parent. At the end of the two-week period she is fully accustomed to the new arrangement.

tional short-term factors. In the area of infant development, we have already made a case for a four-month period when the baby can be at home with a parent or other significant adult. We have also argued that the mother needs at least three to six weeks to recover physically, and that four or five months together allows parent and child to get a good start on the attachment process.

Other short-term aspects are the reactions to strangers and to separation described above. The most sensitive age for these fearful feelings is between six and thirteen months. Therefore, if you have a choice, avoid placing your baby in a new child care arrangement at this time. Because repeated separations are an unavoidable part of nonparental child care, it makes good sense not to introduce such partings during the very stage when your baby would find them most upsetting.

Therefore, unless you can afford to have one of you at home for the first thirteen or fourteen months of the baby's life, the *best* time to introduce your infant to a new child care arrangement is in his fifth or sixth month. The above example has the six-month-old baby beginning that new arrangement part time, with one parent, the mother, employed only twenty hours a week. The infant is introduced to a new caregiver before fear of strangers has become an issue, and the length of time away from the parent is kept to a manageable four to five hours each day. Three months later, when the infant has had ample time to become familiar with the new adult and accustomed to parental departures, both baby and parent shift to full-time schedules. This sort of transition seems reasonable to us, at least until the day when every American working parent has access to four to six months of paid parental leave.

12

Children's Reactions to Child Care

J UST AS YOU BRING various feelings and needs home with you every day when you return from work, so do children returning from child care. These reactions can range from the pent-up emotions resulting from their laboring to be "good" all day to occasional displays of disinterest in you, shown by expressions of annoyance at being separated from you for much of every working day.

Separation Is Hard

As an illustration of one of many issues related to separation that can occur daily, we describe a call received by our local child care resource and referral "warm" line, a noncrisis telephone counseling service provided for parents of children between the ages of zero and twelve:

Mary, the mother of seven-month-old Anna, wanted advice about what to do when she leaves Anna at her child care center each morning. Mary talked about how she hates to hear Anna cry and wants to sneak out of the room when her daughter isn't watching. The caregiver has told her that she has to say good-bye to Anna. Mary wanted to know if this really is good advice. Why should she make Anna cry every morning?

This is a common dilemma for parents, and the caregiver's advice is correct. The warm line counselor told Mary that she has to be sure Anna is in the arms of a caring teacher when her mother leaves, and tell Anna she loves her and will be back at the end of the day. Then Mary should kiss Anna good-bye, wave to her, and leave. A child who is playing or distracted when her mother leaves, then looks up expecting to see her, experiences much more distress than one who goes through a good-bye ritual with her parent. Anna will still be temporarily upset when Mary leaves, but if she is in a good-quality child care situation she'll adapt to the separation faster than her mother will. A child who protests at being left is showing the strength of her attachment, which is a good sign. After all, why should she want to be left behind? It may take ten days or two weeks for Anna to stop crying at Mary's departure, but eventually she'll settle into the new routine.

Separation and Stranger Anxiety

Several different times during their early years, children who are left with child care providers for all or part of a day go through periods of separation anxiety reflecting their developmental stages. The first period of stranger awareness and anxiety usually appears at about six months. Between six and eight months many children begin to protest during any separation. Part of your job is to help your baby adjust to these feelings of anxiety. You and his caregiver must respect his feelings and help him move beyond them. A departure ritual like the one recommended for Mary and Anna helps a lot. Your baby will become familiar with the ritual and find comfort in the predictability of the routine. After a while his protest will be more of a formality than a deeply felt loss.

Many parents like to drop in to visit their children several times a day, especially if they work near the child care site. You must remember that if your child finds it hard to say good-bye once a day, having to repeat that experience several times a day may be too much to handle emotionally. Take the time to work this through with your child's caregiver. You may have to limit one visit to observation, unseen by your child, so that you can see how he is doing without forcing him to experience the discomfort of your leaving without him.

Different Reactions to Different Adults

For some one-year-olds the most threatening "stranger" is one with whom they are somewhat familiar. It might be a grandparent or another relative who sees the child occasionally yet believes that he is on familiar terms with the baby. The best way to support your child in such a situation is to hold her in your arms and ask the visitor to wait for her to initiate the first approach. This may take awhile, but if you are patient, and if the visitor is willing to spend time playing with a toy or other article interesting to the child, she may eventually initiate contact with the newcomer.

As you observe your children, you'll come to learn that different adults trigger different behaviors in them. You may already have noticed these differences in the way your child interacts with each parent. Children tend to be hardest on the parent they feel they can count on the most, traditionally the mother, who carries the main responsibility for child rearing. But in many of today's families fathers share the task equally with their spouses. In such families the father may be the chief target of acting-out and testing behavior. Although it is hard to do, especially after a long day, try to accept this attention as a compliment. Your child feels safe with you and needs an outlet for her stress and pent-up feelings. Young children don't express these feelings in sophisticated ways. However, they do experience anxiety just as we do. When they feel that it is safe to do so, they may simply give up trying to be "big" and fall apart. They need your reassurance that it is all right to let go of their emotions for a while.

Preschool and School-age Separation Anxiety

The initial phase of separation anxiety commonly lasts until a child is eighteen months to two years old. However, there will be later periods when your child does not want you to leave him in child care or send him to school. During the third year this is basically resistance to transition. A child is most likely to be upset when she is being shifted from one group to another in the center, or when her teacher leaves for another job and she must adjust to a strange caregiver. When you know that such changes are about to take place, try to prepare your child by talking about them. Ask her caregiver to help with that preparation by making the upcoming change a topic of normal discussion during the days prior to the shift.

Two-year-olds may even find it hard to move from child care to home at the end of the day. They are so busy searching for stability and predictability that even routine transitions upset them.

A three- or four-year-old might have a "relapse," suddenly crying one morning when you start to leave. He has been fine about your departure for months, then suddenly falls apart again. The cause may be a newcomer to his child care group with whom he doesn't yet feel comfortable or a new and still unfamiliar teacher. Some young children develop social skills slowly and require special help in getting to know new people. The event triggering this upset may originate at home — the arrival of a new brother or sister, for instance. Your older child may wonder why he too isn't allowed to stay at home with his mom or dad and wants to know what goes on when he isn't around to watch. Sometimes your child will fall apart for no discernible reason. When this happens you have to be patient and willing to rebuild your departure routines slowly.

School-age children can develop stomachaches and headaches when they are anxious about going to school. Once you have made sure that there is no medical reason for these symptoms, look for ways to help your child conquer his fears. This can be a long-term project requiring a combination of empathy and firmness. Explain that he has to attend school but that you understand how difficult this is for him. Sit down with him and try to talk about what it is that makes going to school so hard. Perhaps he feels pressured in class or is being teased by a classmate or a group of children is excluding him from their games. You will probably need to involve his teacher as well to get the full picture of what is going on.

The Pressure of Being Good All Day

A familiar sight at pickup time in a child care center is a child on the floor, weeping and wailing as her parent tries to put on her coat and take her home. An insensitive teacher might comment, "Joanie has been so good all day. She never behaves this way here at the center." Of course she doesn't! Her tantrum isn't caused by anger at you for leaving her behind while you go to work, as many parents believe. She has chosen you for this display because she feels secure and loved by you. She has been working so hard to be on her good behavior all day that she just needs to let go in the safety of your presence.

This can happen anytime during the preschool years. Your ten-month-old baby may turn her head away when you come to pick her up one day or hold on to her provider and refuse to come to you. When you cuddle her in your arms, she may fall apart and burst into tears. Don't get upset. Of course you find this disturbing. You don't want to spend your day looking forward to seeing your child only to be greeted with crying and sadness as soon as you walk in the door. But these reactions are normal. Develop a "good-bye child care" ritual. Talk to your child calmly and quietly as you dress her, and wave good-bye to her provider as you leave. Routines are very soothing, for they help children learn what to expect from different people at different times of the day.

Older children are often busily engaged in an activity when you come to pick them up. The best thing to do is to allow them a few minutes of transition time before you rush home. Perhaps you can spend a few minutes involved in the activity with your child, then shift naturally into talk about finishing up and help him put articles away if that has to be done.

Sometimes hearing a short story at the end of the day helps in the shift from child care to home. Some parents borrow story or music audiotapes from their library to play in the car on the way home.

Evening and Weekend Routines Are Important

You may be tempted to use evenings and weekends to make up for the time you miss being with your child during the work week. But remember that everyone, including you, needs time to relax and do nothing. Your child has been busy in child care all day or all week and might need simply to be with you during your hours together. Again, you have to observe him and learn to read his moods and needs. If you can give him your *undivided* attention for even half an hour every weekday evening before he goes to bed, you will be doing much better than most parents in their relationships with their children. Follow your child's lead. Let him decide how to spend your time together. If you have an infant, take the initiative to talk to him, sing to him, read to him, or just hold him while making lots of eye contact. But an older child is ready to lead you to what she wants to do. She may want you to play dress-up, or bake an imaginary pizza, or build a Lego castle, or read a book, or even look something up in the encyclopedia. Be flexible and open to ideas, no matter how silly they seem to you.

Weekend Chores

Weekends can sometimes be a real challenge for you as a working parent. You need to shop, clean, do the laundry, and visit with family and friends, but you also want to spend quality time with your child, who quickly learns what triggers your feelings of guilt. Weekends are when those emotions can really be punishing. Don't let that happen! Stay cool. Remember that firm and caring guidance and discipline strengthen the bond between you and your child. Don't let remorse push you into compromising all your principles. Demonstrate how much your child means to you, but also let her know that work has to be done and that she can help.

Develop family rituals for weekends, events your child can count on and anticipate during the week. If he is three years old or older, invite him to help organize the activity. These routines can be simple projects like fixing Sunday pancakes or walking with you to the corner bakery for fresh bread or running out to the mailbox for the morning newspaper.

The Supermarket Tantrum

Weekends or early evenings are often the only time you have to do your weekly grocery shopping. You are in a store and your daughter spots the cheap plastic toy she has had her eye on for weeks and asks you for it. You don't have the money to spend on a toy that will break immediately, so you say no. Your daughter bursts into tears and throws herself on the floor, kicking and screaming. Although this may be one of your worst nightmares, keep in mind that your child understands your fear, at least at some level, and in some sense is counting on it. It's not that she is cold and calculating; more probably she is tired and vulnerable. But she knows you'd do almost anything to avoid a scene, even buy a plastic toy.

Remember that many of the people in that store have experienced the same kind of situation and are sympathetic toward you. Move your grocery cart to a safe place, scoop your child up in your arms, and find a quiet spot where she, and maybe you, can calm down. Don't give in to her demand or resort to a bribe. Tell her that you understand how much she wants that toy. Explain why you cannot or will not buy it for her. Tell her that you will wait for her to feel better, and then the two of you will finish the grocery shopping and head home. You may regard this as a difficult and time-consuming routine, but your child will soon realize that you won't give in to her manipulation and she'll stop screaming in public.

Tantrums can also occur in the car on your way to or from child care. Follow the same general routine that you would in the store, but remember that you are driving the car! Acknowledge that you know he is upset, and ask what the matter is. It is important always to make sure that he is in his car seat, so that he isn't bouncing around the car in his anger or frustration. You may have to pull over to the side of the road and take him in your arms if he is really distraught. He frequently won't know himself why he is so unhappy, or he can't find the words to tell you. Just plain exhaustion has lowered his ability to handle frustration. A warm caress and soft words can make all the difference.

Why Do They Pick Up Bad Habits?

Suppose your toddler is a biter or has been bitten at day care by another toddler. You think, What is going on here? If your child is the biter, you are totally puzzled over how your peaceful little baby could possibly do something like that to another little human being. If she is on the receiving end, your first reaction may be to find out who did this to your child and hope that the culprit was punished.

Infants and toddlers are what psychologists call sensorimotor learners, discovering the world through their senses of touch and taste. Everything that seems interesting goes into their mouths. Plump cheeks and pudgy arms look very appealing, so into the mouth they go. Biting begins as exploration. The bite does not represent a mean act; it is simply what you do after you put something into your mouth.

Of course, once the other baby or an adult reacts sharply to the biting behavior, other possibilities open up. Biting can become a way of attracting attention or getting a playmate to give up a popular toy.

Biting behavior is common in toddlers, who don't yet have the words or the social skills to get what they want in more acceptable ways. Child care providers need to be most vigilant with children this age, helping them to use the words they are learning and redirecting them if they are heading for another child with their mouth wide open.

Your child is not apt to bite you at home as a way to communicate with you. But sometimes your toddler may bite your finger or the end of your nose in play or just to see what happens. Don't overreact to this kind of behavior. Say that it hurts, adding a firm no-no, but recognize that he is just trying to figure out cause and effect and doesn't really want to harm you.

Here is another Warm Line concern:

Bill calls about his daughter Jane, a three-year-old who started in full-time day care a few months ago. Jane is in a center that assigns three-, four-, and five-year-olds to the same group. Bill is concerned about the new words Jane seems to be picking up at child care. She comes home and uses four-letter words that he and her mother consider street talk! He doesn't even want to repeat them over the phone. Bill can't believe the caregivers allow the children to say such things. Yesterday Jane used one of these words when her mother asked her to help put away her toys. Bill is really upset, both with Jane and with the center staff who allow children to use such filthy language.

It is perfectly normal for preschool children to want to try out "bad" words. When they do, they look at you expectantly, wondering how you will react. Are you going to make it worthwhile for them to repeat this powerful word? Actually, the best way to respond to such testing is with no reaction at all. Sometimes your child will simply run out of energy when you don't do anything, and that's the end of it. If he persists, you may have to tell him that you don't like the word and that you expect him to pay attention to your feelings. Then walk away and ignore him for a little while. The less you make of the incident the better. Children who bring these words into the child care setting learn them from older siblings, from TV, and sometimes from their parents. Within the child care group, using profanity becomes a "naughty" game, which your child's caregiver will do her best to interrupt. You should do the same to make your child understand that you disapprove of such behavior.

Your child will learn hundreds of new words and phrases in child care. Ninety-nine percent of them will expand his vocabulary in positive ways and help him become a better communicator and a happier, more social child.

If your son is in a good-quality child care facility, his overall reaction to the experience will be positive. Sure, there will be ups and downs. We all have our good days and our bad days. But if you express confidence and enthusiasm about the child care provider, and praise your child for managing so well in child care, he will feel free to make the most of the opportunity. Be supportive of his needs, be sensitive to his moods, and above all, be patient.

13

Handling Guilt and Anxiety

S PARENTS you may feel guilty about employing someone outside your family to look after your children. You may also worry about the particular care arrangement you choose and what might happen when you are away from your children. *These feelings are normal!* Some parents experience them more strongly than others, and some report having no guilt or anxiety at all. These typical variations are partly the result of differences in your growing-up experiences and partly because you have access to different kinds of child care.

Guilt and anxiety are like yellow flags or flashing lights. They are messages coming from different parts of your brain, saying, "Be careful!" and "Make sure that you are doing the right thing!" and "Don't do anything that is bad for your child, or for your relationship with your child." But once you have put your child in the hands of a safe and capable child care provider, guilt and anxiety are no longer necessary or helpful. In fact, if you continue to be strongly affected by them once they are no longer of value, those emotions can become a barrier that keeps you from feeling good about yourself. They can also get in the way of relaxed, free-flowing interactions with your child, your partner, your relatives, friends, and workmates, and your child care provider. As a parent who loves your child, you want to find the best possible care for that precious person. That's why you are reading this book. You *are* being conscientious and sensible. Even better, you are learning how to be certain that the child care experience you choose will enrich your child's growth and development. The extra time and energy that you invest in organizing and monitoring your child care arrangements will lessen your anxiety and calm your fears.

Three strategies can help you to leave guilt behind and worry less about your child care setup.

1. Learn the differences between guilt and anxiety.
2. Face these feelings directly by telling yourself and others that you are having them.
3. Take specific, concrete actions designed to lessen these feelings.

The Difference between Guilt and Anxiety

Guilt comes from believing that you are breaking a rule, an agreement, or a promise of some kind, an unwritten vow akin to a law or a religious document. But there is no law or religious tenet against having someone else help you with child care. Indeed, others have been providing parents with child care help for thousands of years. Think of the large extended families of the past, in which aunts, uncles, and grandparents spent almost as much time caring for the children as their own parents did, a situation that is still true in some families. No one has accused the wealthy, who have relied on nannies to raise their children throughout recorded history, of being wrong or immoral. But in present-day America some people believe that they are bad parents if they entrust their children to the care of someone else while they work or attend school.

If that sort of guilt is bothering you, take a minute to get a sense of where those emotions might be coming from. Perhaps one of your parents was always at home during your preschool years and met you at the bus after school. Maybe the adults around you praised stay-at-home moms and criticized mothers with jobs outside the home. Possibly you have good friends who stay home with their children and spend a good bit of time justifying their choice by saying that is best for their kids. Any message telling you that there is a right way and a wrong way, or a good way and a bad way, to bring up children and that you are choosing the wrong way makes you feel guilty.

Anxiety is different. You are anxious because you can't predict or control a part of your life, and you are afraid that it will turn out badly. In this case it is your child care arrangement because you don't know whether it is good for your child. You don't know what is going on when you are away from the child. You worry that you are not in control in these areas.

Confronting Your Feelings

There is nothing wrong or unusual in feeling guilt or anxiety about having someone else look after your child. Think carefully. Is it guilt or anxiety that you are feeling? Maybe a little of each? Don't try to ignore or avoid those emotions. When you know what they are, figure out where they are coming from, what is causing them. Talk about them with other parents, especially parents whose children are in child care. Their similar experiences will help you feel less lonely and may show you ways to put your fears to rest.

Child Care Myths

Guilt related to child care choices is frequently created by people or organizations that use false information as a scare tactic. The following are myths about what could happen to your child in someone else's care while you work outside your home and the truth as we understand it from our own experience and relevant research studies.

Myth 1

Child care is bad for a child's development.

Dozens of studies have been undertaken to discover whether full-day care outside the home is good or bad for preschool children and whether some kinds of care are better than others. We have conducted some of this research ourselves and know most of the other scientists involved. Their results can be boiled down to three basic facts.

- *High-quality* child care is not bad for your child's development, regardless of the child's age.

- Poor-quality child care can interfere with healthy development, especially in an infant or toddler. This is more likely to be true if your family life is also stressful for your child.

- Center care is neither better nor worse for children than family child care or in-home care. In all three settings, it is the quality of the care provided that matters.

Myth 2

Child care makes you less important to your child.

This is just not true! No other person will ever be as important to your child as you are. Parents are the adults a child's life revolves around. Everyone else is extra, people who support and assist your efforts but aren't at the center of your child's life.

If your child care provider is a warm, caring person, your child is quite likely to become attached to her. That's all right! In fact, it's more than all right. It's a healthy sign that your child is developing a secure, trusting relationship. *Remember, this is not a win-lose situation.* Children can become emotionally attached to other people without becoming less attached to you. Suppose your child bonds with your mother or your sister. Would that be *bad*? Most of us are happy when our children can feel secure with and loved by other adults we trust and care about. This is no different. You will continue to be the most important person in your child's world, but she will have a somewhat broader base of trust and caring to build upon, and that is *good*.

Myth 3

You are a bad parent because someone else is the first to witness your child's progress.

So many young mothers or mothers-to-be have told us something like this: "If I knew that someone else [the caregiver at the center or the family child care provider] heard my baby say her first word [take his first step, poop in the potty for the first time, et cetera, et cetera], I would feel soooo guilty!!"

Do you fall into that category? If so, stop and ask yourself why you do. Is there *really* anything so magical about the *first* time your child does something? Or do other people *say* that this is so important to keep you at home with your child or make you feel guilty for going to work?

Why is it that many fathers don't feel guilty when they miss the first word, or the first step, or the first properly deposited poop? Perhaps it is because for a hundred years or more it has been *expected* that they would be at work when those events occurred. They come to realize that it doesn't matter who sees what for the first time. *What matters is when you see these things for the first time and how you express your excitement and pleasure to your child for his great accomplishment.* So your caregiver sees the first step. Big deal! Don't be jealous! Be happy! This is not a competition. You are a team of people working together to care for your child, and you are the member with by far the most influence over the long haul. Relax and enjoy the changes in your child when you experience them without worrying about who saw what first.

Myth 4

Child care robs a child of childhood.

What is childhood? Surely children in different families, growing up in different neighborhoods, from different ethnic and religious backgrounds, experience childhood very differently from one another.

Perhaps what you really mean is that your child's experiences in child care will be quite different from the childhood you experienced. Maybe you have happy memories of the years before school and don't want to deprive your child of that pleasure. Who says that children can't be happy in child care? Anyway, were you *really* always happy at three or four or five, or do you just remember the happy times?

You can influence the pace, rhythm, and content of your child's care experience. If free play and creativity are your idea of childhood, seek a program that emphasizes those activities. If large groups seem too much like school to you, take a good look at family child care with its smaller, mixed-age groupings. Check out the range of options in your community and choose the one that matches your idea of childhood as closely as possible.

Remember, too, that you have complete control over your child's experiences while she is at home with you. Of course, much of that time is taken up with basic care and sleep. But give some thought to how you organize the more flexible times when you and your child can choose how to spend the morning or afternoon. That's when the happy memories from your own childhood can help shape her experience.

Myth 5

Child care produces negative outcomes in children.

"Johnny went to child care, and look how he turned out!" People who want to put down child care can always find a negative example. What does shape the early development of children and how they turn out in the long run? Studies show that child care arrangements have far less impact on these results than the personalities kids are born with, the families they grow up in, and the social and environmental conditions surrounding them — family income, parents' jobs, housing and neighborhood conditions, air and water quality. These circumstances undoubt-edly had much more to do with Johnny's later character and behavior than anything related to his child care arrangement. Yes, children have been abused and neglected by their care providers, but the truth is that such negative experiences are much, much more likely to take place at home than in child care.

How to Feel Less Guilty

There are various ways to hold your guilt feelings down to a tolerable and manageable level.

Be prepared to explain your decision to family and friends. Learn more about the research on the effects on children of having a working parent and being in child care. Those studies tell us that, in general, children whose mothers work outside the home do as well as, and sometimes better than, those whose mothers are homemakers. Good child care has no harmful effects on kids. Poor-quality care can delay develop-ment, especially if the home situation is stressful. Good child care exists in family child care homes as well as in centers, and so does poor-quality care. Arm yourself with these facts and describe them to relatives or friends who are concerned about your decision. If they want more in-formation, give them a copy of the reading list in Appendix H. Empha-size your efforts toward ensuring that your child care arrangement is good. If necessary, make sacrifices to buy the best care you can afford. Drive the old car for a few more years rather than buying a new one. Hold off buying or building a house. This does *not* mean that the most expensive care is necessarily the best, but be prepared to pay more to ensure a better experience for your child. And remember, you do not have to feel guilty as long as you are certain that your child is in good care.

Discuss your feelings with parents who have similar child care setups. It is important to communicate with parents who can sympathize with your feelings. As you hear them explain why they use child care and how it suits them, you will find the words to support your own decision. Being in touch with others who feel good about their child care makes you feel better about yours.

Talk to your provider about your feelings if she seems sympathetic. Many child care center directors and some family child care providers are highly aware of the benefits of child care to both your child and you. You might find it helpful to share your feelings with them. However, studies of child care teacher attitudes do show that, ironically, some teachers disapprove of mothers with young children who work outside the home. These caregivers believe that the parents they serve should be home with their children, not in the workforce. Other providers are of two minds. They think that very young children, especially infants, should be able to spend lots of time at home with a parent during the first couple of years, but condone work after that time. Any teacher or caregiver who increases your guilt about child care is, perhaps unknowingly, doing needless harm. Therefore, our advice is to look for caregivers who respect your decision to work and avoid those who are unwilling to give you that approval.

If family or friends express opinions that make you feel guilty, ask them to stop. You may be spending quite a bit of time with people who feel that you should be at home taking care of your child full time. If so, you have probably heard one or more of the child care myths in one form or another. When a relative or friend makes such a claim, challenge it directly and immediately. Say, "I'm sorry, you are wrong. That is not true. The truth is . . ." By questioning the false information quickly you protect yourself against feeling guilty and send a message that you cannot be influenced by untrue statements. Follow up by asking the person to stop trying to bully you about your decision to work and place your child in care. Say that you have given it a great deal of thought and are doing everything possible to ensure that the arrangement is a good one. By taking a firm, assertive approach, you strengthen your own conviction and announce that interference is unacceptable.

Stop seeing family or friends who are unable or unwilling to support your decision. This most drastic step should be taken only if a person will not back off even after you have warned him that you will not tolerate his laying a guilt trip on you, for friendship is built on support and acceptance. Some parents wish to remain at home while their children are young, and their choice deserves respect and encouragement. You choose to go to work, or may have no alternative, and have arranged for supplementary child care. Your choice also deserves respect and encouragement. Sometimes a relative or friend is unwilling to grant you approval and feels the need to put down your decision. To protect yourself against such abuse, you may have to stop seeing that person for a while. If you make that decision, explain your reason for maintaining distance. That way the person is clear about the behavior you cannot tolerate and can choose to change.

Alleviating Anxiety

The best way to get control over the worry you feel about using child care is to take action. Do something constructive that helps you answer the questions on your mind. Concerns that may seem overwhelming in the abstract become manageable when you replace your fears and fantasies with knowledge and experience. Here are some steps that will help you control your anxiety.

Begin your search for child care early. Rather than sitting around worrying about the future, get out and discover what options are available. Take the bull by the horns! For an infant or toddler, you should actively explore the child care possibilities at least six months before you require the care. Your lead time should be three months for three- to five-year-olds. If you are having many doubts and concerns, start examining the options sooner rather than later — waiting only reduces your choices and reinforces your concerns.

Check out all the possibilities before settling on an arrangement. One reason to start your search early is that it gives you time to challenge your preconceived notions of what kind of care will work best for your family. You may be thinking in terms of a center, but you might be disappointed in the centers in your area. You need time to visit family child care homes. You may be thinking in terms of a nanny. But what if you interview several nanny candidates and are not comfortable with them? Then you should take the time to check out available centers and family-based programs. The more you explore the choices, the better educated you will become, and the better you will feel about your final choice. Sure, it's a lot of work, but your peace of mind is worth the investment.

Take time to make your child's transition into care gradually. In general, parents — and their employers! — and child care providers pay too little attention to the transition from home to child care. During our many visits to Scandinavian child care programs we have been most impressed with the time given to making that shift a smooth one. Parents expect, and are allowed by their employers, to spend part of every day of the first week with their child in the new setting so that he can get used to the new environment and make new friends while the parent provides a secure base. You too can design such a transition for your child by planning ahead. First, arrange for the necessary time off from work, even if you have to take it without pay. Second, work out a plan with your provider so that you both know and are comfortable with the schedule. On the first day, visit for just an hour or so. On the second day, spend thirty to sixty minutes in the setting with your child, then leave for an hour or so before returning to pick him up. Day three might include the same amount of time together in the setting, then leaving the child on his own for the rest of the morning. By day four you and your child are probably ready to have you depart in the morning after a couple of minutes, but you return for the child in midafternoon. The fifth day can then be a successful test of the full-day experience, made easier by the gradual transition. Remember that you are establishing a partnership with your provider. Listen to her and make sure that her knowledge of children and experience with similar situations also helps to guide you in introducing your child to her care.

Admitting that this transition is for your benefit as well as for your child's emotional health and comfort is being honest about yourself. If your child finds it difficult to leave you and spend long hours with comparative strangers, she will let you know by actions that pain you and bring back the guilt or anxiety that you may have experienced during your search for care. A thoughtful, well-planned transition can make life easier for both you and your child.

Make unannounced visits to your child care provider. We can't emphasize strongly enough how important it is, especially during the early weeks and months of an arrangement, to pop in and check it out when you feel like it, even if you don't really believe it's necessary. You will feel better knowing that the provider is doing good work even when she doesn't expect to be observed — it sends the message that you expect good service and are keeping an eye on the situation. Unscheduled visits are as important with nannies and au pairs as with family child care providers and centers. But remember that you will probably have to take your child with you when you leave, especially if you appear during the first couple of months of the new experience. It is too difficult for most young children in a new child care environment to have their parents show up only to turn around and leave them behind. (Of course, you still have to pay for that day of care as with all days off that are not part of your contract.) Also let your provider know when you set up the arrangement that you will pop in unannounced when your work schedule allows so that she can protest if she doesn't like the idea. If her protests seem unjustified, beware! You'll need to evaluate her objections carefully to make sure that they are based on solid child care concerns and not to hide inappropriate behavior.

Question your provider whenever something worries you. When you have worked hard to set up a child care arrangement, of course you want it to work out well. However, you must not allow this desire to keep you from seeing and facing up to problems that may occur. Too often our need to believe that everything is fine keeps us from stepping in when something is making us uncomfortable. But at some level we worry, so that concern nags at us and won't go away.

If something about your child care arrangement confuses you or seems wrong, ask about it immediately. The longer you wait, the more worried you will become, and the harder the problem will be to fix. You don't have to be nasty or mean. Simply say something like, "By the way, I noticed that you do [such and such]. I'm somewhat concerned, because my child . . . Would you please explain why you do it that way?"

Your provider will normally want to know about any concerns you may have. She will either offer you what she believes is a good explanation for her method or approach, or she will try to make changes to meet your needs. If you are not satisfied with her explanation, and she refuses to correct the problem, you must decide whether her behavior or approach is harmful to your child. If in your judgment it is, you must seek a better alternative. The idea of going through the child care search all over again will be painful, but it is far better than worrying about a situation that you are afraid may harm your child.

Reassess your choice of care every three months. One strategy for ensuring that you are being realistic and careful about your child care arrangement is to take time every three or four months to sit down, with your spouse, partner, or a good friend, and ask, "How is this arrangement working out? Is it supporting my child's development? Am I comfortable with it? Is there a better alternative?" Place a reminder to do this on your calendar, perhaps for a Saturday or Sunday when you are not feeling stressed about other matters.

At about the same time, take the opportunity to have a check-in interview with the caregiver. What does she think about the situation? Can she talk about positive developmental changes in your child? Is there anything you can do to make her work easier or to improve the arrangement?

Reexamining your child care regularly gives you confidence that you are on top of the matter. You will feel better even if you should decide to find a different arrangement because you know that you are doing what is best for your child.

At home, set aside time specifically for your child. Finding the best child care arrangement possible and checking up on it regularly goes a long way in relieving your anxiety. But perhaps the single most effective strategy for improving your mental state is to spend as much time as you can interacting directly with your child. During the work week, get up early enough in the morning so that you can spend five or ten relaxed minutes with him while he is waking up. Help him ease into the day at his own pace, even if that sometimes seems agonizingly slow! Allow enough time so that breakfast can be an occasion for you and the child to chat about the day's activities as preparation for those events.

After work, don't exclude your child as you try to unwind behind the newspaper or prepare the evening meal. She will want your attention and may need to "collapse" somehow as a reaction to having worked so hard at being "good" in child care (see Chapter 12). Take a good half hour to help her unwind and get settled. If she is an infant, check her diaper, then set her up in her baby seat so she can watch as you relax for a few minutes or begin to prepare supper. A toddler can be very happy playing with pots and pans on the kitchen floor or with a basket of toys in the living room. Your preschool child can work at the kitchen table with crayons and paper or help to set the table or sit peacefully watching a half-hour video as you do whatever is necessary at that time.

After supper, try to set aside an hour for an activity that you and your child enjoy doing together. If a spouse or partner is available, take turns as lead person during this period so that each of you has a chance to catch your breath and relax. With an infant this activity can be simply smiling and cooing back and forth, bouncing on the knee, holding, and carrying, with much talking along the way so that he hears your voice and feels your presence. Let him signal you that the activity is over by losing interest or falling asleep. You might want to let an older child take the lead in deciding what to do. She may want to reenact something she did earlier in the day, or she might prefer to do something special with you that she can't do at child care. Some children may want to be quite active after supper, while others need cozy one-on-one time with you.

Putting your child to bed is itself an activity. If there are two of you, share as much as possible. When one leads the after-supper activity, the other can be responsible for bedtime. The routines you establish at this hour are very important, because the end of the day is one of the special times you and your child can spend together. A nice, relaxing bath and a bedtime story are two ways to calm him down after an active day in child care. If he is attached to a security blanket or toy, make sure he has it. Such items help him to feel comfortable and to settle down again should he wake up in the middle of the night. Some children like to have a night light burning in their room, while others want the door slightly ajar because it gives them a sense of security to hear the sounds of the household as they nod off.

You may be tempted to be flexible about bedtime hours, letting your child stay up late to make up for your being away all day. *This is a mistake.* Your child needs the comfort of a relatively fixed schedule, even though she may complain about having to go to bed. And you need evening time without the children to rest and recover from the long day. So set a time for bed and stick to it with only minor variations. Your child will sleep better and be in better shape the next morning, and you will appreciate the time you have for yourself.

Weekends are precious times for both you and your child. You have whole days together and can proceed at a more manageable and casual pace. Many young children like to get up at a more leisurely tempo, perhaps having a chance to play around on your bed as you get yourself ready for the day — also more slowly than usual! It's a good idea to plan some activities during the day to give your child something to look forward to, but a certain amount of just hanging out together can lead to nice, spontaneous fun. Don't miss chances to get outdoors for fresh air and exercise. Trips to the park to feed the birds and to the swimming pool in the summer are old favorites. Your child can be quite happy "helping out" with weekend chores like laundry, shopping, and housecleaning. Visiting relatives and friends can be good for everyone involved, but make sure that your child has you to herself for at least part of every weekend day. Bedtime can be more flexible on Saturday night, if you like, but you have to get back to the regular routine on Sunday night in preparation for the work week.

Vacations provide the special opportunities of weekends, only more so. Make them as child oriented as you possibly can. Remember that your children will grow up faster than you can imagine, so take advantage of this time while it is available to you. Your child will probably become adjusted to a different rhythm during vacation, so recognize that he will have to make some adjustments when you resume your regular work schedule. Begin that shift a couple of days before you return to work so that it doesn't come as a complete shock to him.

Guilt and anxiety are normal feelings associated with having children in child care, but you can control and even rid yourself of them if you take the steps outlined here. The good news is that your child can have the best of both worlds — a loving, attentive parent when you are at home and a caring, competent caregiver and teacher when you are at work.

Building Partnerships

14

How to Support Your Child's Caregiver

THIS IS AN EXCITING time! Your child is about to begin child care, giving you a great opportunity to establish a productive relationship with her new caregiver. Because it is so important that this relationship gets off to a good start, you can make it happen easily with a bit of planning and forethought.

If you exert extra effort to support your child's caregiver, you can build a partnership that benefits everyone involved. Your child can feel more secure and ready to learn. You can add at least one new person to your support network and understand your child's daily experience better. Your caregiver can work better with your child if she knows more about you and your family. To achieve these results, you need to treat each other with respect, communicate with honesty and understanding, and work continually on the relationship in order to guarantee that it remains solid.

One of the more hurtful things for a child care provider is a parent who says, "I am paying you for a service. You should appreciate the fact that I place my child in your care. I don't want any involvement beyond dropping him off and picking him up. Do you realize that I spend more than 35 percent of my salary to pay you to care for Jimmy?" Or, "All I want is my money's worth! Considering the huge fees you charge, I don't understand why you don't have plenty of resources available to you. Why do you have to ask me for additional support?" Although it is true that parents have to pay a lot of money for excellent child care, the economics of that care makes such quality expensive. Most individual providers and child care centers barely break even at the end of every week, even though the caregivers are paid far less than nurses or school-teachers or garbage collectors! (See Chapters 16 and 17.) Remember that your provider is a friend and an ally, not a servant or a housekeeper. Think of this as a partnership in which she contributes time, experience, and child care expertise and you contribute money and some social support. The result should be a congenial, constructive relationship that benefits your child greatly in the long run.

Before Your Child Starts in Care

You can attend to a few details that make life much easier for your provider before your child enters a family child care home, a part-day program, or a child care center. Read all the information that the program or provider shares with you. Most group child care programs have parent handbooks that delineate carefully what the program will do for your child and for you, and what you can do for the program. Many family child care providers also have written instructions for parents. These materials usually incorporate the program philosophy, the fee schedule, the program calendar, including hours of operation and days the program is not in session, sickness policies, and a range of other policies — how medication is administered, how the program handles emergencies, and so on. If you have questions, call and ask immediately. You have to be clear about all these topics before your child begins the new experience.

The following information is enormously helpful to your provider. Try to prepare as much of it as possible before your child's first day in care.

- An outline of your work schedule and the phone number where you can normally be reached during the day;

- The emergency phone numbers where your provider can reach your designated contact person if you cannot be reached directly;

- A list of the people who are allowed to pick up your child;

- Labels in *all* your children's clothes, including underwear. (When children get wet and have to remove some of their clothes to be dried, they often don't remember whether their pants were red or orange, or their socks green or striped.)

• A complete set of extra clothes for your child, brought to the facility in a bag;

• A medical checkup for your child, and all the necessary immunizations;

• A list of allergies or other medical problems of which the provider needs to be aware;

• Medical emergency forms, medication forms, and any other forms that the provider has asked you to complete and return;

• Child and family information forms, which provide background information that help your child's caregiver get to know all of you a little better.

You also have to prepare your child emotionally for the start of the new child care arrangement. Your attitude and the feelings you share with your child as you both get ready for the big first day are very important. Do your best to be positive and informative. The older your child is, the more information she will request. Several visits to the child care home or center prior to the "real thing" are a must so that she can become familiar with the new situation. Make sure that she is allowed to bring her special blanket or security object if she has one, to help her get over her initial fears of the unknown. Always be honest about leaving — don't sneak away — and be clear about when you will return. Try to arrange to spend a few days with your child getting used to the new situation (see Chapter 13).

Making Everyday Life Easier for Your Caregiver

• It is a sign of support and respect to read all your caregiver's communications and respond to them promptly. Check your child's bag when he comes home to make sure you receive information that the provider sends with him. These messages can range from the permission slip required for the following week's field trip to a note telling you that another child has chicken pox and your child has been exposed.

• Don't throw away your child's paintings or the illegible scribbles of messages he hands you when you pick him up. This hurts the child's feelings, because he has spent part of the day painting or "writing" with you in mind. The caregiver will have difficulty convincing him to paint or write again if he feels that you don't value his efforts.

• If your daughter is not going to be at child care on a given day, or you will bring her or pick her up earlier or later than usual, let your provider know ahead of time. It is difficult for caregivers to plan outdoor time and small field trips when they have to worry about children who haven't arrived.

• Plan your own day so that you can pick up your child at the time agreed upon with your provider. Family child care providers need to take care of their own families at the end of the day. Centers close, and no one is paid extra to care for your child after closing time. If an emergency forces you to change your plans, inform your provider immediately and make alternative pickup arrangements. At the end of the day, your child will find it difficult to be the only one left with an impatient caregiver, waiting for you to show up. Many children become worried and scared in that situation and cannot be reassured by even the most competent caregiver.

• If you stay at the center or family child care home for a few minutes when you pick up your child at the end of the day, make sure that everyone is clear about who is in charge of your child's care during the changeover. This no-man's land can cause unhappiness and misunderstanding if your provider doesn't know whether you have resumed responsibility, while you may be assuming that she is still in charge. Either way is fine, as long as the two of you agree.

Communicating with Your Caregiver

As a rule, at least one form awaits you at a center, and in some child care homes, each morning when you bring in your child. Some ask you to sign in with your name and the child's name as well as the time of your arrival. The forms for infants or toddlers usually take a little more time to fill out. These forms are designed by the providers themselves as a way of staying in close communication with you. The information sheets should be completed every day, both by you and by your child's caregiver.

You are expected to complete a section about how your child slept the previous night, any unusual events in his life since he was last at child care, and what he has eaten so far that day. Respect the fact that providers have to know this information — it makes sensitive caregiving easier to provide.

Don't use your busy schedule as an excuse to avoid writing a couple of comments. The extra few minutes this takes could make a great deal of difference to the quality of the care your child receives that day. The provider does her part by filling out the rest of the form, describing your child's mood and activities during that day and giving details of feedings, diaper changes, and naps. This regular exchange of information is a great way to build a working relationship with your provider, so don't miss out on it, and be sure to do your part. For an infant or toddler, who can't tell you anything about her activities, this daily information sheet is especially important as it gives you a reasonably complete picture of her day. (See Appendix D for a sample copy of a daily information sheet.)

Some parents feel that caregivers tell them too little about their child's day. If that is your feeling, talk to the caregiver about your desire for more information. Perhaps you can help her find a better system for communicating with the parents whose children she looks after. A blackboard or a large sheet of paper detailing the day's events, posted where all parents can read it as they pick up their children, might help. You might put a small notebook in your child's backpack in which your child's caregiver could write a few sentences to you about your child's day. You could then respond to this information with news about your child's home activities.

When Is My Child Too Sick for Child Care?

One issue that can be a big bone of contention between parents and providers is the sick child problem. Parent handbooks and family child care instructions generally spell out carefully what steps must be taken when the caregiver believes that your child is too sick to attend the program. You may feel that you are in a better position than she to decide when your child is too sick to be away from home. However, your work pressures may cloud your judgment at times, leading you to hope for the best when your child should definitely not be with other children. Your provider has two concerns. First, she knows that when your child is sick, many of the normal activities and routines at child care are too tiring and overwhelming for her. The caregiver's second concern is that interaction with the other children in the setting will spread the infection to them. Although an early morning aspirin may make your child *seem* fever-free and ready for child care, this is in all likelihood a false impression created by a temporary solution. The provider's rule that children with a fever must stay home also protects your child by requiring other parents to keep their sick children at home. So it works both ways for everyone's benefit.

Also be certain that you or a backup person can be reached during the day in case your child suddenly becomes too ill to stay at the facility. Unfortunately, this happens, and when it does your provider must notify you to pick up your child as soon as possible. Don't keep her waiting. Remember that your little boy needs one-on-one love and attention at that point, which the caregiver cannot supply while meeting her responsibility to the other five or six children in her care.

How You Can Help Financially

Hard as it may sometimes be, your prompt payment of your fee is a huge help to your caregiver. Most child care arrangements are small businesses with tight budgets, and every dollar counts. Cash flow needed to run the program depends on having every family pay on time, usually at the beginning of every week. If you have a problem paying, let the center director or your provider know as quickly as possible so that she can help you work out a financing system. Some centers have scholarship funds available for emergency situations. Sometimes communities have scholarship funds for parents who temporarily have problems paying their child care bills. Talk to your provider, who can help you figure out what to do.

Also make sure that you have a written contract with your provider and that you know the days for which she expects you to pay. Most group programs and family child care providers expect you to pay whether or not your child is in care. You also normally pay for legal holidays and days when your child is sick. Some providers allow a certain number of free sick days every year.

You can help your provider financially in ways that don't involve a direct transfer of cash. For instance, most caregivers have wish lists of items they could use in their daily work with the children. What seems like trash to you might be a treasure for the provider. Items like fabric scraps, yarn and ribbons, empty cereal boxes and juice cans, various size boxes with lids, aluminum trays, and clothing that can be used in the dress-up area, as well as clothes that can be used when the children get wet or dirty, are greatly desired by child care providers. When your child has a special day to celebrate, you might want to give a children's book for the center's or provider's collection. Donations of art supplies and weekly snacks are extremely helpful to your provider. You can also contribute services like sewing, painting, typing, repairing toys and equipment, or building new play structures on the playground. Computer time or photocopying can be a big help if you have free access to these services. You might offer to take home dress-up clothes, sheets and blankets, and paint smocks for laundering, thus saving the provider time and money.

Time Is Money

Neither you nor the child care provider has much extra time to spare. Remember this when you want the caregiver's attention as you deliver or pick up your child. She may be busy with several other children, and unable to give you and your problem her undivided attention. Be sensitive to her situation, and try to schedule an appointment to see her at another time or to talk to her on the phone.

Some child care programs ask their caregivers to visit the homes of the children they care for. Although such a visit takes some of your time, it is a great way for you and your child to get to know her caregiver better.

Once you have a year of child care under your belt, you might offer to help parents just joining the program to get better acquainted and more comfortable with the new activities and routines and with other parents. If you have special talents that you would be willing to share with the children, or time to volunteer in the classroom or at the provider's home, your help would be greatly appreciated. Volunteers can often supervise the children during naptime, for instance, enabling the caregiver to go to a staff meeting, an early childhood training session, or a dentist appointment.

Your child always benefits when you become better acquainted with his child care setting. It is so much easier for him to tell you about his day if you are familiar with the space and the people he is talking about. When your son says that he played with Jenny outdoors, for instance, you can ask more relevant questions if you know that there is a cow named Jenny in the field behind your provider's home and that the children talk about Jenny as if she is one of them.

If your provider asks you to read to your child at home or does not allow your child to bring new toys to child care, try to accommodate her. She must consider the needs of the whole program as well as those of your child. Your support of her actions and rules is most important to her, helping to ensure consistency between home and child care.

If you visit the program, be sensitive to its needs. We recall a father at one program who would come in to have lunch with his child. He would sit right in the middle of the room, successfully blocking traffic in every direction. The caregiver was happy to have him there, so she felt a little timid about asking him to move. Eventually she figured out a way to position the table so that he had to sit in a corner, and that solved the traffic problem.

Some children have difficulty with separation and are miserable if their parents come and go many times each day. Be sympathetic to these issues. Check in with the provider about the effects of your visits because she has to cope with the problem when you leave.

Other ways you can help include donating time to drive on a field trip or to help another child get to the program by carpooling. The provider or program may schedule fix-it days when parents can contribute their cleaning, painting, and repair skills for all or part of a weekend day.

Many programs and some family child care providers plan parent education nights or parent socials. Your presence at these occasions shows your child and her caregiver that the program is important to you. They also offer a chance to learn more about caring for children in general and to become more familiar with your child's program.

Attending parent-provider conferences is also important. Some providers like the child to be present, while others prefer to speak with the adults alone. This is another opportunity for face-to-face communication. Be open and honest and listen to your caregiver's issues and concerns without prejudice. If the two of you seem to have diverse child-rearing philosophies, discuss the differences and try to find a compromise. It is most important for your child that the people who care for him agree in principle on issues like guidance and discipline, toilet training, and naptime policies. Consistency gives stability to the child's life and enriches his daily experiences.

Most child care centers and large group programs have an advisory board or a board of directors that sets policy for the program. Parents are valuable resources on these boards, and your input is critical to the development of parent-friendly policies. You can also help with fundraising and by being an advocate for better child care. (See more about advocacy in Chapter 19.)

Little Extras That Count!

Nothing is nicer than a special treat when you least expect it. Surprise your provider once in a while with flowers or a box of chocolates. Or tell her you'll pay for the child care workshop at the resource and referral agency that she is planning to attend the following month. Offer to set up a visit to your workplace for her whole group and to help with the children that day. Make a gift of toys or equipment to the program. Remember her on her birthday. Take extra time to stay and have breakfast with your child one morning. Offer to help your provider at a time convenient for both of you. Write notes to tell her how much you appreciate her and her work with your child.

By developing a positive, supportive working relationship with the caregiver, you make a vital contribution to your child's experience. Active involvement and support may seem both time-consuming and difficult at times, but they are at the heart of high-quality care. A contented and happy caregiver who values her relationship with you will go out of her way to meet your child's needs.

15

The Caregiver as a Family Resource

RINGING UP a child gives you many moments of joy and satisfaction, but it is also very hard work. As a parent you may often wonder whether you are on the right track as you struggle to figure out why your children behave the way they do and how best to respond to those behaviors. All parents feel uncertain and confused at times.

Where do you turn for answers to all your questions? If you have a spouse or partner, you probably start there. Yet he is usually as new at parenting as you are, and won't have all the answers. Relatives or friends, often next in line, can be a great source of advice and reassurance. But in some cases you might not be all that impressed with the way they raised *their* kids, or you don't keep in close touch with them. A pediatrician is another good bet, but if your child is healthy, you won't see her frequently; constant calls to a doctor can be awkward and are not always welcome.

Another possible source of information and ideas about how to understand and work with your child is your child care provider. She has several real advantages as a source of advice and knows your child very well. She has probably known quite a few other children who can be used as a basis for comparison. Any suggestions she offers are based on an understanding of your child's personality and abilities rather than on the simple notion that "it worked for my kids, so it should work for yours."

Throughout this book we stress the importance of building a partnership with your caregiver — supporting her so she feels like an important member of a team working together for the good of your child. If you make an effort to show respect and appreciation for her, she'll probably be willing, even happy, to offer ideas and support when you are concerned about something or need advice.

How Your Provider Can Help

Your provider has several areas of expertise from which she can draw information.

Knowledge of Your Child

Your provider, who spends as many as forty to fifty hours with your child each week, has many opportunities to observe and try out ways to guide, comfort, and teach. Through these experiences she comes to know your child's personality characteristics and areas of strength well. She also learns what kinds of tasks and situations are difficult for him, compared with other children of about the same age. She may discover successful ways of assisting and supporting him that you have not yet found. All this knowledge and information can be valuable to you as a parent. Don't feel bad about the fact that someone else knows your child almost as well as you do. Think of the caregiver-child relationship as a resource, and use it to ease your mind and help your child develop in healthy ways.

Knowledge of Child Development

Child development expertise isn't specific to your child. It is an understanding of how most children develop, what phases and stages they typically go through, and perhaps why certain behaviors and feelings occur when they do. This is not the sort of knowledge people gain just by bringing up their own kids. Once a child care provider has helped many children through their first three or four years, she may have discovered the basic stages in development. But understanding the why behind childhood behaviors and feelings, especially as they change over time, comes from education specifically about early child development based on what scientists have learned through their studies of children at various ages. Your caregiver may have completed a certificate or degree program in early childhood or child development or attended special workshops on child development or simply read books on the subject and applied that learning to the children in her care. Any of these educational experiences helps her to understand your child better and to answer your questions.

In addition, such specialized training introduces providers to methods for guiding and teaching the children how to manage their impulses, behave appropriately with other children, and channel their energies constructively. Trained caregivers know a lot, for instance, about crying as the main mode of communication for infants, how hard it is for toddlers to share toys, and how long preschoolers can be expected to maintain interest in an activity. You, as a parent, can learn a lot from this sort of expertise.

Knowledge of Effective Child-rearing Practices

An understanding of child-rearing practices is different from an education in child development. Child-rearing involves your values about what is good and bad and your beliefs about how your child should behave in certain situations. Child development is about what children are capable of doing at different levels of maturity and how they progress from one phase or stage of development to another. Your child-rearing practices can affect the development of your child, but they are not the same thing. For instance, you may believe that little children shouldn't be allowed to make a mess, especially if they are too young to clean up after themselves properly. So your *practice* is to keep your kids from playing in the mud or running through puddles of water. Because of this belief, you are not likely to buy finger paints for your child. Without mud-pie and finger-painting *experiences*, your child has less opportunity to *develop* certain feelings and concepts, like making shapes as your finger traces them in yellow across the white paper, or the image of "full" as one packs a cup with mud and then lets it pour out onto bare feet. So the limits that you place on your child's experiences — child-rearing practices — determine the developmental opportunities available to your child.

Many child care providers have ideas and suggestions about child-rearing. They often, but certainly not always, are themselves parents who are no different from a relative or a friend — all people who have been through it and are willing to share their experiences and opinions with you. The difference is that the caregives generally know more about child development than your average friend or relative, and that may influence their thinking about child rearing.

For instance, take the issue of whether or not to let a baby cry himself to sleep at night. Maybe your caregiver was told by her mother that you spoil a baby if you pick him up when he cries after being put to bed at night. Perhaps she followed her mother's advice with her first child, but never felt good about it and sneaked in and picked up the child if he cried for long. Then she learned in a child care course that babies who cry for more than a few minutes without falling asleep are uncomfortable and in need of your help and soothing. So with her second child she was more confident about going to her crying child and looking for ways to make her more comfortable. In this case, her child-rearing *practice* was shaped by her knowledge of *child development*. If your child care provider has this combination of child-rearing experience and knowledge of child development, you'll have daily contact with a most useful source of advice and information.

There is room for honest disagreement on many child-rearing issues. Children reared in different ways grow up healthy and happy, within limits. (Obviously, physical and emotional abuse are beyond those limits.) Child care providers have learned how to talk about sensitive subjects in a relaxed and matter-of-fact fashion. They are familiar with children's books that introduce kids to topics like divorce, serious illness, and death in language that young children understand. So when you have child-rearing questions, remember that your provider can offer you another point of view, which may be different from your own, but not necessarily better. She can help you think through your feelings and concerns and offer ideas and suggestions for you to consider.

Knowledge of Community Resources

Good child care providers are usually in touch with other providers, and with the other segments of the community that child care touches, like the schools, family resource programs, and health facilities. Therefore she can be a good source of information when you are wondering what the kindergarten teachers at the local elementary school are like, or which pediatrician to switch to when yours retires, or whether the YWCA is a good place for your four-year-old to take swimming lessons. Think of your provider as part of a network — if she doesn't know the answer to your question, she may well know whom to call for the information you need.

In the case of family child care, in which the group is likely to be small and the age range quite broad, you might want to have your child attend nursery school several mornings or afternoons a week to meet more children her own age. Your provider may know of various nursery schools and be able to suggest a good match. This might also be true of your nanny if she has worked in your area for a good many years.

If your child attends a center, the director probably knows more than your child's caregiver about community resources. She does not ordinarily mind being asked and can be quite helpful.

When to Request Assistance

"Self-sufficiency is best" and "We can make it on our own" are great American myths. Although they may have been functional 150 years ago on the American frontier, and perhaps still make sense for a family living in a back-country cabin in Alaska, they are bad advice for most modern American families. What you need in this cybernetic age is access to good communication! Functioning families are those who are tied in to many outside sources of information and ideas and aren't afraid to ask questions.

Ask When You Have a Child-related Question

You don't have to leap for the phone every time your child coughs or cries. But when he is doing or feeling something that you find puzzling or worrisome, mention it to your caregiver to hear what she thinks. If you are looking for advice on where in the community to find a service or product for your child, feel free to ask whether your provider can suggest where you might find it.

There are also many questions and concerns that your provider doesn't want to be bothered with and doesn't have to know about. You may be annoyed with your spouse or partner or frustrated with a coworker. Perhaps your mother or sister is bugging you about a financial matter. You could probably use advice about how to handle these situations, or at least a chance to let off some steam about them, but don't burden your provider with such personal matters. She may be friendly and helpful, but she isn't your best friend, except in rare cases, or your counselor. Keep your questions focused on your child, and look elsewhere in your network for good listeners and wise counselors who can help with your personal needs and challenges.

Don't get us wrong here. If you have a personal or family problem that *is likely to affect your child,* your provider must know enough about the situation to understand its effects on her behavior and needs. A major conflict between parents, a death in the family, including the dog or the cat, an auto accident, are among the stresses and traumas that affect children deeply. Caregivers need to know the facts of these matters so that they can assist your child through normal reactions of fear, sadness, and misplaced guilt. But the facts are all they require. You can expect their sympathy, but don't ask them to minister to your adult needs or mediate between you and your spouse or other relative. That's not their job.

Ask at a Time Convenient for Your Provider

Your provider's willingness to answer your questions can depend on *when* you ask rather than *what* you ask. Drop-off time in the morning and pickup time at the end of the day are busy periods for her. Many providers would rather be called in the evening than try to listen to you and give a thoughtful answer while keeping an eye on the comings and goings of other children and parents.

The best way to satisfy your desire for an answer while meeting your provider's desire for hassle-free time is to ask her to choose a good time to talk. At drop-off time, for instance, say something brief like, "Sherrice woke up again with bad dreams several times last night. Is there a time when I might get some advice from you about how to handle it?" In this way you are giving your provider an idea of the topic and a chance to pick the time but are not interfering with what she is doing at that moment.

Help Your Provider Expand Knowledge and Skills

By now you can see that your provider is a useful resource only if she has knowledge you lack and time to share that information and experience with you. Perhaps your caregiver hasn't received education or training in child development or child care and doesn't know much about other resources in the local community. We urge you to encourage her — or her director in a center — to enroll in courses and attend workshops that can provide her with that knowledge. If cost is a problem, maybe you and the other parents she serves can join forces to pay all or part of the enrollment fee.

Your Child Receives Better Care

Obviously the main reason you'd like your provider to receive training is so that she can care for your child in safer, more stimulating, and more thoughtful ways. This must be your primary goal, and we know that the right kinds of education and training result in higher-quality care. (See Chapter 3 for more discussion of why training is important.)

You Have Access to Better Information

The other payoff to additional education and training is that your own caregiving can benefit from what your provider learns. Through her new knowledge she is more likely to be able to answer the questions you — and all parents — have about handling your child's behaviors and emotions that trouble you and where to turn for other community resources. If you know that your provider is attending a class or is registered for a workshop and you have a question she can't yet answer, you might ask her to find out about that topic from her instructor or workshop leader. This helps you with your concern and gives her studies more practical significance.

Finding Training Opportunities and Professional Organizations

The best source of information about education and training opportunities in early childhood is your local child care resource and referral agency. You will find an up-to-date list of most of those organizations, with addresses and telephone numbers, by state, in Appendix B. You can also call the Child Care Aware national toll-free parent information line — (800) 424-2246 — to be connected with your local CCR and R. Area colleges, universities, and adult education programs, like a Cooperative Extension office, are also apt to offer education and training in early childhood development.

Providers also gain a great deal of valuable information by joining local provider associations. Perhaps there is a family child care association near you or a local chapter of the National Association for the Education of Young Children. Urge your provider to join these groups and attend their meetings and conferences. There she can learn many valuable new tricks of the trade and make friends who can help her answer your questions about child development, child-rearing, and community resources.

Economic Issues

16

Paying for Child Care

U NLESS YOU ARE very wealthy or very fortunate, paying for child care takes a large slice out of your family budget because in the United States 70 to 75 percent of child care fees are paid directly by parents. This differs from public schools, which are financed with taxes paid by families and individuals without school-age children as well as those whose children are enrolled in the schools.

It is possible to recover part of your payment for child care or to have some of its costs paid by public funds. Take advantage of these ways to save money so that you can buy the best possible care for your child.

How Much Should Good Care Cost?

In 1993, employed mothers with children under age five reported spending an average of $79 per week on child care. Today that figure is probably closer to $90. But this amount isn't much help in planning your budget because costs vary so much by age of child, type of care, and where you live. In rural upstate New York, for example, you may have to pay as little as $60 a week to have your three-year-old cared for in family

> The 70 to 75 percent of U.S. child care costs paid directly by parents represents a before-tax total of more than $25 billion.

child care, while it could cost $240 per week for care of your ten-month-old in a New York City child care center.

The Age of Your Child

The younger your child, the more regular, minute-to-minute attention he needs from a caring adult. This is the reason that licensing regulations require lower ratios of adults to children for infant care than for the care of four-year-olds. In New York State child care centers, each caregiver can look after up to seven four-year-olds, but no more than four infants. Most of your child care fee goes to paying the salary of your caregiver. (See budgets in Chapter 17.) This means that only four families pay the salary of the infant caregiver, while seven share the cost of the person tending to the four-year-olds. You can see, then, that infant care should cost almost twice that of preschoolers, just to ensure that your infant has the proper amount of care and attention.

The Type of Care

If you require child care for one or two children, a nanny costs you the most, followed by an au pair arrangement, center care, and family child care. For three or more children in care, a center is nearly as costly as the nanny or au pair alternative, although it has other advantages (see Chapter 6).

Family child care is a particularly good buy for an infant or a toddler. That type of provider usually charges 25 to 33 percent less to look after an infant than you would pay at a local child care center — if you could find one that accepts infants! Family child care is cheaper because the provider pays herself less than she would earn working in a center, and the costs of maintaining and running her home are lower than the same costs in a center.

In general, profit-making centers are more expensive than non-profit centers. This is *not* because for-profit centers pay their caregivers better. The most recent national comparison found that only 62 percent of the for-profit center budget went to wages, whereas that figure was 79 percent for nonprofit programs.[1] The big cost in profit-making programs is for buildings and grounds, which take about 20 percent of the budget. Because many nonprofit centers have space donated to them, at little or no cost, by schools, churches, and other nonprofit organizations, this expense consumes a relatively small percentage of their overall budgets.

Where You Live

In general, everything costs more in a city than in rural areas. Therefore centers must pay higher salaries and rents, family child care providers must charge more to cover higher costs, and a nanny is more expensive, especially if she doesn't live with you and must pay a high rent. However, cities are also likely to provide more subsidized child care for low-income families. If you are eligible for one of these subsidies (see below), and are able to obtain one (there are usually waiting lists), it may reduce your child care costs considerably.

The Cost of Quality

Does a higher fee always mean better quality in child care? Not necessarily. The programs that charge the lowest fees may also provide care of the lowest quality. But a moderately priced program may do a better job of caring for your child than a top-of-the-line model, *depending on how the money is spent.* That is why you must take time to compare programs carefully. The quality of the caregivers working directly with your child should be your number-one concern.

If you are choosing among centers, look beyond the parent fee in each to see how many children each caregiver is responsible for and how much education and training the caregivers bring to the job. If the choice is between better-paid and more qualified caregivers in a modest physical environment and less-well-paid and qualified caregivers in a beautiful setting, go for the more qualified caregivers. Spend your money on good people. Ten years from now your child will not remember much about the building that housed the program, but will recall with great fondness a special adult and friends made during those early years.

Better-quality family child care costs a good bit more than low-quality family child care, usually because these providers meet the legal regulations mandated by the state in which they operate. But high-quality family child care homes are still a good buy compared with centers, especially if you have an infant or a toddler. Of course, you are buying a different product, with less access to same-age children, often less emphasis on cognitive development, and usually less backup in case of provider illness (see Chapters 5 and 6). If your family child care provider is interested in more education in child development or child care training, offer to cover the cost of enrollment and increase your payments by 5 to 10 percent when she has completed these studies, say, from $90 to $95 per week. (Even if you can't afford to pay for her course, the promise of a fee increase might prompt her to take it anyway.) The added value in improved care and a stronger partnership will more than make up for the increased expense, assuming that you can find the money somewhere else in your budget.

Child Care as a Percentage of Family Income

You should be able to buy good child care for 9 to 10 percent of your before-tax family income. Unfortunately, this is possible only if your income is above about $50,000 a year. For instance, let's assume that you are paying $400 per month for a preschool place in a child care center, which is usually enough for good-quality care. This amounts to $4,800 per year. The following table shows that amount as a percentage of four different annual family incomes.

Annual Income	Percentage to Child Care Costing $4,800 per Year
$15,000	32%
$35,000	14%
$55,000	9%
$75,000	6%

You can see that a family's income has to be close to $50,000 before a $4,800 yearly child care payment represents less than 10 percent of income. And this is with only one child in care! However, you can get some of that money back through a federal tax subsidy available to *all* families (see below).

With an income in the $15,000 range, you can't possibly afford to pay child care costs of $4,800. Fortunately, you can seek public child care subsidies to cover all or some of these expenses (see below). Don't hesitate to use these subsidies if you are eligible. Some parents with higher income receive tax refunds, so why shouldn't you get your share?

If your family income is in the $25,000 to $35,000 range, or if you need care for more than one child and have income below $50,000 to $60,000, good-quality center care may cost more than you feel you can afford. *Don't assume that this is true.* Check it out — you can inquire about fees with a couple of phone calls. There may be centers in your

What do Swedish parents pay for child care? Sweden's child care system is one of the best subsidized in the world. Parent fees vary somewhat from one part of Sweden to another, but in general Swedish parents do not pay more than 10 percent of their income for care. This means that Swedes with lower incomes might pay less than a quarter of the full cost of care, while those with higher incomes pay 50 to 60 percent of the full cost. The fee is usually the same for both center and family child care. The child care costs not covered by parent fees are paid from money collected through national and local income taxes, which are paid by all Swedes, not just those with children of preschool age. Families with more than one child pay only about one percent more of their income for each additional child.

area with sliding fee scales, where wealthy families pay more than the cost of care so that families with lower incomes can enroll their children for less than the full amount. Also give real consideration to a family care provider, especially if your child is under three years old. By using 15 percent of a $25,000 income, you could spend $3,750 on child care, a bit over $70 a week. This is close to the average cost of family child care nationally and about $8.00 a week less than the average cost of family care for infants and toddlers. Again, quality is the key to whether you are spending your money wisely, so check out each provider carefully (see Chapter 5).

Reducing Your Expense

Most modern industrialized societies have public policies that help families with the cost of child care. They recognize that parents work much more efficiently when they can afford to place their children in good-quality child care. Parents with good child care arrangements are absent from work less often and are more productive while on the job than those with inadequate child care.

The United States has two kinds of financial subsidies designed to reduce the overall cost of child care. Although in most cases they are not very generous, compared with the support many European countries provide to parents, they are still better than nothing. *Take advantage of these chances to save money!* You deserve them, for they are part of your rights as hard-working American parents.

Tax-based Subsidies

The federal child and dependent care tax credit allows you to deduct up to 30 percent of the first $2,400 you pay for child care on your federal income tax form. If you have child care costs for two or more children, your savings can be up to 30 percent of the first $4,800 you pay for care. The percentage you can actually deduct depends on your income: the lower it is, the more you can deduct. The table below shows how much you could deduct at four different income levels. This example is based on a married couple filing jointly, with both parents employed and one child in child care.

Adjusted Gross Income	Child Care Credit
$10,000	$720
$20,000	$600
$30,000	$480
$40,000	$480

As you can see, the tax saving is never more than $720 with one child in care, and the upper limit is $1,440 for two or more children. If you owe less than those amounts in overall federal tax, your savings will be lower, because the government won't pay you the difference in cash. Unfortunately, that is likely to be true for the $10,000 example, because standard deductions for that family would add up to more than $9,000, leaving less than $1,000 subject to a tax of less than $150. But suppose you pay $4,800 for the care of one child. If you can deduct the full $720, you can recover 15 percent of the total expense, or about $60 a month. Every little bit helps!

For more detailed information about the child and dependent care tax credit, call the local office of the Internal Revenue Service to request Form 2441 and accompanying instructions. During tax season these forms may be available at your local post office or library. If you have your tax statements prepared professionally, that person can inform you what the deduction comes to at your income level.

At least twenty-two states and the District of Columbia also offer child care tax credit programs. Check with your local child care information and referral agency or any tax preparer to discover whether your state provides this benefit. If it does, you can deduct the same percentage from your state tax return as you do from your federal tax return.

Arkansas, Delaware, the District of Columbia, Hawaii, Iowa, Kansas, Kentucky, Louisiana, Maine, Minnesota, Nebraska, New Mexico, New York, North Carolina, Ohio, Oklahoma, Oregon, and South Carolina offered state tax credits for preschool children in child care in 1994.

The federal government also permits your employer to enable you to pay up to $5,000 of your child care costs in pretax dollars. Check to discover whether your company allows this, and if not, suggest it to the financial officer. Called the Dependent Care Assistance Plan, this program allows you to set aside up to $5,000 of your income to pay for child care. You do not have to pay tax on that income, which results in savings. This plan is not an addition but an alternative to that provided by the child care tax credit.

Public Child Care Subsidies

These subsidies are paid by government to make child care more affordable for low-income families. The money, which comes from a mix of federal, state, and local tax revenues, can be used by parents who are already in the workforce. One such program, the federal Child Development Block Grant, can cover some or most of your child care costs if your family income is less than about $30,000 a year for a family of four. Federal Title XX Day Care Services funds are also available for this purpose, as are many state funds that are available to support part of the cost of child care for low-income families.

If you have been receiving public assistance and are just entering the workforce, there are several subsidy programs designed specifically to help you with that process. These programs, a mix of federal and state funds, cover your child care costs for up to a year after you enter the labor market from public assistance. Federal and state efforts at welfare reform, initiated since 1996, are likely to increase the availability of these funds.

To learn more about whether you are eligible for such subsidies, contact your local child care resource and referral agency. *The programs are not handouts!* They help make up for the fact that low-income families cannot benefit from the federal and state child and dependent care tax credits used by middle- and upper-income families. So if you are eligible for one of these subsidies, go after it. The programs frequently have waiting lists, so look into the possibilities as soon as you can.

Emergency Scholarship Funds

Sometimes you can obtain a scholarship for help during a crisis or an emergency. Some individual centers have scholarship funds, and in other cases the money is available at the community level through your local resource and referral agency. These scholarships are reserved for parents who have financial hardships for reasons beyond their control, like serious illness, fire, separation or divorce, and a housing emergency. The payment is typically for three months or less. It usually covers the majority of the parent fee, with the parent making up the difference.

Spreading Out Your Child Care Expenses

Like your home, your car, and your college education, some or all of your child care costs can be covered by a loan of one kind or another. If you want to spread those expenses over ten years, for instance, instead of absorbing them all as they occur, a loan of some kind can be helpful. Your overall cost will be higher, but a future higher income may make the payments easier to manage. Of course, a relative who is willing to loan you the money at little or no interest might be an excellent option. But pay what you can up front to minimize your debt burden later on.

17

Child Care on a Shoestring

Washington, D.C. (November 30, 1995)

At a rally in front of the White House sponsored by a coalition of 16 national child care organizations, participants are bundled up in coats and hats festooned with shoestrings of every description. "We can't provide child care on a shoestring!" they chant, as speaker after speaker describes how low salaries have become the major barrier to establishment of a stable, well-qualified child care workforce.

— Peggy Hack, "We Can't Provide Child Care on a Shoestring"

*I*N HER SPEECH at that rally, a family child care provider listed some of the myths that surround family child care:

Myth 1. A family child care provider doesn't need much income because she isn't supporting a family.

Myth 2. Anyone can do family child care because education and experience are irrelevant.

Myth 3. Family child care, or "baby-sitting at home," is not serious business.

Myth 4. Family child care providers are like mothers; they just do what comes naturally!

This talented professional then described her qualifications in some detail, giving a lively picture of what a day in her home was really like for the children in her care.

Several child care center teachers also spoke up, describing their frustrations with the low pay, hard work, and long hours. "Where is the evidence that America cares about its children?" they asked. "Quality child care requires well-educated child care workers, but despite our college degrees we are being paid less than animal shelter attendants!"

Well-qualified early childhood professionals are leaving their jobs in increasing numbers, frustrated because they cannot afford to work with young children and provide for their own families at the same time. What would it take to pay these child care providers a reasonable income — a living wage?

Family Child Care Salary: $17,000 a Year

Seventeen thousand dollars a year is not a lot of money in today's economy. Family child care providers are subsidizing their clients' fees by not charging enough to pay themselves a salary commensurate with their education and experience. But $17,000 is $4,000 more than the income of the average American family child care provider. How much do you think you would have to pay in weekly fees to make it possible for your provider to earn this modest salary?

In family child care, her income depends to a large extent on the number of children the provider cares for and how many hours per week each child is in her care. In the example below, we use the budget of a licensed family child care provider with a degree in early childhood education from the local two-year college and many years of experience working with young children and their families. She cares for six children between the ages of three and five full time. She also has several school-age children of her own who are present only in the late afternoons and on school holidays.

Estimated Annual Expenses

Provider's salary	$17,000
Fringe benefits (Social Security, health insurance, etc.)	
30% of salary	5,100
Substitutes	2,400
Food	3,100
Toys, materials, and supplies	1,720
Utilities, repairs, loan interest, furniture, etc.	2,900
License fees, accountant, lawyer, tuition, etc.	1,000
Mileage, postage, field trips, etc.	350
Total Estimated Expense	$33,570

Estimated Annual Income

Tuition per child per week (for an estimated 49 weeks per year to cover unexpected vacancies)	$115
Total Estimated Income	$33,810

As a parent, you would have to pay this provider at least *$115 per week* to guarantee her an annual salary of $17,000 plus benefits and still cover her other expenses. In reality, many family child care providers have no health insurance and pay Social Security and other taxes out of their already meager incomes.

If this provider is caring for children under the age of three, many states allow her to look after only four children at a time. In that scenario her personnel cost would remain the same, $24,500, and her other expenses would drop somewhat, to a total of $30,550. But only four families would share the cost of her salary plus expenses, resulting in a weekly fee of *$156 per child.*

This family child care budget is not extravagant. It does not take into account the wear and tear on the house created by the activities of six energetic preschoolers. The provider is able to care for her own children after school, which saves her some money, and she may also be able to take advantage of the federal food program. But even if the families she serves could afford $156 a week, which very few can, she would still be earning considerably less than the salary of the average American worker.

Some family child care providers employ an assistant so that they can care for as many as twelve children. The budgets for these group family child care homes are similar to the example shown above, with the expense of the second staff member added to the personnel cost. The larger number of paying families compensates for the increased expense. Group family child care homes tend to be a little more expensive than the provider who works alone, probably because their owners feel that they provide more professionalized, higher-quality care to the families they serve.

Although considerably more than most family child care providers earn, an annual salary of $17,000 is inadequate compensation for a well-educated, experienced professional. But an increase in salary to $25,000 would boost the fee for a preschooler to $150 and for an infant or toddler to almost $200 — way out of reach for most parents.

Child Care Center Teacher Salary: $20,000 a Year

A child care center budget is much more complex than that of a family child care home. Distribution of expenses also varies somewhat between profit-making and nonprofit centers. The example below is for a nonprofit center serving 72 toddlers, preschoolers, and school-age children with 14.5 staff members.

Estimated Annual Center Expenses

Personnel

Director and assistant director ($35,000 and $30,000)	$65,000
Clerical staff	17,000
Teachers (11 full-time teachers @ average of $20,000)	220,000
Cook (.5 × $17,000)	8,500
Substitutes (@ $6.00/hour)	13,000
Total Salaries	323,500
Fringe benefits (30% of salaries)	97,050
Total Personnel	$420,550

Nonpersonnel

Contractual expenses like accounting	$4,260
Food	22,000
Supplies (teaching, office, housekeeping)	9,600
Space rental, donated	(57,600)
Building insurance	12,000
Utilities, donated	(7,200)
Furniture and equipment	5,000
Staff development	6,500
Telephone	3,500
Field trips and miscellaneous	2,500
Total Nonpersonnel	$65,360
Total Expenses	485,910 (donated, $64,800)

Estimated Annual Income

Tuition (parent fees and public subsidies)	$467,910
Registration fees	3,500
Federal food program	11,000
Gifts, contributions, etc.	3,500
Total Income	$485,910

Many nonprofit centers are located in space donated by churches, nonprofit organizations, and schools, which often help cover the costs of maintenance and utilities as well. Most nonprofit centers also take advantage of the federal food program, which, like the subsidized school lunch programs, reduces the cost of meals for children from low-income families. In addition, some centers receive money from other government sources (departments of social or child health and welfare services) so that children from low-income families are able to attend. Because most nonprofit child care centers are tax-exempt organizations, they are also eligible to receive contributions from organizations like the United Way and from private citizens interested in a good cause or a tax write-off. All these sources of income and in-kind contributions are reflected in the budget shown above.

To support this budget, the weekly fee would have to be *$200* for a toddler, *$155* for a preschooler, and *$75* for a school-age child, including holiday but not summer vacation care. Most of that money would go straight into salaries; personnel expenses account for 86 percent of this budget.

In this imaginary center, the $20,000 a year its employees earn is not big money, but it is well above the mean wage for a child care center caregiver ($15,000 for teachers and $11,900 for assistant teachers in 1993). Keep this in mind when you think about the weekly fee you pay to your local center. Your child's caregiver is barely scraping by financially, so don't complain when she receives a cost-of-living increase, and do what you can to help make her work satisfying.

Profit-making Child Care Centers

The most prevalent form of profit-making child care is the mom-and-pop center. This type usually began as a family child care home, then expanded into a larger space separate from the owner's house. Many of these centers are struggling to stay afloat, largely because their small size makes them vulnerable to the whims of the marketplace. Nevertheless, 81 percent of all for-profit child care centers were independently operated as recently as 1989.[1]

A newer development has been the growth of child care chains or franchises, corporate enterprises that have become quite common during the past twenty-five years. Many were established in the early 1970s, when construction costs were low. They fall into three general categories based on the numbers of children served nationally: small (1,000–2,500 children); medium (2,500–10,000 children); and large (more than 10,000 children). Most of the growth in this market is through the acquisition of smaller chains or sole proprietorships by the larger chains. At least two of the larger companies work exclusively with employer-sponsored, work-site-based care. The market is dominated by several of the largest franchise operators, each of which provides care to between 100,000 to 150,000 children attending between 750 and 1,100 centers all across the United States.

Because profit-making centers are excluded from many sources of public funds and rarely receive private donations, they must recoup their costs almost exclusively through parent fees. Without access to the donated space and utilities frequently available to nonprofit programs, for-profit centers must expend more money on such nonsalary costs. This means that in order to maintain a modest profit margin of about 5 percent, they must pay their teachers somewhat less than nonprofit centers pay. A study found that labor costs accounted for about 79 percent of nonprofit center budgets and only about 62 percent for profit-making programs.[2] This is significant for you as a parent and consumer, because higher salaries translate into more qualified staff. Lower salaries lead to frequent staff turnover and your child's having to adjust to a new relationship every time her caregiver leaves for a higher-paying job.

One positive trend within the for-profit franchise sector has been a new emphasis on improving the quality of care. Several chains have committed themselves to all their centers earning accreditation by the National Association for the Education of Young Children in the near future. These companies recognize that the biggest threat to their existence lies in unlicensed, low-quality centers that keep parent fees depressed, forcing competitors to lower their fees and the quality of their care. In a welcome departure from past practice, several chains are pushing for more stringent state licensing regulations in order to drive unlicensed operators out of business.

Can We Afford to Pay Staff Properly?

Clearly, all the early childhood practitioners who invest so much in caring for our infants and toddlers, our preschoolers, and our school-age children are entitled to make a living wage. But how can this be accomplished? Parents are already paying a lot for care. Our "ideal" budgets illustrate how much more you would have to pay to compensate your child care providers at the level they deserve and can earn in other professions. But when your family child care provider charges less than that amount, it may well be that she and her family are living without the protection of health insurance. In centers that charge lower fees than those in our example, the teachers you rely on for the healthy development of your child are receiving less than a living wage, and far less than professionals with their education and experience are worth. The result is a high rate of staff turnover and replacements with less education and experience.

The message is simple: better-paid providers deliver higher-quality care. If your child care fee seems unreasonably expensive, don't blame your provider, who is working hard for low pay. Instead, join forces with other parents and providers to do whatever you must to convince employers and policymakers that child care merits more public support. Obviously, other sources of funds must be found to supplement your contributions. Children are our future, and good child care can't be delivered on a shoestring.

Advocacy

18

How to Improve Child Care Conditions

T HE U.S. CHILD CARE SYSTEM is still taking shape, and much remains to be done to improve it. Parents need more choices of higher-quality child care at a more affordable price. Part of this change involves getting employers more involved and bettering state and national child care policies. There are a number of initiatives you can take, as part of your daily life, to enhance your own care arrangement and enrich the whole child care network at the same time. Your personal actions, supplemented by those of hundreds of other parents in your community, will encourage child care providers to do their work with more care and commitment, leading to communitywide upgrading in the use of available human and financial resources. On a larger scale, such combined individual efforts will strengthen the partnership between parents and child care providers that is the hallmark of a responsible, compassionate child- and family-centered community.

Partnership with Your Child Care Provider

A true partnership requires teamwork. When the members share common goals and understand who is to carry out what responsibilities, everyone pulls in the same direction and a great deal is accomplished. The result is satisfaction and a sense of completion for everyone involved. The same is true of your relationship with your child care provider, who wants to do a good job of meeting your needs, but also has a life of her own. You want to make her job as pleasant and fulfilling as possible, but you have to keep your own work and family running smoothly. When both you and your provider meet your obligations, then make that little extra effort, each of you will feel good about your share of the partnership. Both of you will be able to view child care as an enhancement of your daily existence and a support for your families rather than another source of stress and frustration.

Earlier in the book we discussed two obligations related to being on time: picking up your child at the end of each day and paying your parent fee on schedule. They may sound rather minor, but they can lead to major consequences if you ignore them. In both instances, failure to keep your end of the bargain ripples beyond your caregiver to affect others. When you are late at the end of the day, your provider cannot shift to meeting the needs of her own family. When cash flow is disrupted by your late payment, the salaries, rent, heat, light, telephones, food, and equipment that are the lifeblood of the center or family child care home are threatened, affecting the welfare of the caregivers and the other parents. When you meet those basic duties, however, the process of furnishing child care can move forward smoothly. Your provider can concentrate on delivering good care. You feel better, which makes her feel better. The partnership is strengthened and everyone is happier at the end of the day.

We also talked earlier about the improvement in child care quality that results when you keep your provider fully informed and on top of your child's progress at home and aware of anything happening there that might affect her life at child care. This means building a minute or two into your schedule in the morning to pass along information to the caregiver regarding the incidents of your child's weekend or previous evening. A few extra minutes at the end of the day allows your provider to return the favor by sharing insights about the occurrences of your child's day.

Your caregiver can also be much more effective if she knows about dramatic events in your child's life, whether good or bad, happy or sad. Such milestones can range from an exciting birthday party to the death of a favorite pet or a serious and upsetting disagreement between you and your spouse. Your child brings these problems into the child care setting, bottled up inside his head, shaping his behavior, but is unable to verbalize them. Lacking knowledge of these happenings, his caregiver has difficulty interpreting his behavior and responding appropriately. With that knowledge she can not only understand your child's feelings, but may even be able to anticipate them and offer him extra support. Again, immediately sharing this information with your child care provider results in higher-quality care. Over the longer term your provider becomes more competent and content to remain in the child care field.

Another point that we made earlier deserves repetition here. When you nurture a partnership, the little niceties carry special significance. Most of us want and need to believe that we are more than just a cog in a wheel, a tiny piece of a great big, impersonal machine. This is especially true with child care providers, who invest great energy in compassion and concern. Are we purchasing a "service" when we set up child care, or is the goal deeper and more personal than that?

Surely trust and friendship are the desired outcomes in the relationship, although they cannot always be achieved. If the goal is more personal than simply "You work, I pay," the gracious gestures become especially important. A card and perhaps a token gift to celebrate your caregiver's birthday and to show appreciation during holidays take on special significance. So does a note to the center, with a copy to the board of directors, expressing gratitude to your child's caregiver for her extra efforts on your behalf. When she is ill, she will be touched by a phone call or a note to her home saying that she is missed and special. These small courtesies make a big difference. They turn a service provider-client relationship into a friendship, which energizes everyone involved and contributes to the building of a caring community.

Pushing for Quality

Partnership and mutual support lead to greater commitment and caring and motivate both you and your caregiver to work more sensitively and persistently to meet the needs of your child. But commitment and caring are not enough; child care providers and the overall child care system must be challenged to become more knowledgeable about and critical of their policies and practices. Here again, as a parent you can play an important and constructive role by setting high standards and insisting on quality, both during your search for care and once your child is settled in an arrangement. This means, first, becoming knowledgeable yourself about the components of quality care and healthy environments for young children. This book is designed to provide you with that information. Second, it means applauding quality performance and improvements publicly and asking probing questions when you note substandard performance. During your initial search for good care, be honest, but not hurtful, when you encounter situations that don't meet quality standards. Express your concerns, as constructively as possible, to both the care provider and to your local child care resource and referral agency. Once you have chosen an arrangement, continue to ask questions that hold your caregiver to high expectations. A problem-solving approach is often helpful. For instance, when the missing ingredient is education or training, work with your caregiver or her director to locate the necessary educational resources and arrange for the caregiver to have access to them. The pressure created by your insistence on high standards will be felt throughout the child care system and eventually lead to greater investment in child care quality by both the public and the private sectors (see Chapter 19).

It is clear that leadership in the struggle to improve the overall quality of child care will not come from the top; Congress and the federal government have never been willing to take the lead in establishing and achieving quality standards. Therefore pressure must be applied from the bottom, in a grassroots consumer movement of parents who simply refuse to accept mediocre care for their children. This means you. And remember that child care workers are not the problem. They do the best they can under difficult circumstances, including lack of adequate education and training, poor working conditions, and minimal salaries. Parents and providers must become allies in the effort to build a better child care system, which begins when you identify inadequate child care practices and make your concerns public.

Improving Community Supports

The third contribution you can make, in addition to nurturing the partnership with your child care provider and insisting on quality care, is to assist in strengthening the community supports that will lead in turn to improved child care quality and accessibility. They include

- the structures within which your child care takes place — the center with its administrators and governing board, the elementary school housing your after-school program, the settlement house that sponsors your Head Start program.

- the local professional organizations to which your child care provider belongs;

- the institutions and organizations that provide education and training in child development and early childhood to prepare child care workers and to upgrade their skills;

- the child care resource and referral agencies that expand the availability of child care services and link parents with child care options;

- the community college that sponsors, and perhaps subsidizes, a two-year associate's degree in early childhood education;

- local charitable and service organizations like United Way, local churches, and the YWCA, which channel financial and other kinds of support (facilities, equipment, accounting, and so forth) into the local child care system.

As the parent of a child enrolled in a child care program, an adult with a variety of competencies and skills, you can influence these structures of community support in ways that strengthen the local child care system. Take your turn as a member of your child care center governing board or provide leadership in organizing workdays at the center, when walls are painted, furniture cleaned and repaired, and the playground refurbished. Your local child care resource and referral agency is also governed by a board of volunteers — perhaps you have skills that would strengthen its work, for example, accounting, computer systems, fund-raising, long-range planning. You could organize a joint parent–child care provider letter-writing campaign and petition drive directed at the trustees of your local community college, urging the establishment or expansion of a degree program in early childhood education and child care. When making a pledge to United Way, you could direct your contribution to specific child care agencies and organizations and encourage your friends and relatives to do the same.

Some of these volunteer activities are more time-consuming than others. We know that your spare time is precious and that you want to devote much of it to your own family. Yet much can be accomplished without a major time commitment if you make it your business to understand the critical role played by these community organizations and look for opportunities to encourage and support their efforts. Even a good word to your city council representative or a letter of endorsement in support of your center's application for United Way funding makes a difference. You must decide how much time and energy you can afford to invest in improving community supports for the child care providers in your city or town. But do invest something; every little bit helps in ways that you cannot anticipate.

Influencing Community Attitudes

You and other parents are in a better position than anyone else to influence community attitudes toward child care because you rely so heavily on the child care resources available and know how essential those services are to the economic health of your family, local businesses, and the community tax base. Here are two very simple ways of helping to shape those attitudes. First, challenge myths with fact. If your relative, your friend, your employer, your political representative, the local media, or anyone else is reinforcing negative myths about child care (it is bad for children, only bad parents use it, it promotes weak values, it is just another welfare program), step forward and challenge that person or the writer of that newspaper story with facts. Don't allow the voices of ignorance or narrow-mindedness to distort the public understanding that child care is an essential support for working families and that the community must take action to improve it. For instance, if a scandal involving child abuse by a child care worker hits the headlines of your local paper, counter it with a letter to the editor. Point out that the vast majority of child care providers give safe and competent care and outline the steps that parents, other child care providers, and other community groups can do to protect children and their parents against the very rare but extremely destructive child care worker who neglects or abuses her charges.

Second, seize every opportunity to promote good child care with positive examples of how parents, child care providers, and other community agencies and organizations can work together and the excellent outcomes for children that result from these cooperative efforts at community development. Encourage the press to attend events at your child care center. Submit the name of your child care provider as a candidate for public recognition by service organizations. When the children in your child care program create holiday drawings and paintings, convince a local store owner to present their work in his display window with the name of the program prominently featured. There are an endless number of ways to generate positive publicity for child care; all of us simply have to start thinking in those terms and becoming more conscious about and systematic in our advertising strategies.

The actions we have outlined here may appear to be more than you can handle, given all the other demands you face daily. But step back for a minute and think in terms of specifics. Being a good partner to your child care provider just requires careful planning and sufficient communication. Pushing for quality is not hard; you just have to be willing to learn to recognize quality child care and ask questions when you see areas that you believe could be improved. Of course, it is not enough simply to criticize; you must be willing to help find solutions within the limits of your time and energy. That's where helping to improve community supports comes in. Your efforts to influence community attitudes for the better can begin right in your own circle of relatives, neighbors, and friends when you challenge negative myths about child care with proven facts. Your personal actions, combined with similar actions by hundreds of other working parents with young children in your community, will make the neighborhood, village, town, or city where you live a better place in which to bring up healthy, happy, self-confident children.

Your local efforts and those of the rest of us are the starting point for movement toward a better system of child care supports for all families. Together we can create a groundswell, a rallying cry for improvements in the child care services that are so essential to our efforts to be successful parents and efficient workers at the same time. But even as we band together to do more with available resources, we are faced with the reality that those resources are not sufficient. Parents invest billions of dollars in child care nationwide, and your children's caregivers are still poorly paid and work in substandard conditions. Other societies have recognized that parents cannot shoulder the whole burden of financing the child care system of a nation. We too must recognize that just as employers and the general public benefit from the work produced by employed parents, so must they contribute significantly to financing the safe, developmentally enhancing, and affordable child care which makes that labor possible.

It is to the greater involvement of employers in child care issues, the improvement of state and national child care policies, and your role in fostering those changes that we turn in the final chapter.

19

Employers
and Public Policies

AMERICAN CHILD CARE is financed on the backs of working parents and child care providers. Seventy-five percent of the cost of delivering child care, a nationwide total of approximately $24 billion a year, comes directly from you, the parents. Despite your huge direct investment, child care providers' salaries are very, very low, less than those paid to the garbage collectors in your city or town. How can salaries be so low when you are paying so much?

Let's start with your financial burden. If your family income is less than $50,000 and you have one child in care, you can't afford to pay more than 10 percent of your earnings for child care without cutting into the funds you need for housing, food, clothing, and transportation. With two kids in care, you need an income of closer to $100,000 a year to keep your child care costs within 10 percent. Most of us don't make anything like that kind of money, so our costs for care are more like 15 to 25 percent of our income. That often means that if there are two salaries in the family, you spend most of one weekly paycheck just for child care.

How much does child care of reasonably high quality actually cost? Fees in the child care marketplace currently run about $5,000 to $7,000 a year per child, depending on the age of your child, the type of care you choose, and where you live. (See Chapter 17 for more details on cost.) But the child care providers you pay to look after your children are only earning an average of about $15,000 a year in centers and $13,000 if they provide care in their own homes. In fact, if caregivers worked in professions that require no more than their present level of education, they could make an average of $5,000 more per year than they earn in child care. Family child care providers could increase their pay by about $3,000 by changing professions. No wonder so many talented early childhood professionals leave the child care field every year! They can't afford to stay. Those who do stay in child care are keeping your already high costs down by not charging you what they are really worth. If you paid full value for the caregivers you use, both your cost and the quality of the care your child receives would be higher.

Most of you are paying more for care than you can afford, and the people furnishing your child's care are working for about 25 percent less than they would be paid in other jobs. It sounds like a situation in which everybody loses. But is that possible — aren't there some winners out there somewhere?

Who Profits from Child Care Fees?

The biggest winners in the current method of financing child care are the nation's employers. Most American executives can hire parents with preschool children without having to give much thought to who is looking after their kids. They are free to say to the parent, "Child care is up to you. Just make sure that you show up to work on time and work hard. No excuses. I don't want to know about your troubles with your kids. That's not my problem." Employers badly need the skills you bring to them, but most don't want to bear any of the cost you pay to be able to work. So American bosses are profiting from the fact that you pay such a high price for child care and that your caregiver earns so little, especially in comparison with employers in European countries.

Others who benefit from your paying so much for child care are all the Americans without preschool children. You work as hard as you can and pay a large slice of your earnings in federal, state, and local taxes. Your taxes pay for roads, schools, Social Security, military protection, and medical benefits used by millions of people who pay nothing toward the cost of your child care. But without that care you would be out of the labor market, and they couldn't benefit from your tax dollars. So your child care payments are financing the services that flow from a healthy economy for all of us.

How Employers Can Help

Only about 10 percent of the nation's employers offer any sort of child care benefit or service to their employees. Where they do exist, such benefits and services range from counseling and information and referral to child care subsidies and on-site or near-site child care centers. What about the other 90 percent? How can they become involved in reducing your costs and improving the quality of the care your child receives?

There are two general ways that employers can be helpful:

- direct assistance, like paid parental leave, child care subsidies, on- or near-site child care, and financial contributions to the local child care network;

- indirect assistance, including corporate taxes paid to support child care through the tax system, and political action for improved public policies.

Direct Contributions

Paid parental leave would make it more possible for you to care for your own child during the first year of his life. This leave should last for at least four months and be affordable even for low-income parents. It could be financed in various ways, including establishment of parental leave accounts — similar to your Social Security account — to which you would begin to contribute in your first job and continue to pay throughout your child's growing-up years and beyond, as with a college loan. Employers would need government backing in the form of low-income loans for their parent employees (see Indirect Contributions below).

Part-time work schedules would make it possible for you to combine parenting with employment, especially in the first year of your child's life. Such arrangements benefit your employer as well, because they make it more probable that you will bring your valuable skills back into the workplace sooner, reducing reliance on less knowledgeable substitutes. But to be attractive, part-time work opportunities must be accompanied by benefits like prorated health insurance.

On-site or near-site child care is often the first solution parents think of when they consider ways that their employer might be helpful. In fact, this is a good investment only if you are employed by a large company with many employees of child-bearing age. If you work for such a company, having your child in a nearby center can be most attractive, especially if your employer reduces parent fees by subsidizing some of the costs of the program. But the vast majority of U. S. employers operate businesses that are too small to afford such a capital investment, and many parents would prefer to place their children in programs close to home. So we must find ways for employers to help with child care that don't require this kind of investment (see below).

Child care subsidies are funds paid by your employer directly to you or to your child care provider to cover some of your costs. Child care subsidy could be a choice in a cafeteria-style benefits plan. In such a plan you might choose the child care subsidy instead of having your employer contribute to your medical coverage because, for instance, you are covered by your spouse's medical plan. One advantage to such a subsidy is that it benefits your budget directly without requiring your employer the major capital outlay necessary for on-site care.

Contributions to the local child care system can take many different forms. For example, in 1988 the Dayton Hudson corporation (Mervyn's, Target Stores, Dayton's, Hudson's, and Marshall Fields) started Child Care Aware, a national project aimed at developing a family-to-family training program for family child care providers. Since then more than 13,000 care providers in forty communities have been trained through this program. Employers can support a local child care resource and referral agency with financial contributions, thus improving the services their employees receive through that organization. Employers can help to underwrite the expenses of administering the Child Development Associate credential or the cost of a two-year early childhood associate's degree program at a local community college. Each of these investments would strengthen the preparation and continuing education of the professional child care providers tending employees' children.

Indirect Contributions

Tax on profits. Perhaps corporations would prefer to contribute to a general child care fund and allow local and state child care experts to decide how best to allocate those resources in a given community. In the South American country of Colombia, for instance, private companies invest 2 percent of their profits in a national fund, which in turn finances the national preschool program. Corporate taxes also help to finance child care systems in European countries. In the United States these funds might be allocated to the states through a formula based on population, then be made available to counties and cities as local child care block grants.

National lobby for general tax support. Those in the private sector may well feel that they are already paying their share of tax to the federal government and the states. In that case what is needed is a private-sector lobby on behalf of greater investment of those public tax dollars in the parent and provider subsidies, education and training, and resource and referral services described above. Legislators and other public officials would sit up and take notice if the CEOs of the two hundred largest American corporations joined forces in urging Congress, the president, and state legislators to double current investment of tax dollars in support of child care and paid parental leave. A constructive outcome would be a blue-ribbon child care commission created jointly by private-sector leaders, Congress, and the president to make recommendations to Congress regarding increased public-private partnership support for child care policies and programs, including tax credits and parental leave.

How You Can Help

No one knows better than you, as working parents, how much of a difference stable child care support can make in your ability to rear your children effectively while putting forth your best efforts on the job. You must find ways to make your employer aware that quality child care is a major concern and priority for you and that your ability to be an effective worker depends heavily on how secure you can feel about the health and welfare of your child. Obviously you don't want to convey these concerns to your employer in a tone that jeopardizes your future job prospects. But if your interest in your employer's support for child care is expressed in terms of what is best for the company or organization — for example, in reduced turnover, less absenteeism, greater employee loyalty, a more caring image in the community — and you include other parent employees in the process of developing proposals for investment in the child care system, the odds of your finding a sympathetic ear will be enhanced. Always begin with upper-level administrators and leaders who are parents or grandparents themselves, and draw on their knowledge and experience to recruit them as allies in your effort to help the organization become more effective by reducing the stresses associated with child care. By taking these initiatives you will be making life better for many other parents and young children while improving the living conditions of your own family.

The Need for Improved Public Policies

The child care issues that ought to be on your employer's mind are also matters of public policy in the political arena. In candidates running for public office, search for opportunities to test their sensitivity to the needs of working parents. Here are the key policy areas we have been discussing throughout the book. In each area we outline changes that would ease the pressures that plague parents like you. Political candidates should either be actively promoting these policy improvements or arguing intelligently for alternatives that make sense to you in light of your personal experience.

Parental leave has to be available to *all* working parents, not just those in companies with fifty or more employees. The leave period must be lengthened, and there must be enough wage replacement to make leave possible for low- and moderate-income workers. Various financing approaches are possible, including contributions by both employer and employee (see above).

Tax revenues invested in child care must increase at every level of government. You cannot continue to finance 75 percent of child care costs out of your own pocket while most of those who benefit from your work — employers and the public as a whole — pay virtually nothing.

Parent subsidies are one way to invest the additional tax-generated revenue in child care, which could be accomplished most efficiently by improving the *child care tax credit* available to you. These improvements should include

1. doubling the maximum $720 credit allowed per child;
2. maximum child care credit to families with gross incomes up to the average family income in the state or nation and a graduated reduction in credit above that amount;
3. provision of a tax rebate if your tax credit exceeds the amount of tax you owe.

Provider subsidies are another important way of investing additional tax revenues in child care. Resources can be invested directly into improving the quality of child care programs and the system as a whole. Returning money to parents through tax credit provides no guarantee that any of those savings will reach the programs — parents are likely to want to reduce their own child care costs as much as possible. Program directors and the boards to which they report may decide to try to retrieve some of your tax savings by raising their fees, of course. Provider subsidies operate as an alternative to fee increases by making money from the general tax revenues directly available to providers. Legislation can require that these subsidies be used for specific, quality-enhancing purposes, for instance, for provider education and training, caregiver salary increases, facility improvements, and lowering staff-to-child ratios.

Investments in resource and referral agencies are still another important way of allocating increased funds from general tax revenues. We noted above that employers could make this and other quality-enhancing investments directly from their own budgets, but use of general tax revenues spreads the costs more broadly, ensuring participation of all employers and the public as a whole. Specific inclusion of resource and referral organizations is critical, because they furnish several vital services: (1) linking you, the child care consumer, to an array of possible providers; (2) maintaining an adequate supply of child care by recruiting and assisting new providers; (3) delivering to providers pre-service and in-service training, which can lead to their gaining credentials, to maintain and improve the quality of care available to children and their families; and (4) documenting the supply of care and the existing service gaps to assist community and state planners in enhancing the child care support system.

Investments in early childhood education make it possible for young adults to visualize a career of working with young children and to pursue that interest beyond high school. These educational opportunities must be readily accessible to those seeking them in terms of both location and cost. For this reason special emphasis should be placed on two-year degree programs at local community colleges, which are generally part of a state system of higher education. You need to work closely with your state legislators to promote greater investment of state revenues in early childhood education programs within that system.

Regulations have traditionally been the government mechanism used to improve the quality of child care programs. The problem is that implementing stronger regulations costs money. For instance, a change requiring that each center caregiver look after no more than six pre-schoolers instead of seven, or four infants instead of five, means that a center must hire more staff to care for the same number of children, thereby increasing the cost per child by the amount of the added care-giver's salary. Where will that additional money come from? Perhaps it will be generated by lowering the salaries of others on the center staff. But that would lower the quality of care provided by causing some of the best caregivers to leave for better-paying jobs, thus defeating the origi-nal purpose of the stronger regulations. The other likely means of gen-erating more revenue would be by increasing parent fees.

Regulations that promote quality care are essential, but they must be accompanied by greater investment of public funds to pay for the increased costs required to implement them. Greater public investment in the areas outlined above will protect you, the consumer, from having those increased costs simply passed along to you.

Some state legislators are arguing that the best way to lower your child care costs is to make child care regulations less strict. This is a false argument and a bad idea! Sure, weaker regulations might lower your cost a bit, but the biggest effect would be to lower the quality of the care your child would receive. Some advocates of weaker regulations claim that no one has proved that lower-quality care is bad for children. Non-sense! A number of studies show that the personal connection between caregiver and child is weakened, and the child receives less guidance and personal attention when a caregiver must be responsible for more chil-dren in larger groups. You need to protect your child and her provider by advocating against such changes. At the same time, you must de-mand that your elected representatives seek a greater investment of public funds in the child care policies discussed earlier so that you don't have to pay the entire cost of solid child care regulations and good-quality child care out of your own pocket.

After thirty years of work in the areas of early childhood and child care, we have become convinced that further improvements in the quality and availability of child care services require active, sustained political action by those voters with the most to gain from these changes: working parents with preschool and primary school–age children. There are millions of you spread out in every city, town, and village in America. Band together with those dedicated, underpaid people who look after your children while you are working to support your family.

Challenge the employers, the political officials, and the candidates for public office in your local community, your state, and the nation as a whole. Demand that they become more accountable for finding the resources necessary to pay for the child care services that make your work possible and help shape the development of your child. You deserve support from all Americans for the extraordinary efforts you invest and sacrifices you make in order to raise children to become strong, creative, contributing members of our communities. Don't be afraid to insist on this support. You ask not just for yourselves, but for the nation, and for the future of American society. Remember, your children are that future.

Appendixes
Notes
Index

Appendix A: National Support Service Organizations and Agencies for Children in Need of Special Care

American Cleft Palate Association
104 South Estef Dr.
Suite 204
Chapel Hill, NC 27514
(800)242-5338 or (919)933-9044

American Council of the Blind
1155 15th St. N.W., Suite 702
Washington, DC 20005
(800)424-8666

The ARC (a national organization on mental retardation)
National Headquarters
1010 Wayne Ave., Suite 650
Silver Spring, MD 20910
(301)565-3842

Architectural and Transportation Barriers Compliance Board
1331 F St., N.W., Suite 1000
Washington, DC 20004-1111
(800)USA-ABLE or (202)272-5449 (TDD)

The Association for Persons with Severe Handicaps
7010 Roosevelt Way, N.E.
Seattle, WA 98115
(206)523-8446

Autism Society of America
7910 Woodmont Ave., Suite 300
Bethesda, MD 20814
(301)657-0881

The Council for Exceptional Children
1920 Association Dr.
Reston, VA 20191
(703)620-3660

Cystic Fibrosis Foundation
6931 Arlington Rd.
Bethesda, MD 20814
(800)344-4823

Epilepsy Foundation of America
4351 Garden City Dr.
Landover, MD 20785
(800)332-1000

Federation for Children with Special Needs
1135 Tremont St., Suite 420
Boston, MA 02120
(617)482-2915

Learning Disabilities Association of America
4156 Library Rd.
Pittsburgh, PA 15234
(412)341-1515

Muscular Dystrophy Association - USA
National Headquarters
3300 E. Sunrise Drive
Tucson, AZ 85718
(800) 572-1717
http://

Sickle Cell Disease Association
200 Corporate Point, Suite 495
Culver City, CA 90230
(800)421-8453

National Down Syndrome Society
666 Broadway, 8th Floor
New York, NY 10012
(800)221-4602

National Information Center for Children and Youth with Disabilities
P.O. Box 1492
Washington, DC 20013
(800)695-0285

National Parent Network on Disabilities
1130 17th St. NW, Suite 400
Washington, DC 20036
(202)463-2299

Office of the Americans with Disabilities Act
U.S. Department of Justice, Civil Rights Division
P.O. Box 66118
Washington, DC 20035
(202)514-0301 or (202)514-0381 (TDD)

Office of Special Education Programs
U.S. Department of Education
400 Maryland Ave. SW
Switzer Building
Washington, DC 20202
(202)205-5507

Public Access Section
U.S. Department of Justice, Civil Rights Division
P.O. Box 66738
Washington, DC 20035-6738
(800)514-0301 or (800)514-0383 (TDD)

Resources for Children with Special Needs, Inc.
200 Park Ave. South, Suite 816
New York, NY 10003
(212)677-4650

Spina Bifida Association of America
4590 MacArthur Blvd., Suite 250
Washington, DC 20007
(800)621-3141

United Cerebral Palsy Association, Inc.
1660 L St., NW, Suite 700
Washington, DC 20036
(800)872-5827

Appendix B: Child Care Resource and Referral Agencies

Alabama

Ebsco Industries, Inc.
P.O. Box 1943
Birmingham 35201
(205)991-6600

Childcare Resources
1904 First Ave. North
Birmingham 35203
(205)252-1991

Child Development Council
1608 13th Ave. South, Suite 221
Birmingham 35205
(205)933-1095

Community Service Programs of W.
Alabama
203 Cedar Street Square, Suite 3
P.O. Drawer 1027
Demopolis 36732
(334)289-5655

South Central AL Child Care
  Mgmt. Agency, Inc.
P.O. Box 610
101 N. Forest Ave.
Luverne 36049
(334)335-6626

Gulf Regional Child Care
  Management Agency – Early Child
  Care Direction
P.O. Box 16005
601 Bel Air Blvd., Suite 200
Mobile 36616
(334)473-1060

Family Guidance Center of
  Montgomery, Inc.
1230 Perry Hill Rd.
Montgomery 36109
(334)244-0774

U of AL Child Dev. Resources &
  Services
1500 Greensboro Ave., Suite 2
Tuscaloosa 35401
(205)348-2650

Alaska
Child Care Connection
P.O. Box 240008
Anchorage 99524
(907)563-1966

Fairbanks Native Assoc.
Centre for E&CCR&R
911 Cushman St., Suite 206
Fairbanks 99701

Play N Learn, Inc., RD Grant
695 Chena Pump Rd., Suite E
Fairbanks 99709
(907)479-2214

Child Care & Family Resources
419 Sixth St.
Juneau 99801
(907)586-6218

Arizona
Family Service Agency
1530 E. Flower
Phoenix 85014
(602)264-9891

Association for Supportive
Child Care
3910 S. Rural Rd., Suite E
Tempe 85282
(480)829-0500

Griffin Foundation, Inc.
1690 N. Stone Ave., Suite 211
Tucson 85705
(520)740-0041

Child and Family Resources
1030 N. Alverton Way
Tucson 85711
(520)881-8940

Arkansas
White River Planning and
Development District, Inc.
1652 White Dr.
Batesville 72503-4035
(870)793-5233

Arkansas Resource & Referral System
101 East Capitol, Suite 106
Little Rock 72201
(501)682-4891

Center for Effective Parenting
614 East Emma, Suite 113
Springdale 72764
(501)751-6166

California
Community Connection for CC
2000 24th St., Suite 100
Bakersfield 93301
(805)861-5200

Options—A Child Care & Human
Service Agency
304 South 1st St.
Alhambra 91801
(626)284-9935

Child Development Resource Center
809-H Bay Ave.
Capitola 95010
(831)479-5282

Valley Oak Children's Services
287 Rio Lindo Ave.
Chico 95926
(530)895-3572

Equipose CCR&R
P.O. Box 5604
Compton 90224
(310)825-2732

Contra Costa Child Care Council
1035 Detroit Ave., #200
Concord 94518
(925)676-5442

Humboldt Child Care Council
805 7th St.
Eureka 95501
(707)444-8293

Solano Family and Children's
Services
100 Cement Hill Rd., Suite 500
Fairfield, CA 94533
(707)427-6600

Sierra Nevada Children's Services
256 Buena Vista St., Suite 110
Grass Valley 95945
(530)272-8866

River Care Child Care Service
16315 1st St.
Guerneville 95446
(707)869-3613

King County Community Action
1222 West Lacey Blvd., Suite 201
Hanford 93230
(559)582-4386

4C's of Alameda County
22351 City Center Dr., Suite 200
Hayward 94541
(510)582-2182

Child Care Links
1020 Serpentine Dr., Suite 102
Pleasanton 94566
(925)417-8733

Placer Co. Office of Ed.,
    Child Care Services
100 Stone House Ct.
Roseville 95678
(916)784-6060

Crystal Stairs
5200 Century Blvd., Suite 1000
Los Angeles 90045
(323)299-8998

Child and Family Services
425 Shatto Pl.
Los Angeles 90020
(213)351-5602

Community Resources for Children
5 Financial Plaza, Suite 224
Napa 94558
(707) 253-0376

Bananas, Inc.
5232 Claremont
Oakland 94618
(510)658-7101

Family Care, Inc.
5820 Stoneridge Mall Rd., Suite 230
Pleasanton 94688
(925)469-8060

Plumas Rural Services, R&R
536 Jackson St.
Quincy 95971
(530)283-4453

Riverside County Office of
  Education, Children's Services
  Unit, Resource and Referral
3939 13th St.
Riverside 92502
(909)788-6612

HRC Child Care Resources
201 Clinton Rd., Suite 204
Jackson 95642
(209)754-1075

Child Care Resource Service
3333 Camino Del Rio South, #400
San Diego 92108
(619)521-3055

Children's Council of San Francisco
575 Sutter St., 2nd Floor
San Francisco 94102
(415)521-3055

CA CCR&R Network
111 New Montgomery, 7th Fl.
San Francisco 94105
(415)882-0234

Wu Yee Children's Services
888 Clay St.
San Francisco 94108
(415)391-8993

EOC Child Care Resource
  Connection
1030 Southwood Dr.
San Luis Obispo 93401
(805)544-4355

Connections for Children
2701 Ocean Park Blvd., Suite 253
Santa Monica 90405
(310)452-3202

Marin Child Care Council
555 Northgate Dr.
San Rafael 94903
(415)472-1092

Community Child Care Council of
  Sonoma County
396 Tesconi Ct.
Santa Rosa 95401
(707)544-3077

Infant/Child Enrichment Services
14326 Tuolumne Rd.
Sonora 95370
(209)533-0377

Family Resource & Referral Center
509 W. Weber Ave., Suite 101
Stockton 95203
(209)948-1553

North Coast Opportunities
413A N. State St.
Ukiah 95482
(707)462-1954

Human Response Network
P.O. Box 2370
Weaverville 96093
(530)623-2542

Colorado
San Luis Valley Resource & Referral
1011 Main St.
Alamosa 81101
(719)589-1513

City of Boulder Children's Services
2160 Spruce St.
Boulder 80302

Child Care Connections, Inc.
3595 East Fountain Blvd., Suite E-1
Colorado Springs 80910
(719)638-2057

Colorado Office of R&R Agencies
7853 East Arapahoe Rd., Suite 3300
Englewood 80112
(303)290-9088

The Women's Center of Larimer
County
424 Pine St, #102
Ft. Collins 80524
(970)484-1902

Family Resources
13300 W. 6th Ave.
Box 22B
Golden 80401
(303)914-6276

The Resource Center's Child Care
Clearinghouse
1129 Colorado Ave.
Grand Junction 81501
(970)244-3829

Family First Resource & Referral
13300 W. 6th Ave.
Box 22B
Lakewood 80401
(303)914-6307

Child First CCR&R Program
900 West Orman Ave. AB 134
Pueblo 81004
(719)549-3411

Routt County Child Care Network
P.O. Box 775376
Steamboat Springs 80477
(970)879-7330

Rural Communities Resource
Center/ NE Co CCR&R
708 S. Cedar
Yuma 80759
(970)848-3867

Connecticut
United Way of Connecticut/Infoline
1344 Silas Deane Highway
Rocky Hill 06067
(860)571-7500

Delaware
The Family & Workplace Connection
3511 Silverside Rd., Suite 100
Wilmington 19810
(302)479-1679

District of Columbia
Washington Child Development
Council
2121 Decatur Pl. NW
Washington 20008
(202)387-0002

Florida
Florida Children's Forum
2807 Remington Green Circle
Tallahassee 32308
(888)352-2443 – (850)681-7002
http://www.flchild.com

Project Child Care
399 6th Ave. W
Bradenton 34205-8820
(941)745-5949

Child Care Association of Brevard
  County
18 Harrison St.
Cocoa 32922
(321)-634-3500

Child Care Resource & Referral, Inc.
551 SE 8th St., #300
Delray Beach 33483
(800)683-3327 – (561)265-2423

Child Care of Southwest Florida, Inc.
3625 Fowler St.
Ft. Myers 33901
(941)278-4114

Okaloosa Walton Child Care Service
107-A Tupelo Ave.
Fort Walton Beach 32548
(850)833-9330

Early Childhood Resources (Tri
  County)
P.O. Box 368
Lakeland 33802
(863)682-3777

Episcopal Children's Services
100 Blltl Way, Suite 100
Jacksonville 32216
(904)726-1500

Wesley House Child Care
  Coordinating Center
1011 Virginia St.
Key West 33041
(305)296-0235

Metro-Dade Co. Div. Of Child Dev.
  Serv.
111 NW 1st St., #2210, Division 348
Miami 33128
305-633-6481

Child Care of Southwest Florida
231 Airport Rd. South
Naples 33942
(941)218-1002

Family Central
840 Southwest 81st Ave.
North Lauderdale 33068
(954)720-1000

Childhood Development Services,
  Inc.
1601 Northeast 25th Ave., Suite 900
Ocala 34470
(352)629-0055

Child Care Resource Network
230 North Beach St.
Daytona Beach 32114
(800)681-7002

Early Childhood Services, Inc.
450 Jenks Ave.
Panama City 32401
(850)872-7550

Coordinated Child Care of Pinellas,
  Inc.
6698 68th Ave. North, Suite B
Pinellas Park 33781-5061
(727)547-5700

YMCA CCR&R
122 N. Lime Ave.
Sarasota 34237
(800)371-4599 – (941)952-9524

Big Bend 4C
2003 Apalachee Parkway, Suite 206
Tallahassee 32301
(850)627-2128

Child Care Resource and Referral
207 Kelsey La., Suite K
Tampa 33619
(813)744-8941 ext. 229

Curriculum & Instruction, CCS
3310 Forest Hill Blvd., Suite C223
West Palm Beach, FL 33406
(561)434-8252

Georgia
Stepping Stones
P.O. Box 1828
Albany 31702
(912)889-7222

Care Connection
850 College Station Rd., #332
Athens 30605
(706)353-1313

Child Care Solutions (Quality Care
  for Children)
1447 Peachtree St. NE, Suite 700
Atlanta 30309
(404)479-4240

Child Care Connections and R&R
3112 E. Park Ave., Box 2899
Brunswick 31521-2899
(912)261-1844

Child Care Resource and Referral
  Agency of West Central Georgia at
  Thomaston: A Program of Flint
  River Technical College
1533 Highway 19 South
Thomaston 30286-4752
(706)646-6215
(800)613-8546

South Central Georgia CCR&R
P.O. Box 243
Tifton 31793
(888)893-4582
(912)382-9919

Satilla Child Care Resource &
  Referral Agency, Inc.
402 Magnolia St.
Waycross 31501-3429
(912)284-0035

Hawaii
Patch
2828 Pa'a St., Suite 3160
Honolulu 96819
(808)839-1789

Idaho
Child Care Connections
1607 W. Jefferson St.
Boise 83702
(208)342-4453

Child Care Resource Center
1106 Ironwood Dr.
Coeur D'Alene 83814
(208)765-6296

Community Action Agency
124 New 6th St.
Lewiston 83501
(208)746-3351

Western Idaho CAP/CCR&R
315 B South Main
Payette 83661
(208)642-9086

SEICCA/Child Care Resource &
Referral
825 East Bridger
Pocatello 83201
(208)232-1141

South Central District Health
Department: Child Care Link
1020 Washington Street North
Twin Falls 83301-3156
(208)734-5900 ext.255

Illinois
Child Care Resource & Referral
Network
207 W. Jefferson, Suite 301
Bloomington 61701
(309)828-2062

CCR&R Eastern Illinois University
600 Lincoln Ave.
Charleston 61920
(217)581-6698

Child Care Initiatives of Hull House
1880 W. Fullerton, Bldg. A, 2nd
Floor
Chicago 60614
(773)687-4000

Day Care Action Council of Illinois
4753 N. Broadway, Suite 1200
Chicago 60640
(773)561-7900

YMCA of McHenry County
701 Manor St.
Crystal Lake 60014
(815)459-4455

Community Coordinated Child Care
155 North Third St., Suite 300
DeKalb 60115
(815)758-8149

Child Care Connection – Illinois
Central College
1 College Dr.
East Peoria 61635
(309)694-0400

Children's Home & Aid
Society/CCR&R
2133 Johnson Rd., #101
Granite City 62040
(618)452-8900

CCR&R/United Way of Will County
2317 W. Jefferson, Suite 201
Joliet 60435
(815)741-1163

Project Child, Child Care Resource &
Referral
1100B S. 42nd St.
Mt. Vernon 62864
(618)244-2210

Connections Family Referral
2408 Barkdoll
Naperville 60565
(630)778-7916

West Central Child Care Connection
510 Maine, WCU Bldg., Room 610
Quincy 62301
(217)222-2550

Concordia Univ. West Suburban
  Satellite of Cook Co. Child Care
  Resource and Referral
7400 Augusta St.
River Forest 60305
(708)209-3335

YWCA of Rockford CCR&R
4990 East State St.
Rockford 61108
(815)968-9681

Childminders, Inc.
4350 Oakton
Skokie 60076
(847)673-8998

Community Child Care
  Connection, Inc.
1004 N. Milton Ave.
Springfield 62702
(217)525-2863

U. of Illinois Child Care
  Resource Service
905 S. Goodwin, Rm. 174C
Urbana 61801
(217)333-3252

Indiana
Southeastern Indiana EOC
110 Important St.
Aurora 47001
(812)926-1585

Bloomington Day Care Resources
P.O. Box 100, Municipal Building
Bloomington 47402
(812)349-3430

Evansville Area 4C
1100 Lloyd Expressway, Suite 115
Evansville 47708
(812)423-4008

Child Care Answers
615 N. Alabama, Suite 430
Indianapolis 46204
(219)745-0785

Ays-Link
4720 N. Park
Indianapolis 46205
(317)920-3775

Indiana Child Care
  Consultant Services
4345 Kentucky Ave.
Indianapolis 46221
(317)856-4939

YWCA of Indianapolis
4460 Guion Rd.
Indianapolis 46254
(317)299-2750

Community Action
1613 East 8th St.
Jeffersonville 47130
(812)288-6451

Kokomo YWCA
PO Box 1303
Kokomo 46901
(765)459-0314

Tippecanoe Canoe County Child
  Care, Inc.
1200 N. 19th St.
Lafayette 47902
(765)423-4906

HMCC Region IX Child Care
  Resource & Referral
2000 N. Elgin St.
Muncie 47303
(765)284-0887

Orange County Child Care
  Cooperative, Inc.
600 Elm St.
Paoli 47454
(812)723-2273

Community and Family Services
  R&R
521 S. Wayne
Portland 47371
(219)726-9318

Community Coordinated Child Care
  of St. Joseph County
425 N. Michigan, Suite 208
South Bend 46601
(219)289-7815

Community Coordinated Child Care
1901 North 6th St., Suite 600
Terre Haute 47807
(812)232-3952

Wabash Valley Human Services, Inc.
525 North 4th St.
Vincennes 47591
(812)882-7927

Dependent Care Management of
  Indiana
117 S. First St.
Zionsville 46077
(317)873-1420

Iowa
Center for Childcare Resources
1038 Pammel Court
Iowa State University
Ames 50014
(515)294-8833

Child Care Resource & Referral
  Center
611 Northwest St.
Carroll 51401
(712)792-6440

Community Child Care R & R
2804 Eastern Ave.
Davenport 52803
(319)324-1302

CCR&R of Central Iowa
1200 University, Suite F
Des Moines 50314
(515)286-2043

UDMO, Child Care Resource &
  Referral
101 Robins Ave., Box 519
Graettinger 51342
(712)859-3885

Child Care R&R/West Central
  Development Corp.
1105 8th St.
Harlan 51531
(712)755-7381

4C's Community Coordinated
  Child Care
1500 Sycamore St.
Iowa City 52244
(319)338-7684

Mid-Sioux Opportunity, Inc.
418 Marion St., Box 390
Remsen 51050
(712)786-2001

Child Care Resource & Referral of
  Northeast Iowa
P.O. Box 4090
Waterloo 50704
(319)232-6671

Kansas
Reno County Child Care Association
21 West Second St.
Hutchinson 67501
(316)669-0291

Heart of America Family Services
626 Minnesota Ave.
Kansas City 66101
(913)342-1110

Douglas County Child Development
  Assn.
2619 W. 6th St., Suite B
Lawrence 66049
(785)842-9679

University of Kansas Human
  Resources
103 Carruth-O'Leary
Lawrence 66045-1520
(785)825-4626

Day Care Connection
11831 W. 77th
Lenexa 66214
(913)962-2020

Child Care Assn. of Johnson County
7369 W. 97th St.
Overland Park 66212
(913)341-6200

Child Care Resource and Referral
  Center at Parsons
2601 Gabriel, Juap
Parsons 67357
(316)421-6550

YWCA of Salina
651 E. Prescott
Salina 67401
(785)825-4626

ERC, Resource & Referral
1710 SW 10th St.
Topeka 66604
(785)357-5171

Child Care Association of Wichita
1069 Parklane Office Park
Wichita 67218
(316)682-1853

Kentucky
Eastern KY Child Care Coalition
P.O. Box 267
Berea 40403
(606)986-5896

Western KY Univ T/TAS CCR&R
344 Tate Page Hall
1526 Russellville Rd.
Bowling Green 42101
(270)745-4041

Licking Valley CAP, Inc.
203 High St.
Flemingsburg 41041
(606)845-0081

Child Care Council of KY
880 Sparta Court, #100
Lexington 40504
(606)254-0876

Community Coordinated Child Care
1215 South Third St.
Louisville 40203
(502)636-1358

Northeast KY Area Development
  Council
539 Hidgens
Olive Hill 41164
(606)286-4444

Louisiana
Partnerships in Child Care
4521 Jamestown, Suite 13
Baton Rouge 70808
(225)926-8005

Agenda for Children Child Care
  Resources
P.O. Box 51837
New Orleans 70151
(504)586-8509

Northwestern State Univ. Child and
  Family Network
209 Milam, Suite C
Shreveport 71101-7228
(800)796-9080

Maine
Child Care Options
9 Higgins St.
Augusta 04330
(207)626-3410

Penquis Resource Development
  Center
120 Cleveland St.
Bangor 04401
(207)941-2840

Child Care Resources
1025 Waterville Rd.
Waldo 04915
(207)342-5537

Child Care Resource Development
  Center
44 Water St.
Brunswick 04011
(207)725-2413

Child and Family Opportunities
P.O. Box 648
Ellsworth 04605
(207)667-2467

Down East Child Care
Box 280
Millbridge 04658
(800)223-3632 – (207)546-7544

Child Care Connections
307 Cumberland Ave.
P.O. Box 10480
Portland 04104
(207)871-7449
http://www.childcaremaine.org
email: *dbrown@sm38.org*

Carelink Resource Development
  Center
55 Bowdoin St.
Sanford 04073
(207)324-0735

Comm. Concepts, Inc.
  Finders/Seekers
79 Main St.
Auburn 04210
(800)543-7008 – (207)777-1387

Maryland
Maryland Committee for Children,
  Inc.
608 Water St.
Baltimore 21202
(410)752-7588

Baltimore Co. CC Res. Ctr.
AAA Bldg., 1401 Mt. Royal Ave., 3rd
  Floor
Baltimore 21202
(410)752-7588

Child Care Management Resources
5620 Greentree Rd.
Bethesda 20817
(301)897-8272

Child Care Choice
263 West Patrick St.
Frederick 21701
(301)662-4549

Western Maryland Child Care
  Resource Center, Inc.
82 West Washington St., 6th Floor
Hagerstown 21740
(301)733-0000

Prince Georges Child Resource
  Center
9475 Lottsford Rd., Suite 202
Largo 20774
(301)772-8420

Massachusetts
Child Care Search
2352 Main St.
Concord 01742
(978)897-6400

Child Care Choices of Boston
105 Chauncy St.
Boston 02111
(617)542-5437

Home/Health & Child Care Services,
  Inc.
15 Jonathan Dr., #7
Brockton 02301
(508)588-6070

Child Care Resource Center, Inc.
130 Bishop Allen Dr.
Cambridge 02139
(617)547-9861

Child Care Resources
76 Summer St., Suite 345
Fitchburg 01420
(978)343-7395

Child Care Network of Cape Cod &
  Islands
Box 954
Hyannis 02601
(508)778-9470

Child Care Circuit
190 Hampshire St.
Lawrence 01840
(508)686-4288

Child Care Focus/HCAC
56 Vernon St.
Northampton 01060
(413)582-4218

Resources for Child Care
46 Summer St.
Pittsfield 01201
(413)443-7830

Quincy CAP, Community
  Care for Kids
1509 Hancock St.
Quincy 02169
(617)471-6473

Preschool Enrichment Team
293 Bridge St., Suite 322
Springfield 01103
(413)736-3900

PHPCC/Workplace Connections
300 Bear Hill Rd.
Waltham 02154
(617)890-5820

Warmlines Parent Resources
218 Walnut St.
Newtonville 02460
(617)244-6843

Child Care Connection
100 Grove St., Suite 102
Worcester 01605
(508)757-1503

Michigan
Child Advocacy 4C of Central
Michigan
150 W. Center St.
Alma 48801
(517)463-1422

Northeast Michigan Regional 4C
1044 US 23 North
Alpena 49707
(517)354-8089

Macomb County 4C
21885 Dunham Rd.
Verkuilen Bldg., Suite 12
Clinton Township 48036
(810)469-5180

Child Care Coordinating Council
2151 E. Jefferson, Suite 250
Detroit 48207
(313)259-4411

Michigan 4C Association
2875 Northwind Dr., #200
East Lansing 48823
(517)351-4171

Greater Flint/Thumb Area 4C Assn.
1401 South Grand Traverse
Flint 48503
(810)232-0145

Child Care Resources
4 West Oak
Fremont 49412
(231)924-0641

Kent Reg. Community Coordinated
  Child Care
233 East Fulton, #107
Grand Rapids 49503
(616)451-8281

Children's Resource Network – 4C
710 Chicago Dr., Suite 250
Holland 49423
(616)396-8151

Livingston County 4C
121 South Bernard
Howell 48843
(517)548-9112

Office for Young Children,
  Ingham County
P.O. Box 30161
Lansing 48909
(517)887-4319

4C of the Upper Peninsula
104 Coles Dr., Suite F
Marquette 49855
(906)228-3362

Child Care Concepts
1714 Eastman Ave.
Midland 48640
(517)631-8950

Child Care Resources
268-B E. Kilgore Rd.
Portage 49002
(616)349-3296

Northwest Michigan 4C Council
720 S. Elmwood, Suite 4
Traverse City 49684
(231)941-7767

Minnesota
Community Action Council, CCR&R
33 10th Ave. South, Suite 150
Hopkins 55343
(952)933-9639

Anoka County CAP, CCR&R
1201 89th Ave. NE, Suite 345
Blaine 55434
(612)783-4881

Minnesota Child Care
  Innovations, Inc.
900 West 128th, Suite 120G
Burnsville 55337
(612)894-0727

Region 3 Arrowhead CCR&R
320 W. 2nd St., Rm. 309
Duluth 55802
(218)726-2184

CCR&R at Western Community
Action, Inc.
400 W. Main St., Suite 201
Marshall 56258
(507)537-1416

Greater Minneapolis Day Care
  Association
1628 Elliot Ave. South
Minneapolis 55404
(612)341-1177

Early Childhood Resource Center
1600 East Lake St.
Minneapolis 55407
(612)721-0112

Prairie 5 Child Care Resource &
  Referral
7th & Washington, P.O. Box 695
Montevideo 56265
(320)269-6578

Scope Resource Ctr.
560 Dunnell Dr., Suite 204
Owatonna 55060
(507)455-2560

Minnesota CCR&R Network
2116 Campus Dr. SE
Rochester 55060
(651)290-9704

Child Care Resource & Referral, Inc.
126 Wood Lake Dr. SE
Rocheseter 55904
(507)287-2020

CAP Agency
712 Canterbury Rd.
Shakopee 55379
(612)496-2125

Washington County CCR&R
14900 61st St. N
Stillwater 55082
(651)430-6488

Child Care Choices, Inc.
640 54th Ave. N, Suite A
St. Cloud 56303
(320)251-5081

Resources for Child Caring
450 N. Syndicate, Suite 5
St. Paul 55104
(612)641-0305

Childcare Choices, Inc.
770 North Business Hwy. 1, Suite 6
Willmar 56201
(800)221-1421 – (320)214-0030

CCR&R SW Minnesota Opportunity
   Council, Inc.
1106 3rd Ave.
Worthington 56187
(507)376-4195

Mississippi
Mississippi Forum on Children &
   Families, Inc.
737 N. President St.
Jackson 39202
(601)355-4911

Missouri
Child Care Connection
807 Spencer Ave.
Columbia 65203
(800)243-9685

Heart of America Family Services
3217 Broadway, Suite 100
Kansas City 64111
(913)342-1110

Children's Link
P.O. Box 103
Shelbina 63468
(573)588-2533

Child Care Resource & Referral
1910 East Meadowmere
Springfield 65804
(417)887-3545

Northwest Missouri Carefind/YWCA
   CCR&R
304 North 8th
St. Joseph 64501
(816)232-4481

Child Day Care Association
4236 Lindell Blvd.
St. Louis 63108
(314)531-1412

Central Missouri State Univ.
   Grinstead 201; Central Missouri
   State Univ.
Warrensburg 64093
(660)543-4218

Montana
District 7 HRDC
P.O. Box 2016
Billings 59103
(406)248-3325

Child Care Connections
1423 West Babcock
Bozeman 59715
(406)587-7786

Butte 4C's
101 East Broadway
Butte 59701
(406)723-4019

Hi-Line Home Program, Inc.
90 Highway 2 East
Glasgow 59230
(406)228-8275

DEAP Child Care R&R
218 W. Bell
Glendive 59330
(406)365-4909

Family Connections
600 Central Plaza, Suite 225
Great Falls 59401
(406)761-6010

Child Care Link/District IV HRDC
111 11th St. West
Havre 59501-4960
(406)265-6743

Child Care Partnerships
P.O. Box 536
Helena 59624
(406)443-4608

The Nurturing Center
146 Third Ave. West
Kalispell 59901
(406)756-1414

DEAP Child Care R&R
2200 Boxelder
Miles City 59301
(406)232-6034

Child Care Resources
127 E. Main, Suite 314
Missoula 59807
(406)728-6446

Nebraska
Lincoln-Lancaster Health
  Department
3140 N St.
Lincoln 68510
(402)441-8026

Midwest Child Care Association
5015 Dodge St., #2
Omaha 68132
(402)558-6794

Nevada
Child Care Resource Council
1090 S. Rock Blvd.
Reno 89502
(775)856-6210

New Hampshire
Families Matter in Carroll County
Box 892
Center Ossipee 03814
(603)539-8223

Families Matter
170 Kearsarde Rd.
North Conway 03860
(603)356-4739

Child Care Project
6018 McNutt Hall
Hanover 03755
(603)646-3233

Child and Family Service
P.O. Box 448
Manchester 03105
(603)668-1920

RCCAP/Child Care Services
8 Centerville Dr.
Salem 03079
(603)893-8446

New Jersey
Camden County Division for
   Children
Lakeland Rd., Jefferson House
Blackwood 08102
(856)374-6376

Child Care Services of Monmouth
   County, Inc.
30 South St.
Freehold 07728
(732)294-1894

Bergen County Office for Children
21 Main St., Room 202
Hackensack 07601
(201)646-3694

Community Coordinated Child
   Care/Union Co.
225 Long Ave., Bldg. #14
Hillside 07205
(973)923-1433

Children's Home Society of
   New Jersey
761 River Ave., Suite B
Lakewood 08701
(732)905-6363

Info Line of Middlesex Co.
390 George St.
New Brunswick 08901
(908)418-0273

Norwescap, Inc.
186 Holsey Rd., Suite 1
Newton 07860
(973)393-3461

North Jersey 4C's
101 Oliver St.
Paterson 07501
(973)684-1904

Child Care Channels at Catholic
   Charities
700 Sayre Ave.
Phillipsburg 08865
(908)454-2074

Tri-County Child Care
14 New Market St., 2nd Floor
Salem 08079
(856)935-7950

Summit Child Care Centers Corp.
  Care Service
14 Beekman Terrace
Summit 07901
(908)277-2273

Children's Home Society of
  New Jersey
635 South Clinton Ave.
Trenton 08611
(609)695-6274

The Child Care Connection
2425 Pennington Rd.
Trenton 08638
(609)737-9243

Programs for Parents, Inc.
20 Church St.
Montclair 07042
(973)744-4050

New Mexico
Carino CCR&R
1100 Eubank NE, Suite A
Albuquerque 87112
(505)265-8500

Choices for Families, Inc.
2727 San Pedro NE, Suite 113
Albuquerque 87110
(505)884-0208

San Juan College Resource & Referral
  Child Devel. Ctr.
4601 College Blvd.
Farmington 87402
(505)599-0387

Roswell Child Care Resource &
  Referral, Inc.
704 S. Sunset
Roswell 88202-3038
(505)623-9438

Eight Northern Indian Pueblos
  Council, Inc.
P.O. Box 969
San Juan Pueblo 87566
(505)852-4265

Western N.M. Univ. Child Care
  Resource & Referral
  Sechler Hall/12th at Virginia
Silver City 88062
(505)538-6483

New York
Fulmont Devel. Facility
1500 Amsterdam River Front Centre
Amsterdam 12010
(518)842-5713

Steuben Child Care Project
117 E. Steuben St., Suite 11
Bath 14810
(607)776-2126

Broome Co. Child Development
  Council, Inc.
P.O. Box 880
Binghamton 13902-0880
(607)723-8313

C.C. Coalition of Niagara
  Frontier, Inc.
2635 Delaware
Buffalo 14216
(716)877-6666

Child Care Council of Suffolk Old
  Farms School
60 Calvert Ave.
Commack 11725
(631)462-0303

Cortland Area Child Care Council
111 Port Watson St.
Cortland 13045
(607)753-0106

Child Care Network, Inc.
31 Odessa Dr.
East Amherst 14051
(716)639-0717

TLC Child Care Placement and
  Referral Services
19 Eltona Pl.
East Northport 11731
(631)499-7946

Child Care Council of Nassau
  County, Inc.
925 Hepstead Turnpike, Suite 400
Franklin Square 11010
(516)358-9250

LLI National Employee Assistance
  Providers
111 Smithtown Bypass, Suite 119
Hauppage 11788
(631)979-9010

Day Care & CD Council of
  Tompkins County
609 W. Clinton St.
Ithaca 14850
(607)273-0259

Chautauqua Child Care Council
610 W. Third St.
Jamestown 14701
(716)661-9430

Sullivan County Child Care
  Council, Inc.
P.O. Box 864
Liberty 12754
(914)292-7166

Capital District Child Care Coord.
  Council
91 Broadway
Menands 12204
(518)426-7181

Child Care Council of Orange
  County, Inc.
30 Matthews St., Suite 104
Goshen 10924
(914)294-4012

Schuyler Co. CC Coord. Council
310-12 West Main St.
Montour Falls 14865
(607)535-7964

Child Care, Inc.
275 Seventh Ave.
New York 10001
(212)929-7604

Chinese-American Planning Council
365 Broadway St., Ground Floor
New York 10013
(212)941-0030

Committee for Hispanic Children &
  Families
140 West 22nd St., 3rd Floor
New York 10011
(212)206-1090

Cuidando Nuestros Niños
140 West 22nd St.
New York 10011
(212)206-1090

Day Care Council of New York, Inc.
10 East 34th St., 6th Floor
New York 10016
(212)213-2423

Parent Resource Center
3805 Meads Creek Rd.
Painted Post 14870
(607)936-3837

CCCC North County, Inc.
P.O. Box 2640
Plattsburgh 12901
(518)561-4999

Dutchess Co. Child Development
  Council, Inc.
70 Overocker Rd.
Poughkeepsie 12603
(914)473-4141

Western New York Child
  Care Council
595 Blossom Rd., Suite 120
Rochester 14610
(716)654-4720

Ontario/Yates Child Care Council
P.O. Box 594
Rushville 14544
(716)554-6846

Child Care Council of the Finger
  Lakes – Cayuga County
17 East Tennessee St., 4th Floor
Auburn 13021
(315)255-6994

Child Care Council of the Finger
  Lakes – Seneca County
210 Main Street Shop
Waterloo 13165
(315)539-0700

Rockland Council for Young
  Children
185 North Main St.
Spring Valley 10977
(914)425-0009

Onondaga County Child Care
  Council
3175 East Genessee St., Suite 5
Syracuse 13224
(315)446-1220

Child Care Council of
  Westchester, Inc.
470 Mamaroneck Ave., Suite 302
White Plains 10605
(914)761-3456

North Carolina
Stanly County Partnership for
  Children
1000 N. 1st St., Suite 8
Albemarle 28002
(704)982-0286

Buncombe County Child
  Development
50 South French Broad
Asheville 28801
(704)255-5725

Transylvania County
  Child Development
299 South Broad St.
Brevard 28712
(828)884-3116

Child Care Resource & Referral of
  Alamance
711 Hermitage Rd
Burlington 27215
(336)438-2020

Day Care Services Assoc.
P.O. Box 901
Chapel Hill 27514
(919)967-3272

Child Care Resources, Inc.
700 Kenilworth Ave.
Charlotte 28204
(704)376-6697

Child Development Programs
P.S.C. Box 8022
Cherry Point 28533
(919)466-3782

Durham Day Care Council
2634 Chapel Hill Blvd., Suite 100
Durham 27701
(919)403-6950

Pasquotank County CCR&R 1403
Parkview Dr.
Elizabeth City 27909
(919)333-3205

Child Care Solutions
351 Wagoner Dr., Suite 200
Fayetteville 28303
(910)860-2277

Alliance for Children & Youth
P.O. Box 1695
Gastonia 28053-1695

United Child Development Services
1200 Arlington St.
Greensboro 27406
(336)378-7700

Halifax County CCR&R
P.O. Box 402
Halifax 27839
(252)583-2600

The Children's Resource Center
1985 Tate Blvd. SE, Box 17
Hickory 28602
(828)328-8228

Ashe Child Care Resource and
  Referral
P.O. Box 298
Jefferson 28640
(336)246-1900

Choices in Child Care
609 Harper Ave. SW
Lenoir 28645
(828)757-8605

Child Care Directions, Inc.
P.O. Box 911
Laurinburg 28353
(910)276-3367

Harnett County Child Care Resource
  and Referral
P.O. Box 1089
Lillington 27546
(910)893-7597

McDowell Tech. CC/Children's
 Services Net
54 Universal Dr.
Marion 28752
(828)652-6021

Child Care Connections of
 Burke County
P.O. Drawer 630
Morganton 28680
(828)439-2328

Child Care Networks
P.O. Box 1531
Pittsboro 27312
(919)542-6644

Down East Partnership for Children
P.O. Box 1245
Rocky Mount 27802
(919)985-4300

Person County Partnership for
 CCR&R
P.O. Box 1791
Roxboro 27573
(336)599-1240

Child Care Connections
P.O. Box 1739
Shelby 28151
(704)487-9736

Child Care Connections, Inc., of
 Moore Co.
P.O. Box 1139
Southern Pines 28388
(910)944-2443

Family Resources, Inc./Child Care
 Resource & Referral
302 E. Main St.
Spindale 28160
(828)286-3411

Stokes Partnership for Children
P.O. Box 974
Walnut Cove 27052
(336)591-4420

SW Child Dev. Commission
26 W. Webster Rd.
Webster 28788
(828)586-6514

Southeastern Child Care R&R
P.O. Box 151
Whiteville 28472
(910)642-7141

Wilkes Child Care Resource &
 Referral
P.O. Box 788
North Wilkesboro 28659
(336)838-0977

Child Advocacy
 Commission/CCR&R
P.O. Box 4305
Wilmington 28406
(910)791-6270

Work/Family Resource Center, Inc.
322 N. Spring St.
Winston-Salem 27101
(336)761-5100

North Dakota
Tri-Valley Child Care Resource &
  Referral
500 Stanford Rd.
Grand Forks 58208
(701)772-7905

Lutheran Social Services of North
  Dakota
615 South Broadway, Suite L3
Minot 58701-4473
(701)838-7800

Ohio
Info Line, Inc., Child Care
  Connection
474 Grant St.
Akron 44311
(330)376-7706

Child Care Resource Network
1 Pinchot Place
Athens 45701
(740)594-8499

Comprehensive Community
  Child Care
1225 East McMillan St.
Cincinnati 45206
(513)221-0033

Child Care Choices
P.O. Box 439
Circleville 43113
(740)477-1602

Center for Families and Children
1468 W. 9th St., Suite 225
Cleveland 44113
(216)861-0492

Starting Point for CC & Early Ed.
2000 East 9th St., Suite 1400
Cleveland 44115
(216)431-1818

Action for Children
78 Jefferson Ave.
Columbus 43215
(614)224-0222

Northwestern OH Community
  Action Commission
1933 E. Second St.
Defiance 43512
(419)784-2150

Child Care Resource Center
42851 N. Ridge Rd.
Elyria 44035
(440)324-7187

Child Care Choices
P.O. Box 246
Galion 44833
(419)468-7581

Child Carefinder c/o Fairfield Co.
  Dept. of Human Services
121 E. Chestnut St.
Lancaster 43130
(740)653-1701

Apollo Career Center CCR&R
  Services
3325 Shawnee Rd.
Lima 45906
(419)998-2908

Center for Alternative Res. CC
  Connections
35 S. Park Place
Newark 43058
(614)345-6166

Child & Elder Care Insights, Inc.
19111 Detroit Rd., Suite 104
Rocky River 44116
(216)356-2900
(440)356-2900

Child Care Referral Service
217 South Main Ave.
Sidney 45345
(937)498-2169

Child Care Connections
c/o United Way
P.O. Box 59
Springfield 45501
(937)323-1400

Child Care Choices
7390 South State, R. 202
Tipp City 45371
(937)667-1799

YW Child Care Connections
1018 Jefferson Ave.
Toledo 43624
(419)255-5519

Oklahoma
Child Care Finders/N.W. Oklahoma
  R&R Center
2615 East Randolph
Enid 73701
(580)234-3463

Rainbow Fleet/Child Care
  Connection
3024 Paseo
Oklahoma City 73103
(405)521-1426

Child Care Resource Center
1700½ S. Sheridan Rd.
Tulsa 74112
(918)834-2273

Oregon
Child Care Resource Connection
1077 Willamette St.
Eugene 97401
(503)726-3954

Benova, Inc.
1220 SW Morrison, Suite 700
Portland 97205
(503)228-2567

Douglas Co. CCR&R
815 SE Oak
Roseburg 97470
(541)672-7955

Child Care Partners
400 E. Scenic Dr.
The Dalles 97058
(541)298-3107

Pennsylvania
Child Care Information Service
1550 Hanover Ave.
Allentown 18109
(610)820-5333

PROBE
240 South 8th St.
Lebanon 17042
(717)273-2090

Child Care Choices
1233 Locust St., 3rd Fl.
Philadelphia 19107
(215)985-3355

YWCA of Greater Pittsburgh
305 Wood St.
Pittsburgh 15222
(412)255-1453

Child Development & Family
  Council of Centre County, Inc.
2565 Park Center Blvd., Suite 100
State College 16801
(814)238-5480

Child Care Consultants, Inc.
13 West Market St.
York 17401
(717)854-2273

Washington County Day Care
203 Courthouse Square
Washington 15301
(724)228-6969

Rhode Island
Options for Working Parents
30 Exchange Terrace,
  Commerce Center
Providence 02903
(401)272-7510

South Carolina
Family Information Network;
  Clemson Univ.
234 P & A Bldg.
Clemson 29634-0753
(864)656-0110

Interfaith Community Services of
  South Carolina
819 Woodrow St.
Columbia 29205
(803)252-8390

Greenville's Child, Inc.
24 Vardry St., Suite 106
Greenville 29604
(864)467-4800

South Dakota
One Stop Parent Resource Network
730 East Watertown St.
Rapid City 57701
(605)348-9276

Family Resource Network
1000 N. West Avenue, Suite 310
Sioux Falls 57104-1314
(605)334-6646

Tennessee
Family Connection
7227 Winchester Rd., #267
Memphis 38125
(901)358-0604

Child Care Resource & Referral
400 Deadrick St.
Nashville 37248
(615)313-4820

Texas
KidcareFinder.Com
6306 Fair Valley Trail
Austin 78749
(512)892-0342

Austin Families, Inc.
1301 Capital Texas Hwy. S
Building C, Suite 210
Austin 78746
(512)327-7878

Child Care Management Services
1221 River Bend, Suite 209
Dallas 75247
(214)905-2406

Child Care Answers/The Child Care
  Company
1221 River Bend, Suite 250
Dallas 75247
(214)638-8787

El Paso YWCA
1600 N. Brown St.
El Paso 79902
(915)533-7475

Child Care Referral Service
2700 Meacham Blvd.
Ft. Worth 76137
(817)831-2111

Initiatives for Children
8580 Katy Freeway, Suite 220
Houston 77024
(713)365-0313

Children's Enterprises, Inc.
2514 82nd St., Suite G
Lubbock 79410
(806)745-7995

Children's Resource Division, City of
  San Antonio
1222 North Main St., #300
San Antonio 78212

Dependent Care Mgmt. Group, Inc.
130 Lewis St.
San Antonio 78212
(210)225-0276

Utah
Connections for Children
1309 University Circle
Ogden 84408
(801)626-7837

Family Connections R&R Center
UVCC/CEFS Dept.
800 W. 1200 St., MW209B
Orem 84058
(801)222-8220

Child Care R&R – Eastern Region
451 East 400 N, CDB 120
Price 84501
(888)637-4786 – (435)613-5619

Children's Service Society
124 South 400 E, Suite 400
Salt Lake City 84111
(801)355-7444

Five County Child Care Resource
  Center
906 North 1400 W
St. George 84720
(435)628-4843

Vermont
Bennington Co. Child Care
  Association
RR 2, Box 703, East Rd.
Bennington 05201
(802)447-3778

The Family Center of Washington
  County
32 College St., Suite 100
Montpelier 05602
(802)828-8765

Lamoille Family Center
480 Kadys Fall Rd.
Morrisville 05661
(802)888-5229

Child Care Resource & Referral
  Center
181 Commerce St.
Williston 05495
(802)863-3367

Virginia
Office for Children
12011 Government Center
  Parkway, #910
Fairfax 22035
(703)324-8041

The Childcare Network
365 Belle Plains Rd.
Falmouth 22405
(540)373-3275

Childcare Connection
235 Cantrell Ave.
Harrisonburg 22801
(540)433-4531

Child Care Connection of Page
  County
200 Memorial Dr.
Luray 22835
(540)743-1273

Families First, Inc.
530 E. Main St., Suite 520
Richmond 23219
(804)649-8804

Memorial Child Guidance Clinic
5001 W. Broad St., Suite 140
Richmond 23230

Council of Community Services
502 Campbell Ave. SW
Roanoke 24016
(540)985-0131

Child Caring Connection
1461 Richmond Rd.
Williamsburg 23185
(757)229-7940

Washington
Child Care Resources
15015 Main St., Suite 206
Bellevue 98007
(206)865-9920

Child Care and Family Resources
314 East Holly, 2nd Fl.
Bellingham 98225
(360)734-5121

Volunteers of America/CCR&R
P.O. Box 839
Everett 98206-0839
(425)259-3191

Nanny Broker, Inc.
25620 SE 157th St.
Issaquah 98027
(425)392-5681

Family Care Resources
525 East Mission Ave.
Spokane 99202
(509)483-3114

WA State Child Care Resource &
  Referral Network
917 Pacific Ave., Suite 301
Tacoma 98402
(253)383-1735

Educational Services Dist. #112,
  Child Care R&R
2500 NE 65th Ave.
Vancouver 98661
(360)750-7500

Catholic Family & Child Services
23 S. Wenatchee Ave., Suite #210
Wenatchee 98801
(509)662-6761

Child Care Resource & Referral of
  Yakima & Kittitas Counties
5301 Tieton Dr., Suite C
Yakima 98908
(509)965-7100

West Virginia
Link CCR&R
605 9th St., Suite 215
Huntington 25702
(304)523-3417

Burlington United Methodist Family
  Service
RR 3, Box 3122
Keyser 26726
(304)788-2342

Wyoming Co. Opportunity Council,
  Inc./CCR&R
P.O. Box 1509
Oceana 24870
(304)682-8271

Child Care Resource Center
1307 Jacob St.
Wheeling 26003
(304)232-1603

Wisconsin
Child Care R&R Service, Inc.
519 W. Wisconsin Ave.
Appleton 54911
(920)734-0966

Wisconsin Child Care Resource &
  Referral Network, Inc.
1545 E. Broadway Dr.
Appleton 54915
(414)734-1739

Child Care Partnership
R&R/Western Dairyland, EOC, Inc.
221 West Madison St., Suite 110
Eau Claire 54703

Community Coordinated Care
201 W. Walnut, Suite 202
Green Bay 543033
(920)432-8899

NW WI CCR&R
P.O. Box 13230
Hayward 54843
(715)634-2299

South Central CCR&R
1900 Center Ave.
Janesville 53546
(608)741-3426

Family Resource of Lacrosse
122 North 7th Ave.
Lacrosse 54601
(608)784-8125

4C-Community Coordinated Child
  Care
116 E. Pleasant St., Lower Level
Milwaukee 53212
(414)562-2650

CCR&R of Fon Du Lac, Green Lake
& Winnebago Co.
683 N. Main, Suite F
Oshkosh 54901
(920)426-8920

Family Connections R&R
1930 North Eighth St.
Sheboygan 53081
(920)457-1999

Mid-Wisconsin Child Care Resource
  & Referral
23 Park Ridge Dr., Suite 11
Stevens Point 54481
(715)342-1788

CCR&R of Racine & Kenosha, Inc.
9400 Durand Ave.
Sturtevant 53177
(262)884-9890

Child Care Connection
301½ Grand Ave.
Wausau 54403
(715)848-5297

Child Care Resource and Referral of
  Central Wisconsin
210 East Jackson St.
Wisconsin Rapids 54494
(715)423-4114

Wyoming
Children's Nutrition Service
P.O. Box 2455
Casper 82602
(307)266-1236

Wyoming P.A.R.E.N.T.
1050 N. 3rd, Suite C
Laramie 82070
(307)635-2272

C

Appendix C: Family Child Care Forms and Checklists

Telephone Contact Form

Name of provider _____ Telephone no._____

Address_____

Space available for child the age of mine when I need it?   Yes ___ No ___

Number and ages of children cared for now _____

_____

Number of children enrolled full time _____

Licensed or certified?   Yes ___   No ___

Working toward license?   Yes ___   No ___

How many years providing care?_____

Fee (hourly, daily, weekly) _____

Names of two references (and phone numbers, if possible)

_____

_____

Comments:

_____

_____

Questions for References

Provider's Name _____ Date _____

Name of Reference _____

Address _____ Phone _____

How long was or has your child been with (provider)? _____

How old was your child when she or he started in this care? _____

What did you like about the care offered by (provider)? _____

_____

_____

Were there aspects of this care that made you unhappy? _____

_____

_____

How easy is it to approach (provider) about problems? _____

_____

How flexible is (the provider)? _____

_____

What words would you use to explain how (provider) deals with children? _____

_____

_____

_____

Does (provider) organize activities for children? Please describe some of those
activities._____

_____

_____

Does (provider) also care for her own children? How does that work out? _____

_____

Knowing what you do now, would you choose (provider) again? _____

_____

_____

- A home with one provider should have no more than six children, including the provider's own children. No more than two of these children should be under age two.

- A group home with two or more adult providers should have no more than twelve children, including those of the providers. No more than four of these children should be under age two.

- A family child care provider should be at least eighteen years old.

- The provider must have at least basic training in first aid, safety, and child development.

Family Child Care Checklist

Name of Provider_____

Address_____

Date_____

Yes	No	
		Basic Information
___	___	Program licensed?
___	___	Hours compatible with work?
___	___	Affordable weekly rate?
		Health and Safety
___	___	Is the home secure?
___	___	Is the home well maintained?
___	___	Working smoke detectors/fire extinguishers?
___	___	Electrical outlets covered?
___	___	Safe windows/gated stairs?
___	___	Medicines/cleaning agents locked away?
___	___	Clear emergency exits?
___	___	Kitchen/bathroom sanitary?
___	___	Play area clean and uncluttered?
		Indoor Play Area
___	___	Are toys safe and appropriate?
___	___	Is there adequate space for children to play?
___	___	Is a variety of toys/materials available?
___	___	Can children be seen easily?
___	___	Is there adequate lighting/windows/ventilation?
___	___	Are bathrooms accessible?
___	___	Is there space for personal belongings?
		Outdoor Play Area
___	___	Is it enclosed and secure?
___	___	Is it free of hard ground surfaces and rocks?
___	___	Are climbers, swings, slides, safe and supervised?
___	___	Can children be seen easily?
___	___	Is it uncluttered so children can run?
		Nap Area
___	___	Individual cots/cribs?
___	___	Cots and cribs clean and in good order?
___	___	Quiet location but can be observed?
___	___	Evacuation plan clearly posted?

Yes No

Care Providers

— — Do the children seem happy around the provider?

— — Is the provider in good physical condition and able to keep up with the children?

— — Is the provider warm and affectionate?

— — Is the provider positive and open?

— — Is the provider willing to talk to you?

— — Does the provider invite you to drop in whenever you wish?

— — Does the provider seem organized?

— — Does the provider seem genuinely to like children?

— — Does the provider maintain discipline by careful supervision, clear limits, and explanations that the children can understand?

— — Does the provider avoid conflicts between children by listening and watching carefully, then stepping in early to prevent violence?

— — Does the provider use praise and attention to encourage cooperation and helpfulness?

If Working with Infants and Toddlers

— — Does the provider respond quickly to signs of unhappiness or distress?

— — Does the provider hold infants and toddlers often and in caring ways?

— — Are babies who are too young to hold their bottles fed in the arms of the provider?

— — Does the provider talk directly to the infants and toddlers, responding to their sounds and vocalizations?

— — Does the provider set limits consistently and gently?

— — Does the provider allow children to explore, and give help when needed?

— — Are babies allowed to nap when they are tired?

— — Does the provider wash her hands after every diaper change and before feedings?

Program

— — Is there a clear daily schedule?

— — Are activities varied and age-appropriate?

— — Does the provider serve nutritious meals and snacks?

— — Is there a program policy on discipline?

Parent-Provider Child Care Contract

I. The following contract is between:

1. _____

    Mother/legal guardian   Home phone   Work phone

_____

    Home address   Mailing address if different

_____

    Employer/school name and address

and

2. _____

    Father/legal guardian   Home phone   Work phone

_____

    Home address   Mailing address if different

_____

    Employer/school name and address

3. _____

    Child care provider   Phone

_____

    Address

for the care of:

4. _____

    Child's name and birth date   Child's name and birth date

_____

    Child's name and birth date   Child's name and birth date

5. _____

    Start date of this contract   End date of this contract
                                    (may be renewed at this
                                    time if all parties agree)

II. Standard Rates and Payment Policies:

1. A deposit of $ _____ is required. It will be applied to the last week's payment or to the termination notice period if proper notice is not given. (See V., Termination procedure.)

2. The pay will be $ _____ per hour or $ _____ per day or $ _____ per week. Child care will be provided:

Mon. Tues. Wed. Thur. Fri. Sat. Sun. Hours: _____
(circle appropriate days)

3. Payment is due ❒ weekly   ❒ bi-weekly   ❒ other _____

every _____.   (day of week)

4. The provider will provide: ❒ Breakfast   ❒ Morning snack   ❒ Lunch
❒ Afternoon snack   ❒ Dinner

(check all that apply)

The provider is ❒ informal   ❒ registered with state   ❒ licensed with state Provider will notify parent/guardian in writing if status changes. If registered or licensed, provider will comply with all day care regulations and will make a copy of the regulations available to the parent/guardian upon request.

5. The parent/guardian will provide: ❒ Formula   ❒ Infant food   ❒ Diapers (type _____) and wipes

❒ Change of clothes   ❒ Other _____ or will pay an additional weekly fee of $ _____ to cover _____. Other special arrangements: _____

Parent/guardian must supply a current medical form, completed by the child's doctor and updated annually.

III. Rates for holidays, absences, vacations, overtime:
1. Care will not be provided, but payment is due, on the following holidays when they occur on a day the child(ren) is/are regularly scheduled for care:

2. The provider will be notified by _____ (time) if the child(ren) will be absent. Policy for payment for absences is:

3. Fees and policies for provider's vacation:_____

4. Fees and policies for parent/guardian's vacation:_____

5. If the provider is unable to provide care because of illness or emergency, the policy is: _____

_____

6. If the parent/guardian drops off the child earlier or picks up later than the times specified in II, 2, the following overtime rate will be charged:

$_____per _____ or portion thereof.

IV. Damages:

The policy on damage caused by the child(ren) while in the provider's care unless caused by the negligence of the provider is:

_____

(This does not apply to normal wear and tear on toys or furniture, only to damage.)

V. Termination procedure:

This contract may be terminated by either parent/guardian or provider by giving _____ weeks' written notice. The provider may terminate the contract without notice if the parent/guardian is more than _____ week(s) late with scheduled pay-ments. Parent/guardian may terminate the contract without notice if the provider does not comply with day care regulations. Changes to the contract, desired by either provider or parent/guardian, must be made in writing and acknowledged in writing by the other parties at least two (2) weeks before the desired change takes effect. A new contract may be signed at this time to reflect the changes.

V. Signatures:

By signing this contract, all parties agree to all of the above terms and policies, including financial responsibility for care provided. The provider is responsible for giving/sending all signers a copy of the signed contract.

_____

Provider's signature   Date

_____

Mother/legal guardian signature   Date

_____

Father/legal guardian signature   Date

Co-signer's signature (required if parent/legal guardian is under 18   Date
years old. Co-signer must be 18 or older and by signing assumes
financial responsibility in case the parent fails to pay for care provided.)

About the Child

The following general information about your child will help your child's care-giver provide a safe and comfortable experience for your child. *Make sure that you update this form if the information changes.*

Child's name _____Date of birth_____

Home address_____Home phone_____

(circle one if appropriate)

Address and phone no. of father/mother if different from above_____

_____

Child will be dropped off at day care home at _____ AM/PM and picked up by

_____ AM/PM

School child attends (for school-age child care)_____

Teacher's name_____ Grade/room no._____

Phone no. of school_____ School bus no._____

Parent/Guardian Information:

Name_____Title/position_____

Employer or school_____Phone_____

Address_____

Days and hours of employment_____

Name_____ Title/position_____

Employer or school_____ Phone_____

Address_____

Days and hours of employment_____

Where else might parents or guardians be reached?_____

Emergency Phone Numbers:

In case of an emergency (e.g., child becomes ill, needs transportation home) and the parent cannot be reached, please list two other people who may be called for assistance. Select people who live in the area and have transportation. Make sure you discuss these responsibilities with them.

Name_____Phone_____

Name_____Phone_____

Persons authorized to pick up the child (besides parents):

Name_____Phone_____

Name_____Phone_____

Family Information:
Names and ages of siblings_____

_____

Other family/household information_____

_____

Family pets_____

Medical Information:
Insurance company_____ID/group no._____

Child's doctor_____Phone_____

Address_____

Child's dentist_____Child's orthodontist_____

Address_____Address_____

Phone_____Phone_____

Please list any allergies or chronic illnesses your child has, including the symptoms and what needs to be done to help care for them:

_____

_____

Miscellaneous Information:

Please list foods that your child particularly likes or dislikes_____

_____

Please give any special information about your child that might be helpful, such as information about nap arrangements, special fears, special words for urination or bowel movements, favorite activities, and so forth.

_____

Consent for Emergency Treatment of
Minors in Absence of Parent(s) or Legal Guardians

Name of child_____Age_____Birthdate_____

Home address_____Phone_____

Phone Number for Parents/Guardians During Child's School Hours

_____

(phone number)   (name)   (relationship to child)

_____

(phone number)   (name)   (relationship to child)

Insurance Information

Insurance Co._____Contract No._____

Address_____Subscriber_____

Authorization for Treatment of a Minor

We, the undersigned, are the legal guardians of_____.

In the event that we cannot be contacted, we give consent and authorization for emergency medical, dental, or surgical treatment that is deemed necessary, by emergency medical personnel or hospital physicians, for the best interest of our child's health and safety. We request, that in our absence the health care provider discuss the matter with at least one of the persons designated below.

1. _____

(name)   (phone number)   (relationship to child)

2. _____

(name)   (phone number)   (relationship to child)

3. Teachers/director of the early childhood program in which my child is currently enrolled.

The period of time over which this authorization exists is as follows:

_____(date) to_____(date)

_____

(signature of guardian)   (date)   (signature of guardian)   (date)

Please refer to the attached medical history.

Emergency Medical Information

Child's doctor_____Phone number_____

Child's dentist_____Phone number_____

Is the child allergic to any medications?   Yes _____   No _____

If yes, please list:_____

Any other allergies?_____

_____

Is the child taking any medications?   Yes _____   No _____

If yes, please list the name and dosage:_____

Is the child currently up to date with immunizations?   Yes _____
No _____

Please describe medical history or other pertinent facts that should be known
before treating your child:_____

_____

_____

_____

_____
(Signature of Guardian)   (Date)

_____
(Signature of Guardian)   (Date)

Appendix D: Center Care Forms and Checklists

Sample Daily Information Sheet for Parents and Caregivers

Parent Report:

_____

Baby's name   Date

Food: What, how much, and when did your baby eat or drink last?

_____

What   Amount   Time

Sleep: How long did your baby sleep last night?_____

What time did your baby get up this morning?_____

Did your baby sleep well? _____ If no, what seemed to be the problem?

_____

Mood: What is your baby's mood today?_____

Other information that will help us take better care of your baby today:_____

_____

_____

_____

_____

Center Report:

Your baby ate:

	When	What	Comments
Snack			
Lunch			
Snack			
Other			

Your baby slept from: ____ to: ____ and from: ____ to: ____ and from: ____ to: ____

Diaper changes: No. wet _____; B.M.s _____; _____; _____; _____;

Comments:_____

Your baby's activities and the caretakers' observations.

_____

_____

_____

_____

General disposition:_____

Center Telephone Survey Form

Center name   Date of call

Location   Name of director

Ages of children served   Hours care provided

Is this a year-round program?_____

Will there be an opening when we require care?_____

Is the center licensed?_____What are the fees?_____

Number of children per adult in our child's age group:_____

Total number of children in our child's age group:_____

Qualifications of caregiving staff_____

_____

When is a good time to visit?_____

Center Child Care Checklist

Name of center_____

Address_____

Date_____

Yes No   **Basic Information**

___ ___   Program licensed?

___ ___   Hours compatible with work?

___ ___   Affordable rates?

     Health and Safety

___ ___   Is the facility secure?

___ ___   Is the facility well maintained?

___ ___   Working smoke detectors/fire extinguishers?

___ ___   Electrical outlets covered?

___ ___   Safe windows/gated stairs?

___ ___   Medicines/cleaning agents locked away?

___ ___   Clear emergency exits?

___ ___   Kitchen/bathrooms sanitary?

___ ___   Indoor and outdoor play areas?

___ ___   Play areas clean and uncluttered?

     Indoor Play Area

___ ___   Are toys safe and appropriate?

___ ___   Is there adequate space for children to play?

___ ___   Is there a variety of toys/materials available?

___ ___   Can children be seen easily?

___ ___   Is there adequate lighting/windows/ventilation?

___ ___   Are bathrooms accessible?

___ ___   Is there space for personal belongings?

___ ___   Is there room for both active and quiet play?

     Outdoor Play Area

___ ___   Is it enclosed and secure?

___ ___   Is it free of rocks and other safety hazards?

___ ___   Are climbers, swings, slides, safe and supervised?

___ ___   Are there soft surfaces under outdoor equipment?

___ ___   Can children be seen easily?

___ ___   Uncluttered areas so children can run?

___ ___   Space for quiet and active play?

___ ___   Does the area have regular maintenance inspections?

Yes No

Nap Area

—— —— Individual cots/cribs?

—— —— Cots and cribs are clean and in good order?

—— —— Quiet location but can be observed?

—— —— Evacuation plan clearly posted?

Caregivers

—— —— Do the children seem happy around the providers?

—— —— Are the caregivers in good physical condition and able to keep up with the children?

—— —— Are the caregivers warm and affectionate?

—— —— Are the caregivers positive and open?

—— —— Are the caregivers willing to talk to you?

—— —— Do the caregivers invite you to drop in?

—— —— Do the caregivers seem organized?

—— —— Do the caregivers seem genuinely to like children?

—— —— Do the caregivers focus on and interact mostly with the children, rather than chatting with one another?

—— —— Is discipline maintained by careful supervision, clear limits, and explanations that the child can understand?

—— —— Do caregivers avoid conflicts between children by listening and watching carefully, then stepping in early to prevent violence?

—— —— Do caregivers use praise and attention to encourage cooperation and helpfulness?

—— —— Do the caregivers work as a team?

If Working with Infants and Toddlers

—— —— Do caregivers respond quickly to signs of unhappiness or distress?

—— —— Do caregivers hold infants and toddlers often and in caring ways?

—— —— Are babies too young to hold their bottles fed in the arms of caregivers?

—— —— Do caregivers talk directly to the infants and toddlers, and respond to their sounds and vocalizations?

—— —— Do caregivers set limits consistently and gently?

—— —— Do caregivers allow children to explore, and give help when needed?

—— —— Are babies allowed to nap when they are tired?

Yes No

___ ___ Do caregivers wash their hands after every diaper change and before feedings?

Program and Administrative Structure

___ ___ Is there a clear daily schedule?

___ ___ Are activities varied and age-appropriate?

___ ___ Are the meals and snacks nutritious?

___ ___ Is there a program policy on discipline?

___ ___ Is there a program philosophy about children?

___ ___ Is there an active board of directors with parent representatives?

___ ___ Are parents welcome to visit any time they wish?

Director Interview

Name of director   Date

Name of center

Center address

Center phone   Director phone

What year did the center open for business?_____

Is your license current? When was the last licensing visit?_____

How long have your teachers/caregivers been with you? How many have left in the past six months?_____

_____

_____

What is the calendar for the center___holidays, vacations?_____

_____

_____

_____

What is your policy regarding sick children?_____

_____

_____

_____

_____

How many children would be in my child's group? How many adults are with that group?

_____

What is the education and training background of the person who would care for my child?

_____

_____

_____

What about first-aid training, in case of illness or accident?_____

_____

Do you have specific policies regarding (choose those relevant for your child):
   Pacifiers and personal security objects, for example, blankets? _____

_____

   Bottles?_____

_____

   Toilet training?_____

_____

   Discipline?_____

_____

_____

   Bringing toys to the center?_____

_____

What is the fee for a child the age of mine?_____

What is the payment schedule?_____

Are parents expected to pay any other expenses?_____

May I have a copy of your parent contract?

What are your policies regarding meals and snacks?_____

_____

_____

If meals are served: May I see a weekly menu?_____

How do you feel about parent-teacher communications?_____

_____

Do you have any policies that encourage communication?_____

_____

_____

_____

Are there other ways that parents can be involved in the center?_____

_____

_____

_____

Questions specific to your child's particular needs, for example, food allergies, sleep requirements, personality._____

_____

_____

_____

_____

About the Child

The following general information about your child will help your child's care-giver provide a safe and comfortable experience for your child. *Make sure that you update this form if the information changes.*

Child's name _____ Date of birth_____

Home address_____ Home phone_____

(circle one if appropriate)

Address and phone no. of father/mother if different from above_____
_____

Child will be dropped off at day care at _____ AM/PM and picked up by _____ AM/PM

School child attends (for school-age child care)_____

Teacher's name_____ Grade/room no._____

Phone no. of school_____ School bus no._____

Parent/Guardian Information:

Name_____Title/position_____

Employer or school_____Phone_____

Address_____

Days and hours of employment_____

Name_____ Title/position_____

Employer or school_____ Phone_____

Address_____

Days and hours of employment_____

Where else might parents or guardians be reached?_____

Emergency Phone Numbers:

In case of an emergency (e.g., child becomes ill, needs transportation home) and the parent cannot be reached, please list two other people who may be called for assistance. Select people who live in the area and have transportation. Make sure you discuss these responsibilities with them.

Name_____Phone_____

Name_____Phone_____

Persons authorized to pick up the child (besides parents):

Name_____Phone_____

Name_____Phone_____

Family Information:

Names and ages of siblings_____

_____

Other family/household information_____

_____

Family pets_____

Medical Information:

Insurance company_____ID/group no._____

Child's doctor_____Phone_____

Address_____

Child's dentist_____Child's orthodontist_____

Address_____Address_____

Phone_____Phone_____

Please list any allergies or chronic illnesses your child has, including the symptoms and what needs to be done to help care for them:

_____

Miscellaneous Information:

Please list foods that your child particularly likes or dislikes_____

_____

Please give any special information about your child that might be helpful, such as information about nap arrangements, special fears, special words for urination or bowel movements, favorite activities, and so forth.

Appendix E: Part-Day Program Form

Nursery School Checklist for Parents

Nursery school programs run for up to three hours a day. They are not subject to regulation or inspection by any public health, social services, or education official. In most states, nursery school staff, like public school teachers, are not cleared through a state central register for child abuse and maltreatment. Check if this is true in your state. The ultimate responsibility for your child's safety and well-being is *yours*.

When you visit a nursery school, take your time and ask plenty of questions. You may want to inquire about some of the items on this checklist. In addition, you should be able to answer yes to these questions about your final choice:

• Do you feel that being in this setting will be a happy experience for your child?
• Do you feel you will be able to develop a relaxed, sharing relationship with the teacher?

Name of nursery school

Address

Phone number   Date visited

Business Practices

___Fees?

___Total enrollment of children?

___Schedule: What hours, days, does school operate?_____

___Does it follow public school calendar or go year round?_____

Indoor Space

___Warm, clean, dry?

___Adequate space?

___Friendly, colorful, inviting?

___Bathroom?

___Natural light/windows/screens against insects?

___Two (2) exits from each floor?

Outdoor Space

___Well-drained yard?

___Accessible?

___Free of hazards?

___Fenced or with natural borders?

___What equipment is available?_____

_____

Safety

___Building safe and maintained?

___Smoke detectors?

___First-aid kit in easily accessible place?

___Fire extinguisher; all know how to use it?

___Working phone, emergency numbers posted nearby?

___Evacuation plan and fire-drill plan?

___No peeling paint or plaster? No lead-based paint?

___Any pet friendly, in good health, and properly cared for?

___All cleaning supplies safely stored away from children?

Appendix F: In-Home Care Forms and Checklists

National Au Pair Placement Agencies

Seven national au pair agencies have permission from the federal government to bring au pairs into the United States.

Au Pair Care
1 Post Street, Suite 700
San Francisco, California 94104
  or
17 Neperan Rd.
Tarrytown-on-Hudson, N.Y. 10591
(800) 428-7247

World Learning/Au Pair/Homestay
  USA
1015 15th Street, N.W., Suite 750
Washington, D.C. 20005
(202) 408-5380

Au Pair in America
102 Greenwich Avenue
Greenwich, Connecticut 06830
(800) 727-2437

Au Pair Programme USA
36 South State, Suite 3000
Salt Lake City, Utah 84111
(801) 255-7722

EF Au Pair
1 Memorial Drive
Cambridge, Massachusetts 02142
(800) 333-6056

EurAuPair
250 North Coast Highway
Laguna Beach, California 92651
(800) 333-3804

InterExchange
356 West 34th St.
New York, New York 10001
(212) 924-0446

Sample Telephone Contact Form: Nanny and Au Pair

_____

Date of phone contact

_____

Name of applicant   Telephone no.

_____

Address

Tell applicant the number and ages of your children.

Give a brief description of the position, including work hours, pay, and benefits.

Please tell me about your educational background._____

_____

_____

How many years of experience do you have in the child care field?_____

Please give a brief description of this experience._____

_____

_____

_____

_____

Why do you want this job?_____

_____

_____

Please tell me why you left your last position._____

_____

What are your plans for the future?_____

_____

Please give me the names and phone numbers of two references.

_____

_____

Do you have any questions we can clear up now on the phone?_____

_____

_____

_____

_____

Comments:_____

_____

_____

_____

_____

_____

Do I want to interview this applicant in person? _____ Yes _____ No

Date, time and, place of interview_____

Sample Questions for Reference Check of
In-Home Child Care Provider

_____

Date of reference interview

_____

Name of reference   Relationship to applicant

_____

Reference address   Phone no.

Applicant's name_____

Employment dates and salary_____

Why did applicant leave?_____

Did the applicant live with you, and if so, how did she fit into your family?_____

_____

_____

Please describe her duties and her ability to perform them._____

_____

_____

_____

_____

Please describe her strengths

_____

_____

and weaknesses.

_____

_____

Additional comments?_____

Nanny and Au Pair Sample Interview Questions

If at all possible, you should conduct this interview in person. You will probably have to interview prospective au pairs by telephone, since those young people cannot enter this country unless they have already secured a position.

_____

Date of reference interview

_____

Applicant's name

_____

Address   Phone

Describe the position to the applicant. Tell her about your children, their ages, and what you require in relation to their care. Spell out any other duties you expect her to perform (cooking, housecleaning, washing clothes, transportation, etc.). Show her through your house to give her an idea of what her job will entail. If she is going to live with you, show her the room she will occupy. Set forth her hours of work, salary, and benefits. Be as clear as you can about your expectations.

Have you any questions about the position and what is required of you?_____

_____

_____

Please describe your background (personal, educational)._____

_____

_____

_____

How would you occupy my child on a typical day?_____

_____

_____

_____

_____

What methods of discipline do you use?_____

_____

_____

_____

"Sarah" is two years old and "Peter" is five; please give me examples of activities you'd plan for them._____

_____

_____

_____

_____

_____

Have you ever had to handle a medical or other emergency? If yes, please describe. If no, how would you handle one?_____

_____

_____

_____

Are there any reasons why you would not be able to perform your duties in this job?

_____

_____

Do you have any questions for me at this point?

I'd like you to spend a few hours interacting with my child(ren) as part of this interview. Observation comments:_____

_____

_____

_____

_____

Other comments:_____

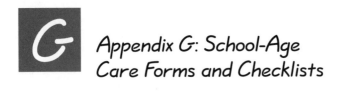

Appendix G: School-Age Care Forms and Checklists

SACC Telephone Survey Form

SACC program name   Date of call

Location   Name of director

Ages of children served   Hours of care provided

Days program does *not* operate_____

Do you provide transportation from my child's school to program?_____

Will there be an opening when we require care? _____

What are the fees? _____

Is part-time care available? _____ If yes, how does it work?_____

Is the program licensed/registered?_____

Ages of children in my child's group?_____

Number of children per staff in my child's group?_____

Total number of children in my child's group?_____

Are age groups ever mixed? _____ Please describe. _____

Qualifications of program staff?_____

_____

Tell me briefly about your program philosophy._____

_____

_____

_____

_____

Names and phone numbers of references (parents of children who are attend-ing or have attended the program)?_____

_____

_____

When is a good time to visit?_____

Sample Questions for Visit to School-Age Child Care or Camp

Consider these key questions as you visit potential school-age child care programs and camps:

1. How will the program match up with your child's personality?
   With his interests?
   With his likes and dislikes?

2. What is the underlying program philosophy?
   Is the emphasis on cooperative play or on primarily competitive games, or on a balance of the two approaches?

3. Does the staff show respect for the children?
   In what way?

4. What is the approach to discipline?
   Are the children allowed to help set the rules for individual and group behavior?

5. What is the physical layout of the program?
   Is it open and flexible?
   Is it designed to keep the children stimulated and occupied?
   Are there spaces for retiring with a good book and relaxing?
   Is there a place to do homework undisturbed?
   Is there space for running around and getting rid of extra energy?

6. What foods are on the menu?
   Do the plans include nutritious meals and snacks that are appropriate for children of this age group?

7. Are the activities geared toward the differing developmental levels of the children in the group?

8. Are the materials and equipment available for self-selection?
   Are they safe and interesting to children the age of your child?

9. If your child has special needs, can the program accommodate them?

10. Make sure that you check all the standard health and safety issues:
    - cleanliness of bathrooms and kitchen
    - health policies
    - staff training in CPR and first aid
    - fire-drill practice

Use the school-age child care checklist as another tool for your program visit.

School-Age Child Care/Camp Checklist

Name of program_____

Address_____

Date_____

Yes No

___ ___   Program licensed?

___ ___   Hours compatible with work?

___ ___   Affordable rates?

___ ___   Transportation available, safe, and convenient?

                Health and Safety

___ ___   Is the facility secure?

___ ___   Is the facility well maintained?

___ ___   Working smoke detectors/fire extinguishers?

___ ___   Electrical outlets covered?

___ ___   Safe windows and stairs?

___ ___   Medicines/cleaning agents locked away?

___ ___   Clear emergency exits?

___ ___   Kitchen/bathroom sanitary?

___ ___   Play area clean and uncluttered?

___ ___   Staff trained in first aid and CPR?

___ ___   Are fire drills held regularly?

                Outdoor Play Area

___ ___   Is it enclosed and secure?

___ ___   Is it free of hard ground surfaces and rocks?

___ ___   Are climbers, swings, slides, safe and supervised?

___ ___   Can children be seen easily?

___ ___   Uncluttered so children can run?

___ ___   Are there large open areas for ball games, etc.?

___ ___   Is there an undeveloped area for exploration and discovery?

                Indoor Play Area

___ ___   Are toys and materials safe and appropriate?

___ ___   Is there adequate space for children to play?

___ ___   Is a variety of toys/materials available?

___ ___   Are activities progressive according to age?

___ ___   Can children be seen easily?

___ ___   Is there adequate lighting/windows/ventilation?

Yes No

___ ___ Are bathrooms accessible?

___ ___ Is there space for personal belongings?

___ ___ Is an area designated for doing homework?

School-Age Program Staff

___ ___ Do the children seem happy around the staff?

___ ___ Are the staff members in good physical condition and able to keep up with the children?

___ ___ Are the staff members warm and affectionate?

___ ___ Are the staff members positive and open?

___ ___ Is the staff willing to talk to you?

___ ___ Does the staff invite you to drop in whenever you like?

___ ___ Does the staff seem organized?

___ ___ Do the staff members seem genuinely to like children?

___ ___ Do staff members avoid conflicts between children by listening and watching carefully, then stepping in early to prevent violence?

___ ___ Do staff members use praise and attention to encourage cooperation and helpfulness?

___ ___ Does the staff work well as a team?

___ ___ Have you checked the age and training of staff members?

Program and Administrative Structure

___ ___ Is there a clear daily schedule?

___ ___ Are activities varied and age-appropriate?

___ ___ Does the program offer a variety of field trips?

___ ___ Are nutritious meals and snacks offered?

___ ___ Is there a discipline policy?

___ ___ Are children allowed to help set rules for individual and group behavior?

___ ___ Is there a program philosophy about children?

___ ___ Does the program encourage active parent involvement?

___ ___ Does the program have a specific focus? If so what is it?_____

Additional Questions for Camp

___ ___ Are lifeguards on duty at the waterfront?

___ ___ Is there adequate nighttime supervision of the children?

___ ___ Is your transportation safe and reliable?

Sample Interview Questions for Camp or SACC Director

When visiting a residential camp and interviewing the camp director, you need to ask additional questions.

1. What is the program's or camp's overall philosophy?_____

_____

2. What are the educational backgrounds of the director and the staff?_____

_____

3. How old are the counselors?_____

_____

4. What kinds of special training in the care of school-age children have they received?_____

_____

5. What is the ratio of adults to children?_____

_____

6. What about special safety issues such as:
   - medical staff on call?_____
   - lifeguards on duty at the waterfront?_____
   - nighttime supervision of the children?_____
   - CPR and first-aid training for staff?_____

7. What kinds of vehicles are used for transportation?_____
   - What condition are they in?_____

_____

8. What happens during a typical day at the program?_____

9. Ask for the names of at least three families whose children attended the program or camp during the previous year or summer.
   - If at all possible, include at least one family whose name you obtained on your own.

10. Call references right away.
   - Speak to the parents and if possible to the children who attended the program or camp.
   - What did the parents and children like most about the program?
   - What did they like least?
   - Would they recommend the program to friends?

H Appendix H: Suggested Reading and Other Resources

Bergstrom, Joan. *School's Out — Now What? Creative Choices for Your Child.* Berkeley: Ten Speed Press, 1984.

Brazelton, T. Berry. *Touchpoints: Your Child's Emotional and Behavioral Development.* Reading, Mass.: Addison-Wesley, 1992.

Bredekamp, Sue, and Carol Copple, eds. *Developmentally Appropriate Practice in Early Childhood Programs.* Washington, D.C.: National Association for the Education of Young Children, 1996.

Dynerman, Susan. *Are Our Kids All Right? Answers to the Tough Questions about Child Care Today.* Princeton: Peterson's, 1994.

Greenman, Jim, and Anne Stonehouse. *Prime Times: A Handbook for Excellence in Infant and Toddler Care.* St. Paul: Redleaf Press, 1996.

Platt, Elizabeth Balliett. *Scenes from Day Care. How Teachers Teach and What Children Learn.* New York: Teachers College Press, 1991.

Shelov, Steven P., ed., et al. *Caring for Your Baby and Young Child: Birth to Age Five.* New York: Bantam (American Academy of Pediatrics), 1991.

Child Care Action Campaign (CCAC) promotes high-quality child care at an affordable price through public education, research, and advocacy. The organization provides useful child care information to parents, employers, and policymakers. CCAC can be reached at 330 Seventh Avenue, Seventeenth Floor, New York, N.Y. 10001-5010, telephone (212) 239-0138.

Child Care Aware has a toll-free telephone line — (800) 424-2246 — for parents who wish to obtain free information about how to contact their nearest child care resource and referral agency. We endorse this service highly and encourage parents to take advantage of it.

Child Care Information Exchange, a magazine for child care center directors, a very useful resource, is published by Exchange Press, Inc., 17916 N.E. 103d Court, Redmond, Washington 98052-3243, telephone (800) 221-2864.

The National Association for the Education of Young Children publication *Young Children* is an extremely valuable resource. NAEYC can be reached at 1834 Connecticut Avenue, N.W., Washington, D.C. 20009-5786, telephone (800) 424-2460.

Appendix I: Questions for Potential Family Child Care Providers

---

Should You Become a Family Child Care Provider?

Be Clear about Your Objectives

- Do you enjoy working with children and want to invest your energies and talents in that direction?
- What challenges and satisfactions are you looking for? Will being a family child care provider help you understand your own children better? Will the extra income make you more secure? Do you really want the responsibility of caring for someone else's children?
- Do you know enough about children's growth and development to do a good job?
- Can you be with children long hours and still be able to give each child the attention and affection he or she needs?
- Are you in good health? Do you have the physical strength and stamina that caring for children requires?
- Can you care for other people's children and still have time and energy for your own family?
- Can you understand and respect other families so as not to become overinvolved with their children or make judgments about their family lifestyle?
- How do you really feel about mothers and fathers who leave their children with someone else for all or part of the day?
- Are you flexible enough to handle the surprises that come when young children are around? Can you handle accidents and emergencies calmly and efficiently?
- Are you willing to rearrange your house and your routines to meet

the needs of children?
- Do you expect to stay in business long enough to provide the continuity of care that young children need? Can you continue to offer care until the children and their families no longer need it?

Consider Your Family
- Do you have a warm family life that will give children the feeling that they are welcome and secure?
- Do your family members enjoy children? Are they willing to share their home and belongings? Are they willing to share your attention?
- Does your family understand that although the family child care business will bring in extra income, it will take a lot of your time and energy? Are they willing to help? Will they accept changes in the house and household routines?
- Will having young children in the house disturb your family? Will your older children be able to find privacy for studying or having friends in? Will older relatives be able to stand the commotion of having children around? Will a family member who works at night be able to sleep through the daytime noise of children's activities?

Source: Polly Spedding, *Child Care Notebook* (Ithaca, N.Y.: Cornell Cooperative Extension, Media Services, 1992).

Notes

Chapter 3

1. Marcy Whitebook, Carollee Howes, and Deborah Phillips, *The National Child Care Staffing Study: Who Cares? Child Care Teachers and the Quality of Care in America* (Oakland, Calif.: The Child Care Employee Project, 1989); Cost, Quality, and Child Outcomes Study Team, *Cost, Quality, and Child Outcomes in Child Care Centers,* Public Report, 2d ed. (Denver: Economics Department, University of Colorado at Denver, 1995); Ellen Galinsky, Carollee Howes, Susan Kontos, and Marybeth Shinn, *The Study of Children in Family Child Care and Relative Care: Highlights of Findings* (New York: Families and Work Institute, 1994).

2. Galinsky et al., *The Study of Children in Family Child Care and Relative Care,* and Ellen Galinsky, Carollee Howes, and Susan Kontos, *The Family Child Care Training Study: Highlights of Findings* (New York: Families and Work Institute, 1995).

3. Hedy Nai-Lin Chang, Amy Muckelroy, and Dora Pulido-Tobiassen, *Looking In, Looking Out: Redefining Child Care and Early Education in a Diverse Society* (San Francisco: California Tomorrow, 1996), 15. See also the California Tomorrow publication *Affirming Children's Roots: Cultural and Linguistic Diversity in Early Care and Education,* California Tomorrow, Fort Mason Center, Building B, San Francisco, California, telephone (415) 441-7631.

Chapter 5

1. Ellen Galinsky, Carollee Howes, and Susan Kontos, *The Family Child Care Training Study: Highlights of Findings* (New York: Families and Work Institute, 1995).

2. Ellen Galinsky, Carollee Howes, Susan Kontos, and Marybeth Shinn, *The Study of Children in Family Child Care and Relative Care: Highlights of Findings* (New York: Families and Work Institute, 1994).

3. These standards are in Judith Berezin, *The Complete Guide to Choosing Child Care* (New York: Random House, 1990), 62, which is out of print. Contact the National Association for Family Child Care, 725 15th Street, N.W., Suite 505, Washington, D.C. 20005, telephone (800) 359-3817.

4. These lists were adapted from Berezin, *The Complete Guide to Choosing Child Care,* 70–72.

5. Susan Dynerman, *Are Our Kids All Right? Answers to the Tough Questions about Child Care Today* (Princeton: Peterson's, 1994), 243.

Chapter 6

1. *Happy Day Playschool Parent Handbook (1996–1997): Our Goals and Philosophy* (Ithaca, N.Y.: Happy Day Playschool, 1996).

2. *CAPCO Head Start Program of Cortland County,* brochure, fall 1996 (Cortland County, N.Y.: Cortland County Head Start, 1996).

3. *Ithaca Community Childcare Center (IC3) Parent Handbook: "Mission, Values and Vision Statement"* (Ithaca, N.Y.: Ithaca Community Childcare Center, rev. September 1995).

4. Sue Bredekamp, ed., *Accreditation Criteria and Guidelines of the National Academy of Early Childhood Programs* (Washington, D.C.: National Association for the Education of Young Children, 1984), Table 2, 24.

5. Data compiled from *The State of America's Children, 1997 Yearbook* (Washington, D.C.: The Children's Defense Fund, 1997), Table B8, 104.

6. Ibid.

7. Ibid.

Chapter 7

1. Ellen Galinsky and William H. Hooks, *The New Extended Family* (Boston: Houghton Mifflin, 1977), 35–49.

Chapter 8

1. "Rules and Regulations," *Federal Register* 60, no. 31 (February 15, 1995), 8549–8553.

Chapter 9

Epigraph: Joan M. Bergstrom, *School's Out — Now What?* (Berkeley: Ten Speed Press, 1984), 15.

1. American Camping Association, *The Guide to Accredited Camps* (Martinsville, Ind.: American Camping Association [5000 State Road 67 North, Martinsville 46151-7902], n.d.).

Chapter 16

1. From Suzanne Helburn and Carollee Howes, "Child Care Cost and Quality," *The Future of Children* 6, no. 2 (Summer/Fall 1996), Table 3, 73; published by the Center for the Future of Children, David and Lucile Packard Foundation, 300 Second Street, Suite 102, Los Altos, California 94022.

Chapter 17

Epigraph: Peggy Hack, "We Can't Provide Child Care on a Shoestring!" — a speech given at a rally in front of the White House, November 30, 1995, in "Rights, Raises, Respect," *National Center for Early Childhood Workforce 1*, no. 1 (Spring/Summer 1996), 12.

1. Roger Neugebauer, "How's Business? Status Report #9 on For Profit Child Care," *Child Care Information Exchange*, no. 108 (March/April 1996), 64.

2. Suzanne Helburn and Carollee Howes, "Child Care Cost and Quality," *The Future of Children 6*, no. 2 (Summer/Fall 1996), Table 3, 73.

Index

Adult-to-child ratio, 78
    age of child and, 228
    best and worst states, 80, 90, 92
    center-based care, 11, 79, 80, 90,
        91–92
    family/group family care, 57, 64–65
    infant, 11, 79, 80, 228
    part-time care, 111, 114
    preschoolers, 91–92
    recommendations, 77, 106, 137
    school-age, 137, 142
    toddler, 90
    See also Group size, recommended
Advertising for child care, 41
After-school programs. *See* School-age
    child care
Age of child
    and adult-to-child ratio require-
        ments, 228
    and age mix, 50–51, 58, 80, 165
    and cost of care, 228
    and form of quality care, 78
    infant, for start of supplementary
        care, 181–83
American Civil Liberties Union, 122
American Council of Nanny Schools
    (ACNS), 19, 123, 125–26

Americans with Disabilities Act (1990),
    9
Anxiety. *See* Guilt and anxiety (of parents);
    Separation anxiety; Stranger anxiety
Assertive persistence, 4
Au pair, 10, 14, 18, 120–21, 129–34
    background and training, 132
    cost, 18, 121, 133, 228
    finding and hiring, 132–33
        forms and checklists, 326–32
    placement agencies, 326
    regulations on, 31, 129, 130–32
    and school-age children, 144
    unannounced visits to, 200

Baby sitters, 122–23, 144
Bad habits, 190–91
Bank Street Co-op, 112–13
Bedtimes, 203
Bergstrom, Joan M., 135
Big Brother/Big Sister programs, 143
Bredekamp, Sue, 137
Bright Horizons child care, 76

Caregiver or teacher
    age of, 65
    backup for, 55–56, 58, 86

Caregiver or teacher *(cont'd.)*
  -child ratio, *see* Adult-to-child ratio
  communicating with, 210–11,
    214–15, 247
    asking questions of, 201, 220–21
    information needed by or useful
      to, 208–9, 246–47, 321–23
  contract with, 70–71, 212, 303–6
  discipline by, *see* Discipline
  distinction between, 93
  education of, *see* Education/training
    of care provider
  on family child care checklist, 62–63
  as family resource, 216–23
  financial help for, *see* Cost of care
  get-acquainted visit (of child) to, 63,
    69, 209
  how to judge, 52–53, 62–63, 104–5
  interview with, 67–69
  as key to quality care, 27
  parental support of, parents as part-
    ners with, *see* Parent involvement
  staff qualifications and practices,
    83–85, 89–91, 95–97, 138–41
  staff schedules, 98
  staff turnover, 97–98, 106
  substitute, 79, 98
  unannounced visits to, *see* Visits
  wages of, *see* Cost of care
  See also Au pair; Nanny
Care in someone else's home, 15–17.
    See also Family child care homes
    (single provider); Group family
    child care homes (two or more
    providers)
Care in your own home, 10, 17–19,
    120–34
  combined with other care, 14, 117
  continuity of, 30
  disadvantages of, 121–22
  newborn, 169–83
  play groups, 110

school-age children, 144
unannounced visits, 29, 129
See also Au pair; Nanny
Center-based care, 10, 11–15
  adult-to-child ratio, 11, 79, 80, 90,
    91–92
  choosing center, 100–108
  cost of, 47, 58, 108, 228, 229
    salary, 238–41
  disadvantages of, 79, 86, 91
  financing of, 12
  forms and checklists, 103–5, 312–23
  infants in, 10, 11, 19, 79–85, 100,
    104–5
  interviewing director, 106–7,
    318–20
  parent involvement in, 82, 89,
    98–100
  philosophy and policies of, 73–76,
    99, 215
  preschoolers in, 20, 91–97
  profit and nonprofit, *see* Child care
    centers
  regulation of, 78 (*see also* State-
    regulated standards)
  school-age children in, 10, 12, 15,
    19–20, 136, 142–44
  staff qualifications and practices,
    83–85, 89–91, 95–97, 106–7, 111,
    138–41
  staff schedules, 98
  staff turnover, 97–98, 106
  supporting provider, 207–15
  toddlers in, 10, 19, 85–91, 100,
    104–5
  unannounced visits to, 100, 200
  Yellow Pages listings, 40–41, 42
Center Child Care Checklist, 103–5
Certification, 54–55. *See also* State-
    regulated standards
Checklists
  au pair, 327–32

family child care, 298–311
    center, 312–23
    nannies, 327–28, 330–32
    nursery school, 324–25
    school-age child care, 333–38
Child abuse, 29, 69–70
Child care
    before child starts, 208–9
    child's reactions to, 184–91
    child's transition to, 199–200
    child too sick for, 211–12
    creating alternative forms, 155–66
    employer-supported or -sponsored,
        19–20, 254–56
    establishing your own service,
        164–66, 340–41
    how to improve conditions, 245–51,
        256–57
    how to locate and choose, 38–44,
        73–108, 155–63
        beginning search, 100, 199
        reassessing choice, 201–2
        sources of information, 156
    of newborn, 169–83 (see also
        Infants)
    parents as partners in, see Parent
        involvement
    paying for, see Cost of care
    public policies concerning, 257–60
    three-family system, 162–63
    See also entries for different types of
        care
Child Care Aware project, 42, 156, 222,
    255
Child care centers, 11–12
    nonprofit, 12, 143–44, 228, 239
    popularity of, 12
    proprietary (for profit), 12, 99, 228,
        239–41
        franchised chains, 12, 76, 240–41
    See also Center-based care
Child care myths, 194–97, 198, 235, 250

Child care resource and referral (CCR
    and R) agencies, 42–44, 58–59,
    70, 116–17, 156, 165
    state-by-state list of, 267–97
Child development. See Developmental
    stage
Child Development Associate creden-
    tial, 115, 116, 255
Child Development Block Grant, 233
Child-rearing practices, caregiver's
    knowledge of, 218–19
Children's Discovery Centers, 12
Children's World Learning Centers, 12,
    76
Church-based centers, 12–13, 31, 136, 143
    day camps of, 147
Cleanliness. See Physical environment
Colombia preschool program, 255
Community centers, SACC programs
    in, 143–44
Community resources, caretaker's
    knowledge of, 219–20
Community supports and attitudes,
    how to improve, 248–51
Consent forms. See Emergency consent
    forms
Continuity of care. See Quality care
Contract, 303–6
Contract with provider, 70–71, 212,
    303–6
Cooperative Extension Service, 156, 222
Cost of care, 106, 108, 227–41
    age of child and, 228
    alternative arrangement, 161
    au pair or nanny, 18, 121, 125, 133,
        144, 228, 229
    caregivers' wages, 208, 228, 236–41,
        252–53
    employers' assistance with, 19–20,
        254–56
    family/group family vs. center, 47,
        58, 212, 228, 229

Cost of care *(cont'd.)*
  financial help for provider, 47, 54,
    212–13, 222, 229–30, 257–58
  financing of centers, 12
  group size and, 228, 259
  income-eligibility requirements, 10,
    13, 115
  parental co-op programs, 114
  parental leave costs vs., 181
  partial recovery of, 4, 227
  percentage of family income,
    230–31, 252
  and quality, 229–30
  "on a shoestring," 235–41
  spreading out, 234
  subsidies or tax credits available for,
    229, 231–34, 255, 257, 258
  summer camp (day and residential),
    147–48
  type of care and, 228
  voucher programs, 19, 20
  where you live and, 227–28, 229
Cost of implementing regulations,
  258–59
Cost of parental leave, 178–81
Criminal background, checking for,
  69–70, 78
Cultural experience, 35–36
Curriculum
  church-operated program, 12
  family child care, 53
  High/Scope, 20
  kindergarten, 14
  lab school, 15
  meaning of, 34–35
  Montessori, 21
  parent cooperatives, 13
  Waldorf, 21

Day camps. *See* Summer camps
Day care centers. *See* Child care
  centers

Dayton Hudson corporation, 255
Developmental stage, 8–9
  caregiver's knowledge of, 68,
    217–18, 219
  and kindergarten, 14
  newborn, 171–72, 173–74, 181–82
  school-age (middle childhood), 138,
    139–40
Disabilities
  federal acts concerning, 9
  Head Start program and, 13
Disability insurance (for pregnancy),
  176–77, 179, 180, 181
Discipline
  flexibility of, 107
  physical, 66, 68
  "time-out," 96, 107
Disease, susceptibility to. *See* Illness
Dynerman, Susan, 71

Education/training of care provider
  au pair, 132
  in center care, 83, 91, 95, 106–7, 111
  Child Development Associate cre-
    dential, 115, 116, 255
  in family/group family child care,
    53–54, 57, 65
  financing of, 54, 222, 230
  guidelines for, 65, 78
  Head Start, 115, 116
  in infant care, 83
  investments in, 258
  lack of child-related, 32, 48, 106
  nanny, 19, 125–26
  opportunities for, source of infor-
    mation about, 222–23
  part-time care, 111, 114
  in school-age care, 138, 142
  toddler teacher, 91
  value of, 32–33, 35, 53–54, 55, 222
Emergency care
  in part-day care situation, 116, 144

pickup arrangements, 210
    when care provider is ill, 55–56
Emergency consent forms, 310–311
Emergency scholarship funds, 234. *See also* Cost of care
Employers
    care supported or sponsored by, 19–20, 254–56
    and parental leave, *see* Parental leave policies
Environment. *See* Physical environment
Evening routines, 188, 202–3
Extended-day programs. *See* Part-day care

Family and Medical Leave Act, 176, 179
Family Child Care Checklist, 61–63
Family child care homes (single provider), 10, 15–16, 47–57, 117
    age of provider, 65
    backup for, 55–56, 142
    continuity of care, 30, 56–57
    cost, 47, 212, 228, 229
        salary, 236–37
    curriculum, 53
    disadvantages of, 47–48, 141–42
    group size, 50–51, 64
    how to select, 58–70
        forms and checklists, 298–312
    regulation of, 15, 16, 47, 54–55, 142
    reserving space, 58
    school-age children in, 10, 47, 50–51, 141–42
    setting up your own, 164–66, 340–41
    supporting provider, 54, 207–15
    training for care provider, 53–54, 65
    visits to (in selecting), 61–66
    visits to (unannounced), 200
    written agreement with, 70–71
Family participation in program, 21.
        See also Parent-run cooperatives; Parents; Relatives

Father
    child's behavior toward, 186
    new, 170, 174–75
    parental leave for, 176–82 *passim*
    See also Parents
Federal Register, 130
Federal Title XX Day Care Services, 233
First-aid training, 16, 33, 65, 150
Flexibility of care, 16, 17, 47, 107, 109
Forms, 298, 299–300, 307–9, 312–13, 314, 321–23, 327–28, 333–34
Friends and neighbors, in creating child care arrangement, 158–61
Full-time care, 10
    for infants, 182
    vs. part-time, 9
    for preschoolers, 91

Group family child care homes (two or more providers), 10, 16–17, 57–58
    cost of, 58, 212, 237
    group size, 57, 64–65
    how to select, 58–70
    philosophy and policies of, 57, 215
    regulation of, 16–17, 57
    supporting provider, 207–15
    visits to (in selecting), 61–66
    written agreement with, 70–71
Group size
    and cost of care, 228, 259
    recommended, 32, 78, 106, 137
    family/group family child care, 50–51, 57, 64–65
    infants and toddlers, 32, 50
    preschoolers, 50, 91–92
    school-age children, 50, 137
    state regulations concerning, 16–17, 157, 165, 228, 259
Guide to Accredited Camps, The, 147
Guilt and anxiety (of parents), 192–94
    child care myths and, 194–97, 198
    how to alleviate, 197–204

Hack, Peggy, 235
Handicaps. *See* Disabilities
Happy Day Playschool, 74, 75
Head Start programs, 13–14, 114–16,
    118–19, 248
    combined with other care, 20, 109,
        115
    funding of, 115–16
    income eligibility requirements, 10,
        13, 115
    philosophy of, 74–77, 115
High/Scope curriculum, 20
Home care. *See* Care in someone else's
    home; Care in your own home

Illness
    child too sick for care program,
        211–12
    of provider, backup for, 55–56, 58,
        86
    susceptibility of child to disease, 16,
        47, 79
Income. *See* Cost of care
Individuals with Disabilities Education
    Act, 9
Infants
    adult-to-child ratio, 11, 79, 80, 228
    age of, for start of supplementary
        care, 181–83
    in center care, 10, 11, 19, 79–85,
        100, 104–5
    communicating with caregiver
        about, 210–11
    cost of care, 228, 229, 237
    at end of day in care, 187–88, 202
    family home care for, 10, 50
    group size recommendations, 32, 50
    Head Start program for, 115
    home care for, 18
    judging caregiver, 63, 104–5
    newborn, 169–83
    starting search for care, 100, 199

    stranger and separation anxiety of,
        172, 181–86 *passim*
    in three-family system, 163
Internal Revenue Service, 125, 232
International Association of Nannies, 126
Interviewing
    care provider (in selecting family
        child care home), 67–69
    director of center-based care, 106–7,
        318–20
Investment of tax revenues, 258. *See
    also* Taxes
Isolating child (as punishment), 66, 68,
    96
Ithaca Community Childcare Center,
    75, 76

KinderCare Learning Centers, 12, 76
Kindergarten programs, 10, 14, 15,
    136
    adult-to-child ratio in, 77

Laboratory ("lab") schools, 14–15
Language
    "bad," 191
    second, encouragement of, 35–36
    toddlers' development of, 90
La Petite Academy, 12, 76
Latchkey children, 144–46. *See also*
    School-age child care (SACC)
Licensing, 54–55
    as indicator of quality, 105
    for infant care, 79
    for part-time care, 112, 114
    for school-age programs, 138
    See also State-regulated standards

Montessori, Maria, 21
Montessori schools, 20–21, 76
Mother, new
    emotional relationship with new-
        born, 170–71

expectations of, 169
maternity leave, 173, 176–81, 182
time for, 173, 182
See also Parents
Mother's helpers, 123

Nanny, 10, 14, 18–19, 117, 120–22,
    123–29
cost, 121, 125, 133, 228, 229
duties, 123–24
education, training, and experience,
    19, 125–26
finding and hiring, 126–29
    forms and checklists, 326–28,
    330–32
hours of work, 124–25
and school-age children, 144
Social Security and unemployment
    taxes for, 125
unannounced visits to, 129, 200
Naps and naptime, 66, 82, 88–89, 94,
    95
area for, 62, 104
enforced, 26, 88
nursery schools and, 110–11
and visit to care center, 102
National Association of Child Care
    Resource and Referral Agencies
    (NACCRRA), 42
National Association for the Educa-
    tion of Young Children
    (NAEYC), 32, 75, 77, 78, 106,
    137, 223, 240
National Association for Family Child
    Care, 64
Newborn, 169–83
emotional relationship with, 170–71
key phases in development of,
    171–72
time spent with, 172–76
See also Infants
Nonprofit centers. *See* Child care centers

Nursery schools, 10, 14, 110–12, 117
checklist, 324–25
extended-day programs, 14, 112
philosophy of, 117
regulation/nonregulation of, 14, 31,
    109

Outdoor space. *See* Physical environment

Parental leave policies, 176–78, 183, 254
cost of, 178–81
need for improved, 257
Scandinavian, 182, 199–200
Parent involvement, 199–200
in center care, 82, 89, 98–100
in family/group family care, 54, 57,
    65
in improving conditions, 245–60
parent-provider conferences,
    214–15
parent-provider partnership, 36–37,
    245–51
in part-day program, 115
in SACC programs, 140–41
support of caregiver, 54, 57, 207–15,
    217, 221–23
See also Parent-run cooperatives
Parent-Provider Family Child Care
    Contract, 71, 303–6
Parent-run cooperatives, 10, 13, 99,
    109, 112–14, 117–18
Bank Street Co-op, 112–13
differing philosophies of, 118
extended-day programs, 114
three-family system, 162–63
Parents
guilt and anxiety of, 192–204
new, 169–83
as partners with care providers, *see*
    Parent involvement
tax credits for, 232–33, 257, 258 (*see*
    also Cost of care)

Part-day care, 109–19
avoiding "patchwork," 116
choosing, 116–17
extended-day programs, 14, 112, 114, 116
program form, 324–25
for school-age children, *see* School-age child care (SACC)
state regulation of, 109, 112, 114
See also Part-time care
Part-time care, 10–11
arrangements combined, 10–11, 14, 20, 109–16 *passim*, 144
vs. full-time, 9
for newborn, 179
See also Part-day care
Part-time work schedule (for parents), 180, 254
Perry Pre-School Program (Ypsilanti, Michigan), 20
Personality of child
caretaker's knowledge of, 217
in choosing care, 8
Physical discipline. *See* Discipline
Physical environment
checking on, 62, 66, 103–4, 105
cleanliness of, 26, 51, 85, 87, 150
family child care, 51–52, 62
for infant care, 79–83
outdoor, 29, 52, 62, 83, 89, 94, 104, 105, 139
for preschoolers, 93–94
quality, 34
regulations centered on, 31, 78
safety of, 28–30, 51–52, 55, 62, 78, 137, 150
for school-age children, 137, 139
space requirements, 78, 137, 157
of summer camp or program, 150
for toddlers, 86–89
Physical privacy, 66, 97
Pickup time, 187–88, 210

Play groups, 109, 110, 117
Pre-kindergarten (Pre-K) programs, 10, 20
Preschoolers
Colombian program, 255
cost of care, 237
full-time or center care for, 10, 20, 91–97
group size recommendations, 50, 91–92
separation anxiety of, 186–87
Proprietary (for-profit) centers. *See* Child care centers
Provider. *See* Caregiver or teacher
Public child care subsidies, 233–34. *See also* Cost of care
Public policies, need for improvement of, 257–60
Public schools, SAAC programs at, 142–43

Quality care, 23–37
age of child and, 78
caregiver/teacher as key to, 27
continuity, 30, 37, 56–57, 98, 106
cost, 229–30
curriculum, 34–35
definition of, 25, 27
for infants, 78, 82
judging, 23–26
licensing as indicator of, 105
not guaranteed by CCR R agencies, 44
parents and providers as partners, *see* Parent involvement
physical environment, 34
predictors of, 31–33
race, culture, and language, 35–36
respectful, 28
safe and secure, 28–30, 37, 51–52 (*see also* Safety)
standards of, 31, 55 (*see also* State-regulated standards)

See also Education/training of care provider

Racial experience, 35–36
Reference checks
    of family-based providers, 58–61, 329
    of SACC program or camp, 151
Registration standards, 54–55, 157. *See also* State-regulated standards
Regulations
    cost of implementing, 258–59
    federal (au pair), 129, 130, 132
    state, *see* State-regulated standards
Relatives
    care by, 10, 17, 18, 39, 56, 146
    in creating child care arrangement, 158–61
Religious institutions. *See* Church-based centers
Resource and referral agency. *See* Child care resource and referral (CCRR) agencies
Respect for children, 26, 28, 96
Responsibility for care, 4, 106, 119, 142
    at pickup time, 210
    See also Parent involvement
Right to care, 4

"Safe houses," 146
Safety. *See* Physical environment
Scandinavia, 83, 182, 199. *See also* Swedish national child care program
School-age child care (SACC), 10, 135–54
    center-based, 10, 12, 15, 19–20, 136, 142–44
    employer-supported or -sponsored, 19
    family/group family care, 10, 47, 50–51, 141–42
    forms and checklists, 333–38

group size recommendations, 50, 137
    at home, 144
    legal requirements, 137–38, 141, 142
    parent involvement in, 140–41
    school-based, 142–43
    self-care or latchkey children, 144–46
    and separation anxiety, 187
    staff qualifications and practices, 138–41
    in summer months, 147–54
    See also Kindergarten
Search strategies, 38–44
    early start, 100, 199
    formal approaches, 42–44
    informal approaches, 38–41
Separation anxiety
    infant, 172, 181, 182, 184, 185
    preschool and school-age, 186–87
Sexual contact, inappropriate, 66
Single provider. *See* Family child care homes
Space requirements. *See* Physical environment
Special support services, 9, 96
    nationwide listing, 263–66
Staff. *See* Caregiver or teacher
State-regulated standards
    for center-based care, 11–12, 13, 17, 73, 76–78, 241
    exemption from or lack of, 13, 16, 142, 157, 165, 241
        family home care, 47, 55
        own home care, 31, 163
        part-day care, 109, 114
    for family child care, 15, 16, 47, 54–55, 142
    group size, 16–17, 157, 165, 228, 259
    and inspection of facilities, 78
    minimum, 11–12, 31, 44, 54–55, 77, 78, 79
    nursery school, 112

State-regulated standards *(cont'd.)*
  safety, 78, 137
  school-age children, 137–38, 141,
    142
  See also Licensing
Steiner, Rudolf, 21
Stranger anxiety (infant), 172, 181, 182,
  185–86
Subsidies. *See* Cost of care
Summer camps
  checklist, 152–54
  choosing, 148–54
  day, 147, 152
  and parent involvement, 140
  regulations on, 138
  residential, 147–48, 152
  visiting (to select), 150–51, 335–38
Summer vacation. *See* Vacation time
Supermarket tantrum, 189
Swedish national child care program,
  162, 163, 182, 231

Tantrums, 189–90
Taxes
  corporate, funding child care,
    255–56
  investment of tax revenues, 258
  Social Security and unemployment
    (for nanny), 125
  supporting child care, need for, 256,
    257, 258
  tax credits for child care costs,
    232–33, 257, 258
Teacher. *See* Caregiver or teacher
Telephone screening
  of au pair applicants, 132–33
  of candidates for alternative child
    care arrangement, 160
  of center-based care, 101–2
  of family-based providers, 58–60,
    64
  of nanny applicants, 127

of summer SACC program or camp,
  148–49
Three-family system, 162–63
"Time out." *See* Discipline
Toddlers
  in center care, 10, 19, 85–91, 100,
    104–5
  communicating with caregiver
    about, 210–11
  cost of care, 229, 237
  family home care for, 10, 50
  group size recommendations, 32,
    50
  Head Start program for, 115
  home care for, 18
  judging care, 63, 104–5
  and separation anxiety, 172
  starting search for care, 100, 199
  in three-family system, 163
Toilet training, 87–88, 107
  as eligibility for enrollment, 111
Training. *See* Education/training of
  care provider
TV watching, 69, 141
Two or more providers. *See* Group
  family child care homes

Unannounced visits. *See* Visits
United States Information Agency
  (USIA), 129, 130, 131
United Way, 249
University Extension Services, 156

Vacation time
  children's adjustment to, 203–4
  for parents, and parental leave,
    177–78, 180
  for school-age children, 147–54
Verbal aggression by caregiver, 27, 68,
  84
Visits
  of caregiver to child's home, 213

to child at care site, limits on, 102, 185, 214
to child care centers (when making selection), 79–81, 83–85, 88, 90, 93–94, 100, 102–5
to family child care homes (when making selection), 61–66
get-acquainted (of child), 63, 69, 209
unannounced, to child care program, 29, 100, 129, 200–201
Volunteer activities, 213, 249–50

Voucher program, 19, 20

Waldorf Schools or programs, 21, 76
Walkers or jumpers (for infants), 81
Weekends, 188–90, 203
Weikart, David, 20

Yellow Pages, child care programs listed in, 40–41, 42, 116, 132
YMCAs and YWCAs (the Ys), 136, 142, 143, 147, 249